THE ECONOMICS OF REAL PROPERTY

By the same author

BASIC ECONOMICS

BASIC ECONOMICS WORKBOOK

ELEMENTARY ECONOMICS

WORKBOOK FOR ELEMENTARY ECONOMICS

INTERMEDIATE ECONOMICS

MULTIPLE CHOICE QUESTIONS FOR
INTERMEDIATE ECONOMICS

THE BRITISH CONSTITUTION (*with L. Bather*)

HOW BRITAIN IS GOVERNED

WORKBOOK FOR HOW BRITAIN IS GOVERNED

PRODUCING AND SPENDING (*with M. Harvey*)

MODERN ECONOMICS (*Third Edition*)

MODERN ECONOMICS STUDENT'S NOTEBOOK

MODERN ECONOMICS: STUDY GUIDE
AND WORKBOOK (*with M. K. Johnson*)

INTRODUCTION TO MACRO-ECONOMICS
(*with M. K. Johnson*)

INTRODUCTION TO MACRO-ECONOMICS:
A WORKBOOK (*with M. K. Johnson*)

GOVERNMENT AND PEOPLE (*with M. Harvey*)

THE ORGANISATION IN ITS ENVIRONMENT

THE ORGANISATION IN ITS ENVIRONMENT:
ASSIGNMENTS FOR BEC COURSES
(*with J. Chilver*)

The Economics of Real Property

J. Harvey

B.Sc. (Econ.), Dip. Ed. (Oxford)
Visiting Lecturer, University of Reading

First published 1981 by
THE MACMILLAN PRESS LTD
London and Basingstoke
Companies and representatives throughout the world

ISBN 0 333 31828 5   (hard cover)
ISBN 0 333 31829 3 (paper cover)

Filmset by
Vantage Photosetting
Southampton and London

Printed in Hong Kong

I am the basis of all wealth, the heritage of the wise, the thrifty and prudent.

I am the poor man's joy and comfort, the rich man's prize, the right hand of capital, the silent partner of many thousands of successful men.

I am the solace of the widow, the comfort of old age, the cornerstone of security against misfortune and want. I am handed down to children, through generations, as a thing of greatest worth.

I am the choicest fruit of toil. Credit respects me. Yet I am humble. I stand before every man, bidding him know me for what I am and possess me.

I grow and increase in value through countless days. Though I seem dormant, my worth increases, never failing, never ceasing, time is my aid and population heaps up my gain. Fire and the elements I defy, for they cannot destroy me.

My possessors learn to believe in me; invariably they become envied. While all things wither and decay, I survive. The centuries find me younger, increasing with strength.

The thriftless speak ill of me. The charlatans of finance attack me. I am trustworthy. I am sound. Unfailingly I triumph and detractors are disproved.

Minerals and oils come from me. I am producer of food, the basis for ships and factories, the foundation of banks.

Yet I am so common that thousands, unthinking and unknowingly, pass by me.

I am land.

Lou Scott, *What is Real Estate?*

Contents

Preface

In recent years much attention has been directed to the nature of our environment in its various aspects – town planning, adequate open spaces providing recreational and cultural facilities, housing, inner-city decay, pollution, noise, architectural harmony, conservation, and so on. Our environment today is the result of a combination of economic, sociological, aesthetic and political influences. This book concentrates on the economic factors which have to be taken into account. While it recognises the importance of the other influences, its central theme is that, instead of economics being relegated to a secondary role often called upon to appraise and analyse only after basic decisions have been taken, the economist should be integrated into the decision-making process from the beginning, for his approach is of vital importance.

Since land and buildings are scarce resources, it is essential that they are used as efficiently as possible. This is the starting-point of the economist, and his task is, by applying economic analysis, to formulate principles necessary for the efficient use of land resources and thereby to suggest ways in which the existing allocation might be improved.

Thus the book follows the accepted procedure of first building abstract models, from which are derived the essential conditions for the efficient allocation of resources, and then proceeds to examine the assumptions which are essential for this most efficient situation to be achieved. Using this theoretical analysis, it goes on to consider how, in the British context, the conclusions derived from the model can be applied to the allocation of real property resources – land and buildings.

In Britain's mixed economy real property resources are mainly distributed by market forces. Initially, therefore, the book examines the market solution, its strengths and weaknesses, both in the way in which it functions and the institutions through which it works. Subjects covered are the nature of the market, the determination of real property prices, investment in real property assets, property development in both the private and public sectors, the construction industry and housing policy.

While passing references are made to possible government adjustments to the market solution, the main discussion of government policy is reserved for the final chapter. This considers the impact on land resources of government macro policy and the strengths and weaknesses of influencing the allocation of resources through taxation and subsidies, planning controls and public ownership. It must be emphasised, however, that the economist can only define the economic issues involved. For instance, he is limited in what he can say about the redistributive, sociological, aesthetic and even the political effects. Different strategies have different economic results – and while the economist can indicate these, the final choice of policy must rest with the politician.

Although the emphasis is on theoretical economic analysis, the discussion is made as practical as possible by being conducted in the context of the real property market in Britain and by being supplemented by empirical studies and selected statistics.

The main aim of the book is to provide a text for the student following courses in estate management, surveying, valuation, town planning, housing administration, geography and environmental subjects. While it does assume some knowledge of basic economic theory, this is no more than is required for most first-year courses for professional examinations. But the book should be of interest to those already actively engaged in professions relating to the land, in that it demonstrates how economics can provide a useful tool in the solution of practical problems. More hopefully, where decisions are subject to or are influenced by politicians or public administrators, it is trusted that what economics reveals may cause them to reflect on the full implications of their selected policies.

Of the many people – fellow-lecturers and students – who have contributed to the ideas expressed in this book, the outstanding influence has been the late Professor F. G. Pennance, a pioneer in applying economic analysis in the field of land use. He is remembered as a true friend and a wise counsellor, always encouraging, suggesting improvements and offering penetrating criticism and alternatives, backed by a sound professional training and long experience in teaching. Many past students of the College of Estate Management, the University of Reading and the University of Aberdeen who had the privilege of attending his tutorials must, like me, now appreciate the contribution which sound economics can make to the principles which should guide the improvement of our environment.

J.H.

ACKNOWLEDGEMENTS
The author and publishers wish to thank the Controller of HMSO for permission to reproduce extracts from official publications, and also Allsop & Co. for permission to include Table 5.2.

1

Economic Efficiency through the Price System

I WELFARE AND ECONOMIC EFFICIENCY

Maximising welfare

We can start with the proposition that society's aim is to maximise its welfare. Two factors which will influence welfare are: (a) the way society uses its limited resources; and (b) the distribution of income between members of society.

The first is the subject-matter of positive economics; it is possible to analyse it scientifically. Economic efficiency is achieved when society has secured the best allocation of its limited resources, in the sense that the maximum possible satisfaction is obtained. In other words, there is the greatest difference between benefit and cost.

The second, the distribution of income, does not lend itself to scientific analysis. The reason is that the satisfaction a person derives from his income is, like love and pain, personal to the individual and cannot be measured on any objective scale. Taking a small amount of income from the rich man and giving it to a poor man may increase welfare since the former's loss may be little compared with the latter's gain. But we can never be sure: since we cannot measure welfare ordinally, interpersonal comparisons are impossible. Thus, while distributional efficiency is necessary to maximise welfare, it cannot be dealt with scientifically. Decisions on income redistribution are left to the subjective decisions of the politician.

This book is concerned with economic efficiency, with particular reference to the allocation of land resources, more generally referred to as *real property*. This does not mean that we shall ignore the redistribution of income. Politicians carry out such redistribution in the field of real property, both directly through taxation, e.g. income tax, capital transfer tax and development land tax, and indirectly by intervening in the free operation of the price system, e.g. rent control, subsidies to council housing and pressure on building societies to keep mortgage rates low. What the economist has to point out is how such redistributive measures may affect economic efficiency. The politician can then weigh the balance of advantage.

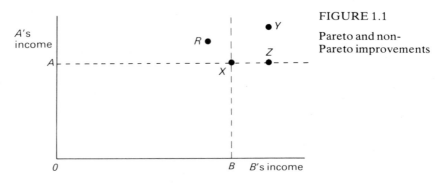

FIGURE 1.1

Pareto and non-Pareto improvements

Pareto optimality

In discussing economic efficiency, therefore, the economist side-steps the distributional problem which may result from a reallocation of resources (see pp. 139–40). He does this by adopting the narrow Pareto-optimality condition: welfare is maximised when no one can be made better off without somebody else being made worse off. Thus any improvement in economic efficiency which involves nobody losing will represent an increase in welfare.

For instance, in Figure 1.1 we start from the initial income position X, with A's income equal to OA and B's equal to OB. A movement to Y would represent an increase in welfare for both A and B; a movement to Z would increase B's welfare without reducing A's. Both Y and Z therefore represent Pareto improvements. It is impossible, however, to say whether position R represents an over-all gain or loss since A's income has increased but B's has fallen.

II CONDITIONS NECESSARY FOR PARETO OPTIMALITY

The weakness of the Pareto-optimality condition is that its application is limited to cases where only gainers and no losers result from a reallocation of resources. Even so, it does enable us to specify three conditions which must be fulfilled for economic efficiency. First, no improvement can be achieved by an exchange of goods between persons. Second, no increase in output can be obtained by producers substituting one factor for another. Third, from the maximum over-all output of goods which can be obtained when society's limited resources are combined efficiently, that assortment is produced which gives society the greatest possible satisfaction. We shall examine each in turn.

We simplify the exposition by assuming: (a) resources consist of a limited quantity of land and capital; (b) two goods are produced, food and manufactured goods.

FIGURE 1.2

Indifference maps of
consumers *A* and *B*

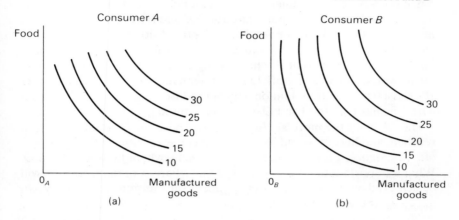

Consumer *A*

Food

30
25
20
15
10

0_A Manufactured
                                        goods
          (a)

Consumer *B*

Food

30
25
20
15
10

0_B Manufactured
                                        goods
          (b)

(1) *Exchange efficiency*

Figures 1.2(a) and 1.2(b) represent the 'indifference maps' of consumers
A and *B* respectively. Each indifference curve shows combinations of
food and manufactured goods which yield equivalent satisfaction, and the
further the indifference curve is from the origin, the greater the satisfaction obtained, as shown by the unspecified units, 10, 15, etc. Note that the
indifference curve is convex to the origin. This denotes a diminishing
marginal rate of substitution, an increasing amount of one good having to
be given up in order to obtain an additional unit of another. It assumes
that there is no 'conspicuous consumption' when people buy goods simply
to impress others.

We can depict the preferences of *A* and *B* in an 'Edgeworth box' (see
Figure 1.3). *B*'s indifference map is rotated 180°, so that the origin is O_B.

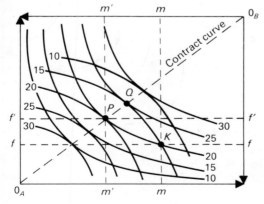

FIGURE 1.3

Efficiency in
exchange

The length of the vertical side of the box denotes the maximum food available to be exchanged, and the horizontal side the maximum amount of manufactured goods.

Suppose A and B commence with an initial distribution at K, where A has $O_A f$ food and $O_A m$ manufactured goods, and B has $O_B f$ food and $O_B m$ manufactured goods. K is not a Pareto-optimal situation. A could move along his indifference curve substituting food for manufactured goods until he reached the point P, where, being on the same indifference curve 20, he would feel no worse off. On the other hand, this exchange increases B's satisfaction, putting him on a higher indifference curve 20 (from 15) where he has $O_B f'$ food and $O_B m'$ manufactured goods.

Had A been the more skilful bargainer, position Q could have been reached, and here A would have been on curve 25 without B being worse off. In practice, they are likely to end up somewhere between P and Q. What is important to note, however, is that a Pareto-optimal position will be achieved only when the marginal rate of substitution between any two goods is the same for each consumer, as at P and Q where their indifference curves are tangential. Indeed, it is possible to find such a point for all combinations of food and manufactured goods. A line joining these points, the thick broken line, is known as a 'contract curve', and Pareto optimality will only hold provided that the division of available goods between consumers is on this curve.

(2) *Factor-combination efficiency*

We can use the same technique to specify an efficiency condition for combining factors of production. In Figures 1.4(a) and 1.4(b) we have

FIGURE 1.4
Combinations of land and capital to produce food and manufactured goods

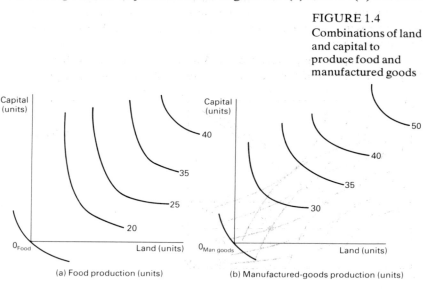

(a) Food production (units)   (b) Manufactured-goods production (units)

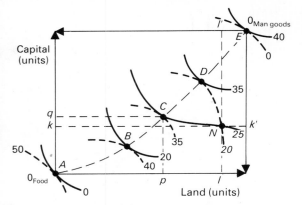

FIGURE 1.5

Efficiency in factor
combination

isoquants showing how two factors, land and capital, can be combined to
produce given quantities of food and manufactured goods respectively.
Note that the isoquants are convex to the origin. This denotes a diminishing marginal rate of technical substitution between factors, an increasing
amount of one factor being needed to compensate for the loss of a unit of
the other factor if the same quantity of output is to be produced.

Again, these isoquant maps can be combined in an Edgeworth box by
rotating the manufactured goods origin through 180° (see Figure 1.5).
The length of the vertical side represents the amount of capital available,
and the horizontal side the maximum amount of land.

Assume initially that production is at N, with $O_F l$ land and $O_F k$ capital
used to produce 25 units of food, and $O_M l'$ land and $O_M k'$ capital used to
produce 20 units of manufactured goods. N is not an efficient situation.
By transferring land from food to manufactured-goods production and
capital from manufactured-goods to food production, we can move to C
(with a net gain of 15 units of manufactured goods), or to D (with a net
gain of 10 units of food), or to an in-between position (showing some net
gain of both manufactured goods and food).

Thus a Pareto-optimal position will be achieved only when the marginal rate of technical substitution between factors is the same in each use
and for all producers. As before, we can obtain a contract curve joining all
points for all combinations of land and capital where this condition holds.
Pareto optimality requires that, according to the assortment of goods
required, factors must be combined on the appropriate point on the
contract curve, otherwise society can be better off by a reshuffling of
resources.

(3) *Economic efficiency*

From Figure 1.5 we can derive the various combinations of food and
manufactured goods which it is possible to obtain from the limited supply
of land and capital. These outputs are achieved only if land and capital are

The Economics of Real Property

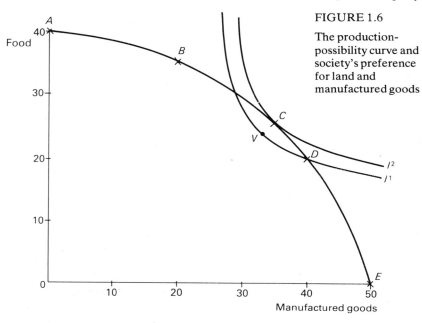

FIGURE 1.6

The production-possibility curve and society's preference for land and manufactured goods

combined efficiently: that is, each combination of land and capital must be found on the contract curve.

For the various points *A* to *E* on the contract curve, we obtain the following outputs:

	Food (units)	*Manufactured goods (units)*
A	0	50
B	20	40
C	25	35
D	35	20
E	40	0

Figure 1.6 graphs these outputs, smoothing them in the curve *AE*. This represents a production-possibility curve for this society. Any point within the production-possibility curve, for example *V*, is not a Pareto optimum because it is *technically* inefficient, as more of both goods can be obtained with the limited land and capital resources.

But while *technical efficiency* is a necessary condition for Pareto optimality, it is not sufficient. *Economic efficiency* requires that the actual product-mix is the one which gives society maximum satisfaction. We therefore have to relate the production-possibility curve to society's preferences.

Ignoring the conceptual difficulties involved, let I^1 and I^2 represent two indifference curves of society. While a product-mix D is on the production-possibility curve, it does not maximise society's welfare, since by producing more food and less manufactured goods a higher indifference curve I^2 can be attained at C, where the indifference curve and production-possibility curve just touch. We therefore have a third condition of Pareto optimality: consumers' marginal rate of substitution between products must equal the marginal rate of transformation between products.

III ACHIEVING THE CONDITIONS OF ECONOMIC EFFICIENCY

Alternative methods

In our model, society maximises welfare when 25 units of food and 35 units of manufactured goods are produced. Thus in Figure 1.5 the optimum allocation of resources is achieved when $O_F p$ land and $O_F q$ capital are used to grow food, and the remainder produce manufactured goods.

Broadly speaking there are two methods by which the above resource allocation can be carried out: government fiat and the price system. While the former can overcome certain defects in the price system, for example the external effects (social benefits and social costs) of private decisions would be 'internalised', it faces formidable difficulties. Not only does it have to assess people's preferences, but it has the gigantic administrative task of allocating resources in the optimum proportions to produce the goods and services preferred.

In contrast, the price system assumes that the individual is the sole judge of his welfare and that, both as a consumer and as a producer, he acts through markets to maximise that welfare. Economic efficiency is achieved through Adam Smith's 'hidden hand'. As we shall see, however, this will only apply when many rigorous conditions prevail. Nevertheless, since in Britain's mixed economy, and particularly in the real property market, most decisions are taken through the price system, we shall concentrate on this.

Pareto optimality through the price system

Exchange efficiency is achieved by the consumer relating his preferences to market prices in order to maximise satisfaction from his limited resources.

In a perfect market a single price is established at which food and

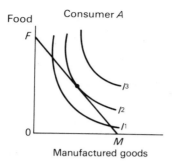

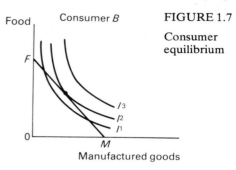

FIGURE 1.7

Consumer
equilibrium

manufactured goods can be exchanged. In Figure 1.7 the distance of the line *FM* from the origin indicates the limit of consumer *A*'s resources, his budget-possibility curve. The slope of this budget line reflects the relative prices of food and manufactured goods. Consumer *A* will maximise his welfare when the budget price line touches the highest possible indifference curve. Here the marginal rate of substitution of food for manufactured goods is equal to their relative prices.

But since there is a single market price at which food exchanges for manufactured goods, and consumer *B* adopts the same course, it follows that the marginal rate of substitution of food for manufactured goods is the same for each consumer. Thus the condition for exchange efficiency is satisfied.

Put in Marshallian terms the equilibrium condition in spending on goods occurs when, for all consumers,

$$\frac{\text{Marginal utility of food}}{\text{Marginal utility of manufactured goods}} = \frac{\text{Price of food}}{\text{Price of manufactured goods}}$$

A similar argument can be applied to factor combinations – *technical efficiency*. Individual producers combine land and capital to obtain maximum output from a limited budget. Demand and supply in the factor market will establish a price at which land and capital are exchanged, the demand for each factor being dependent upon the price of the finished product. The food producer therefore employs those quantities of land and capital where the marginal rate of technical substitution equals their relative price. But since there is only one price at which land exchanges for capital, and since the manufactured-goods producer adopts the same profit-maximising course, it follows that the marginal rate of technical substitution of land for capital is the same in the production of both food and manufactured goods. Thus the condition for factor-combination efficiency is achieved.

Put in Marshallian terms, the equilibrium condition in combining factors occurs when, in all uses and for all producers,

$$\frac{\text{Marginal physical product of land}}{\text{Marginal physical product of manufactured goods}} = \frac{\text{Price of land}}{\text{Price of manufactured goods}}$$

How *economic efficiency* is achieved through the price system is more easily explained by translating the production-possibility curve into Marshallian terms.

As we have seen, there is a single price in the market at which food is exchanged against manufactured goods. The production-possibility curve shows, for any combination, the rate at which food can be transformed into manufactured goods. This transformation rate can be referred to as the *opportunity cost*, which, in perfect competition, is reflected in marginal costs (given no external costs). Thus the rate of transformation at any point on the production-possibility curve equals

$$\frac{\text{Marginal cost of food}}{\text{Marginal cost of manufactured goods}}$$

However, in perfect competition, a farmer growing food will produce that output where the price of food (P_f) equals the marginal cost of a unit of food (MC_f). Similarly, the output of manufactured goods will be where the price of manufactured goods (P_m) equals the marginal cost of a unit of manufactured goods (MC_m).

Since we are dealing with equalities, we can divide the first equation by the second, giving

$$\frac{P_f}{P_m} = \frac{MC_f}{MC_m}$$

That is, the relative price of food and manufactured goods is equal to the marginal rate of transformation between food and manufactured goods. But equilibrium for both consumers A and B is where the relative price of food and manufactured goods is equal to the marginal rate of substitution of manufactured goods for food. Thus the condition for economic efficiency is fulfilled.

In the simple Marshallian formulation, we have:

$$\frac{MU_f}{MU_m} = \frac{P_f}{P_m} = \frac{MC_f}{MC_m}$$

IV CONDITIONS NECESSARY FOR ECONOMIC EFFICIENCY THROUGH THE PRICE SYSTEM

The careful reader will have noticed that before commencing the above outline of the working of the price system no assumptions were made.

This was done deliberately in order not to interrupt the flow of the main argument. Our analysis, however, implicitly assumed that certain conditions held, particularly perfect competition, the absence of 'spillover' benefits and costs (often referred to as 'externalities'), and the ability of the market mechanism to supply all goods and services provided society is able and willing to pay the necessary costs. We shall examine each in turn.

Perfect competition

Prices established in the market not only reflect consumers' preferences but provide the signals upon which producers act. But in order that such market prices really do reflect consumers' satisfaction and producers' costs, certain requirements have to be met:

(1) *There must be a perfect market*, so that any price differences are quickly eliminated. Consumers and producers must seek to maximise utility and profits respectively and, in doing so, be unhampered by legal and other constraints.

(2) *There must be perfect knowledge* of any price differences which temporarily exist in the market, by consumers as they satisfy their wants, and by producers in deciding what to produce and in combining factors of production. Moreover, there should be no costs of obtaining knowledge, no ostentatious buying and no 'brain-washing' advertising. In practice, personal judgements have to be made where market criteria are not available, e.g. in estimating the plans of other producers. Such uncertainty means that Adam Smith's 'hidden hand' is likely to act only through a process of trial and error.

Given conditions (1) and (2) there will be common prices throughout the market for each product or factor of production.

(3) $P = MR = MC$. Producers maximise profits by producing that output where marginal revenue equals marginal cost ($MR = MC$). But this will only represent economic efficiency if marginal revenue equals price ($MR = P$), since production must proceed to the point where the satisfaction which the consumer derives from an additional unit of the good equals the cost to society of producing that unit, that is $P = MC$.

However, price will only equal marginal revenue under conditions of perfect competition (see Figure 1.8(a)). Here the producer is a 'price-taker', accepting the market price as given. For this situation to occur there must be many producers each supplying so small a quantity to the market that no single producer can influence the market price. Furthermore, there must be freedom of entry into the industry. Similar conditions must apply in selling factors of production.

In contrast, where there is imperfect competition, marginal revenue is less than price (see Figure 1.8(b)). This means that output is less, OM_1,

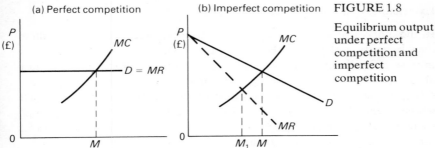

(a) Perfect competition (b) Imperfect competition FIGURE 1.8

Equilibrium output under perfect competition and imperfect competition

than that at which consumers' satisfaction from an additional unit equals the cost of producing it, *OM*. There is thus a sub-optimal allocation of resources.

(4) *There must be increasing costs.* For perfect competition to exist, the *MC* curve must be rising to cut the horizontal demand curve from below (see Figure 1.8(a)). However, certain industries, chiefly those that have to produce on a large scale, have decreasing costs at the relevant part of the demand curve. Thus to obtain an equilibrium output the marginal revenue curve must be sloping down if it is to be cut by the *MC* curve (see Figure 1.9). Here again, the price system cannot fulfil the conditions of economic efficiency, for price, *OP*, is greater than marginal cost, *OC*.

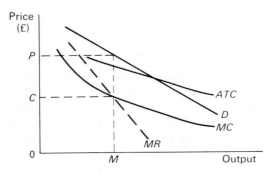

FIGURE 1.9

Equilibrium output under conditions of decreasing cost

(5) *There must be perfect mobility of factors of production.* The price system operates only imperfectly if factors of production do not move in response to changes in relative prices. Time is usually necessary for such mobility to occur, and this is particularly so with real property resources where leases have to expire and sites assembled before redevelopment can take place.

Immobility may also be one of the reasons for imperfect competition, for instance allowing the owner of a site vital for a proposed development to exercise monopoly powers.

Externalities: spillover benefits and costs

In the market private consumers and producers seek to maximise their own benefits and profits. However, this assumes that their decisions impose no indirect benefits or costs on others. In practice, this is not always so. Flowers in people's gardens may give pleasure to the passer-by; the design of a new house may destroy the architectural harmony of a whole street. Both private and spillover benefits and costs are all part of social benefits and true opportunity costs and as such should be allowed for in the decision-making process.

Unemployment also affects society's estimates of costs, for, from society's point of view, activating unemployed resources normally involves no cost.

Community goods and services

The price system we have described implicitly assumes that all economic goods are capable of being priced in the market. But this is possible only if people who are unwilling to pay the price for a good or service can be excluded from enjoying it. With some goods and services, however, for example defence, street-lighting, common land and National Trust open spaces, it is impossible or impractical to exclude people by charging a price, since anybody can be a 'free-rider'. Such goods, from which the community benefits, have therefore to be provided collectively, and financed, not by charging individuals as they use them, but by subscription (e.g. The Royal Society for the Protection of Birds), advertising and sponsorship (e.g. commercial television) or, more usually, by taxation (e.g. defence, street-lighting, common land). Indeed, as we shall see in Chapter 13, a Pareto improvement may be effected by providing collectively, rather than privately, goods where exclusion *is* possible. While the cost of such 'collective' goods may be covered by making a charge, they are more often treated as free goods, being paid for from the proceeds of taxation.

Other weaknesses of the price system

It is necessary to mention briefly some other weaknesses of the price system.

First, the above is essentially a purely static theory. Economic decisions also span time, so that a choice has to be made between present and future benefits. This involves accuracy in estimating such future benefits and costs, and is thus likely to conflict with our previous condition of perfect knowledge. Consideration of allocating resources over time, however, will be postponed to Chapter 10.

Second, the price system cannot guarantee full employment, while decisions are influenced by inflation expectations. With the first, government action is demanded politically; with the second miscalculation can distort resource allocation.

Third, the price system only operates within the existing distribution of income. There are as many Pareto-optimal situations as there are possible distributions of income. But, as we have seen, redistribution of income is ultimately a political decision.

Using the price system

The above qualifications imply that the market economy is unlikely to be fully efficient in allocating resources. On the other hand, allocation by government fiat in a 'command economy' can present even greater problems. At least the market system does start with the advantage that economic decisions are based on prices which reflect, albeit somewhat imperfectly, consumers' preferences and relative costs.

This points to the compromise of a 'mixed economy'. This uses the price system as the basis for allocating resources, but, recognising its defects, relies on the government to provide, as far as possible, the conditions necessary for its efficient functioning (see Chapter 13).

Such is the approach of this book. Allocation of real property is still mainly through the market system. We examine this system and analyse its efficiency in the light of economic principles and the institutional background. We then examine the rationale of government interference in the market, assessing where possible the extent to which improvements are achieved.

FURTHER READING

J. Harvey, *Modern Economics*, 3rd edn (London: Macmillan, 1977) chs 5, 10, 11.

K. Lancaster, *Introduction to Modern Micro-economics*, 2nd edn (Chicago: Rand McNally, 1974) ch. 10.

E. Nevin, *Textbook of Economic Analysis*, 4th edn (London: Macmillan, 1976) chs 4, 5.

2
Characteristics of the Real Property Market

I   IS THERE A REAL PROPERTY MARKET?

What is a market?

Modern economies are often referred to as 'exchange economies'. Instead of people producing directly for their own wants, they specialise in production in order to increase total output. Thus both factors of production and final products are exchanged. Exchanges take place because both buyers and sellers benefit from them (see Figure 1.3).

To effect exchanges, buyers and sellers must be put in touch with one another. Any arrangement for doing this can be termed 'the market'. Such a market may be formal, as with the Stock Exchange and organised produce markets, or informal, as with dealings in foreign currencies over the telephone.

In the market economy exchanges take place on the basis of prices determined in the market by the interaction of demand and supply. Because the formation of price is central to the functions of the market, we can define a market as *any arrangement by which buyers and sellers are brought together to fix a price at which goods can be exchanged.*

Allocating land resources and real property through the price mechanism therefore immediately poses three questions:

(1)   In what sense is there a 'real property market'?
(2)   How perfect is the market in registering changes in demand and supply for the same kind of property by means of changes in a common price?
(3)   How does the market function through price changes to bring demand and supply into equilibrium (a) in the short run; and (b) in the long run?

The first two questions will be answered in this chapter, the third in Chapter 3.

The meaning of 'the real property market'

Real property refers to a particular type of good – land, or resources embodied in land. The point is that neither is physically movable. This characteristic distinguishes it from labour and capital and from other consumer goods and services, including furniture, antiques and works of art (often referred to as 'chattels' and frequently the concern of valuers and estate agents).

Although the resources embodied in land are not movable, they are a form of property which can be owned by some person or institution. Moreover, exchanges in them take place. There is thus a real property market, the arrangement by which buyers and sellers of virgin land, agricultural estates, industrial buildings, offices, shops and houses are brought together to determine a price at which the particular property can be exchanged. Sometimes the market is formal (e.g. the London Auction Market), sometimes informal (e.g. introductions by estate agents, deals between principals). Indeed, it is not possible to distinguish the means by which people are informed from 'the market'. Much real property, as with consumer goods and labour, is advertised in journals (e.g. the *Estates Gazette* and *Daltons Weekly*) and newspapers, all of which can therefore be said to be part of the market. Thus 'the real property market' is simply an omnibus term covering all transactions in real property. Yet, as we shall see, it is possible to distinguish sub-markets according to special characteristics, e.g. City of London office blocks, prime shop properties, houses in a given locality, with each fulfilling, albeit perhaps imperfectly, the basic functions of a market.

Real property rights

At this point it is essential to emphasise that what the real property market actually deals in is 'property rights', often referred to as 'interests'. In this, however, it is no different from any other market. I may, for instance, go to Burton or Hepworth and purchase a suit. In this case the suit is handed over to me and I am given the exclusive right to wear it as long as I wish, and even to part with that right by selling it to somebody else. Alternatively, I could hire a suit from Moss Bros. Here my right to wear the suit would be restricted to a specified period and subject to conditions regarding damage, etc. In the first case there is little formal definition of my right: the suit is simply handed over to me upon payment for it. On the other hand, when I hire a suit my restricted rights are more likely to be clearly defined in a written agreement which, by implication, also excludes Moss Bros from letting anybody else wear the suit during the specified period.

Similarly with real property – here it is not possible to hand over land and buildings in the same way as would be the case with movable goods. It is much more obvious, therefore, that it is 'rights' which are dealt in, especially as, accompanying the transaction, there is a written statement defining the exact rights which are being transferred. In short, the real property market deals in the rights relating to real property rather than in the land and buildings themselves.

With real property, too, the separation of rights is more usual than with personal property. The largest collection of rights which a person can hold in real property is 'fee simple absolute': that is, the unencumbered freehold. But all the rights inherent in the ownership of 'fee simple absolute' can be separated and transferred individually to other people. Thus a lease may be granted to a person to erect a building on a plot of land and to enjoy the rights to this building and land for a ninety-nine-year period on payment of a specified yearly sum to the lessor. Provided the terms of the lease are fulfilled, the lessor's rights are, for ninety-nine years, now restricted to the receipt of a freehold ground rent. The freehold has thus been divided into two interests: the leasehold and the freehold ground rent. In any given land resource different people may have many different rights, for example a freehold ground rent, a head-lease, a sub-lease, a mortgage, a rent charge, and so on.

It is worth noting that the exact rights transferred can be finely adjusted according to the individual preferences of the seller or buyer, e.g. by a restrictive covenant. Such a fine differentiation to meet the individual preferences of sellers and buyers is achieved automatically through the free-market mechanism simply by adjusting the price to take account of them.

Four aspects of real property rights need emphasis. First, within his rights the 'fee simple absolute' owner can possess, use, abuse and even destroy his real property. He can sell rights in such a way as to restrict their future use (e.g. by covenant), or he can bequeath them to distant heirs. Even so, his rights are limited: (i) he can only use his property subject to other people's property rights (e.g. easements may exist giving other persons 'ancient lights', or the right to take drains or pipe water across his freehold interest); (ii) he is subject to the legal restraints imposed by planning Acts, building regulations and similar legislation.

Second, an interest comes into existence simply because a bundle of certain rights is wanted. But no rights would be wanted unless their owner can exclude others from them. What, for example, would you give for fishing rights in a country where poaching was no offence and suffered no penalty? Thus the concept of *rights* is essentially a legal one: it presupposes that there is a sovereign power which will, if necessary, protect the rights vested in the owner. Moreover, being a legal concept, a right must be clearly defined. This implies limitations to the right. Thus a right is merely exclusive, not absolute or unlimited – even a 'fee simple absolute'. In fact, different rights are really only differences in 'exclusiveness'.

Third, where rights are well defined and the costs of negotiating and enforcing contracts are small compared with the benefits of the transaction, an exchange system based on prices works smoothly. Economic theory tends to assume these conditions. At times, however, the failure to define rights unambiguously may lead to economic inefficiency. Thus it is generally felt that low-income persons should enjoy some form of housing subsidy. In practice, however, this right has not been made explicit. It has been attached, not as intended to the person, but to the occupation of a particular property, e.g. a rent-controlled flat (where the landlord virtually subsidises the tenant) or a council house. This right is not transferable to another property and, as a result, people occupying rent-controlled accommodation are restricted in their mobility as compared with owner-occupiers.

Fourth, because real property is durable, the rights existing in real property have a long time scale. Moreover, no problem of storing such rights exists, though there may be management costs. Real property rights, like stocks and shares, are therefore demanded as investment assets (see Chapter 5). Indeed, the real property market can now be regarded as a part of the wider investment asset market, its significance in this respect having increased in recent years.

II THE EFFICIENCY OF THE REAL PROPERTY MARKET

The nature of the real property market

Since the market is essential to the functioning of the price system, a defective market mechanism will impair the efficiency with which resources are allocated through the price system. We therefore have to ask: How efficient is the real property market in registering the effect on price of changes in demand and supply?

The efficiency of a market depends on both technical and economic characteristics.

(1) *Technical characteristics*

Physical conditions should be such that price differences for the same commodity in different parts of the market are eliminated easily and quickly. This comes about by buyers moving to cheaper parts of the market and sellers moving to the dearer. For this to happen, however, both buyers and sellers must have up-to-date knowledge of the prices ruling in different parts of the market and base their actions solely on these prices. Moreover, dealing costs should be small relative to the value of the transaction.

Now, when we look at the real property market, we find factors which not only make it difficult to obtain up-to-date knowledge but which lead to dealing costs being relatively high. As regards the first, knowledge tends to be obtained infrequently and is limited geographically. Most occupiers (as distinct from investors) move in response to changes in family circumstances, income or business conditions. Only rarely do they move for the sole purpose of making a gain from a price or rent difference. Moreover, with occupational interests, buyers tend to have a demand which is essentially local, either because their knowledge of the prospects of their business is confined to a particular district or because, as workers, they have to be within easy travelling distance of their place of work. On the other hand, for a holiday or retirement residence people in Britain may compare prices in Cornwall, Spain or the Bahamas. Here the cost and time involved in travelling to work no longer count.

Nor do we overcome the difficulty of lack of knowledge simply by saying that it can be overcome by paying for advice. Because of differences of site, construction and age, most units of real property have special characteristics, making 'grading', the most efficient form of description, difficult. Of course, some interests, e.g. freehold ground rents, can be described accurately. Others, such as houses, shops, offices or industrial premises, may have labels attached according to the physical characteristics of the structure (e.g. high- or low-rise, in good repair or in need of modernisation, a large or small number of units) or by location (e.g. city centre or suburban, London or provincial). Indeed, it is possible to say what price a special location will fetch fairly accurately. Thus a standard shop unit (one with a frontage of twenty feet or less) commands a rent of about £60,000 a year in Oxford Street, £35,000 in Regent Street, and £25,000 in Bond Street and Kensington High Street. Yet even within these 'grades' individual properties have their own characteristics. Nor, owing to their great heterogeneity, can a professional valuer fully assess their respective merits. To some degree, therefore, his valuation is subjective. Thus, unlike transport costs, costs of obtaining knowledge are not absolutely certain, and a purchaser would normally go to the trouble of making a personal inspection and discussing with his professional adviser the weight to be given to special characteristics.

This does not, however, diminish the role played by valuers and agents in the property market. Indeed, where knowledge is difficult to obtain, their specialised functions assume an even greater importance for the smooth working of the market, since they provide information on the availability, type and price of properties, assist or conduct negotiations, arrange finance and insurance, and collaborate with conveyancers.

In addition to the costs of obtaining knowledge, there are the legal costs and stamp duties incurred in the actual transfer. Except for the difficulty mentioned above regarding the uncertainty of information costs, the cost of obtaining knowledge, estate agents' fees and legal costs involved in the actual transfer are, in principle, no different from the costs usually incurred in transporting goods within the market. Thus they have the same effect as transport costs: if they are high relative to the value of the commodity dealt in, they tend to separate markets geographically, or, at least, to reduce their sensitivity to small changes in demand and supply.

In practice, therefore, the real property market is not one market but is divided into a number of separate markets. Moreover, while some markets are quite distinct (e.g. urban housing and Scottish grouse moors), others are intimately related and overlapping (e.g. houses and shops can be sold for both occupation and investment). Some, where institutional investment demand dominates, are national (even international) in coverage (e.g. offices and prime shop property). Others, where demand is local, tend to be divided geographically into sub-markets (e.g. owner-occupied houses and seaside hotels). Moreover, even within these markets or sub-markets, differences in rent (i.e. price) persist, changes in demand not being fully effective until leases have expired.

Nevertheless, all markets and sub-markets have this in common – the commodity traded in is *real property rights*, even though such rights can take a variety of forms.

(2) *Economic characteristics*
In addition to its physical features, we must examine the market's economic characteristics, particularly as regards the extent to which competition prevails. We have to ask: Is there freedom of entry into the market? Does the market consist of many buyers and sellers, each so small that no one can exert monopsony or monopoly powers?

Generally speaking, there is freedom of entry into real property markets, resulting in many buyers and many sellers. But we must also recognise that certain conditions make it easier for an owner to gain some monopolistic control. Such conditions are: (i) the geographical divisions of the market lead to imperfect competition through local markets; (ii) the imperfection of the capital market may prevent some would-be buyers from borrowing the large sums required for certain purchases, e.g. multi-storey office blocks; (iii) the spatial fixity of real property puts certain site-owners in a strong position relative to a buyer. Consider, for instance, a developer who has purchased every freehold interest except one in a given district. The owner of the outstanding site, realising that his land is essential to the completion of the development, can exploit his monopoly power by demanding a price far in excess of that paid for other similar sites, and so virtually secure all the developer's super-normal profit from the scheme.

Conclusions

Prices are the signals which indicate changes in the conditions of demand and supply. In their turn supply and demand adjust to these signals (see Chapter 3).

Where knowledge of market conditions is defective, the price signals work at less than full efficiency, and adjustments in supply and demand are sluggish. Relatively high costs of dealing, incurred either in obtaining knowledge or in the necessary legal procedures, restrict the extent to which small signals can motivate response. Furthermore, any limitation of the market localises demand and supply, making it easier for imperfect competition to exist.

Our examination of the real property market suggests how it might be improved. Any institution or government action which serves to make knowledge better or more readily available is likely to be beneficial. Under this heading we would include professional associations which prescribe standards of competence in valuers; universities, polytechnics and professional bodies which develop improved methods of valuation; and estate agents, newspapers and journals which advertise current prices. Similarly, any move which reduces the legal costs of transfer can help the market to respond to small changes in price. Thus the government could lay down maximum scale fees for legal work, encourage competition between solicitors, simplify procedures, e.g. through a central land registry, and reduce stamp duties.

Where imperfect competition exists in the market, there is an even stronger case for government intervention. Economic analysis shows that, where a monopoly is set up mainly for marketing purposes, the economies of rationalisation tend to fade into the background. The same applies to real property firms, e.g. land speculators, who seek to secure monopoly selling powers. Thus in our earlier example of a property owner obstructing comprehensive development by demanding a price above the competitive one, the government can use powers of compulsory purchase to overcome the defects of the price mechanism.

We must not overemphasise the barriers in the real property market. Better knowledge can result from the increasing mobility of people and funds, and from the more sophisticated methods of calculating values. And, by and large, prices do respond, albeit somewhat sluggishly, to changes in market conditions; *given sufficient time*, the necessary adjustments to supply and demand do take place. How these adjustments come about through the mechanism of the market will now be examined.

FURTHER READING

R. Barlowe, *Land Resource Economics* (Englewood Cliffs, N.J.: Prentice-Hall, 1958) ch. 7.

E. Fisher and M. Fisher, *Urban Real Estate* (New York: Holt, 1954) chs 9–17.

J. Harvey, *Modern Economics*, 3rd edn (London: Macmillan, 1977) pp. 49–57.

R. Turvey, *The Economics of Real Property* (London: Allen & Unwin, 1957) ch. 1.

A. M. Weimer and H. Hoyt, *Principles of Real Estate*, 4th edn (New York: Ronald Press, 1954) ch. 20.

3

Functions of the Real Property Market

I DEALINGS IN REAL PROPERTY INTERESTS

Classification of interests

While a fuller description of the characteristics of the various types of property interests is given in Chapter 5, it is useful to indicate here the main categories:

(1) *Freeholds* (FHs) involve the holder in the full financial risks of ownership. Thus if rents rise through inflation, a freehold interest provides a hedge against inflation.

(2) *Leaseholds* occur where a freeholder grants a lease for a number of years, during which time he parts with some of his equity interest in exchange for a premium and/or for a regular fixed money income. Thus leaseholds are equivalent to fixed money interest-bearing bonds, though they assume a greater equity interest as the lease nears its reversion date.

(3) *Freehold ground rents* (FGRs) are paid on long leases of undeveloped land. Certainty of payment means that FGRs are similar to an investment in gilt-edged securities.

(4) *Mortgages* are long-term money loans against the security of property. Since interest and capital repayment in money terms are fairly certain, mortgages can be regarded as almost equivalent to debentures and medium-term government bonds.

Who deals in real property interests?

Buyers and sellers of real property can be divided into occupiers and investors.

Occupiers demand property either as a consumer good (e.g. a house, garage, mooring rights), or as a producer good (e.g. a shop, farm, office, factory). As a consumer good, property is wanted for the satisfaction it yields directly, and demand varies with tastes, income, etc. As a producer good, the demand is derived from the contribution it makes to production, and thus depends upon its marginal revenue productivity. It should be noted that occupiers are found in both the private and public sectors.

Thus the Property Services Agency has a portfolio of property for occupation – defence establishments, offices, warehouses, etc. (Chapters 4 and 11 analyse the main factors affecting the occupation demand for different types of property.)

Investors regard property primarily as an alternative to other types of investment asset. But, as we shall see in Chapter 5, investment demand cannot be completely separated from occupation demand. Not only is investment in real property possible because some occupiers prefer to rent rather than to buy their premises, but the amount of rent paid will affect the capital value of the interest.

In discussing the functions of the market we give examples from both occupation and investment dealings since they differ as regards the major considerations affecting demand and supply.

II FUNCTIONS OF THE REAL PROPERTY MARKET

In any market a price of a good is established which reflects current conditions of demand and supply. But the market does more than *indicate*. Because buyers and sellers respond to these price signals, it also *motivates*. In short, the price system functions through the market.

Thus we can break down the functions of the real property market as follows:

(1) *To allocate existing real property resources and interests*

Because land resources are scarce (that is, not unlimited in supply), they have to be allocated between the various uses and people wanting them. This is achieved by arriving at the *equilibrium* market price – the price which equates the resources (or interests) being offered for sale with what people wish to buy. Thus the market reflects preferences and allocates available supply accordingly. The tendency is to assume static conditions in a perfectly competitive market.

Let us illustrate by looking at the market from the point of view of investors. Different people prefer different types of interest. A retired person, for instance, is likely to choose the high and certain income of a FGR. On the other hand, an insurance company which emphasises its 'with-profits' bonuses will want the capital growth associated with freeholds. We can illustrate by means of an 'Edgeworth-box' diagram (see Figure 3.1).

Assume a supply of FGRs equal to OX and of FHs equal to OY. The indifference curves of the retired person are shown by the thinner lines; those of the insurance company (rotated 180°) by the bolder lines. The shapes of these indifference curves reflect the preferences of each as between FGRs and FHs.

FIGURE 3.1

Increased satisfaction
through the exchange
of real property
interests

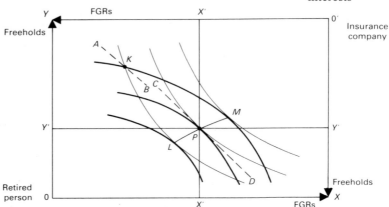

Suppose we start from an initial position K, with the current relative
price at which FGRs exchange for FHs represented by the slope of the
line AB. The insurance company has more FGRs than FHs; the retired
person more FHs.

This will not be an equilibrium market situation. The insurance company values FHs relative to FRGs more highly than the market (as shown
by the slope of AB). It will therefore exchange some of its FGRs for FHs
with the retired person. As it does so, the rate at which FGRs exchange
for FHs falls. Equilibrium will occur on the contract curve at a point
between L and M. This point will be the position where for *both* the
retired person and the insurance company the marginal rate of substitution of FGRs for FHs is equal to the market rate at which FHs exchange
for FGRs. Suppose this rate of exchange is represented by the slope of the
line CD. Then the equilibrium position will be P. Thus exchange in the
market has: (i) allocated supply so that the retired person has OY' FHs
and OX' FGRs, and the insurance company has $O'Y'$ FHs and $O'X'$
FGRs; (ii) made both the retired person and the insurance company
better off since at P each is on a higher indifference curve than at K.

(2) To indicate changes in demand for land resources and interests

If, for instance, house occupiers switch their demand from rented to
owner-occupied houses, this will be shown (see Figure 3.2), other things
being equal, by a relative rise in the price of houses for owner-occupation,
up from OP to OP_1, compared with houses for renting, *down* from OR to
OR_1.

FIGURE 3.2

A change in demand
from rented to
owner-occupied
houses

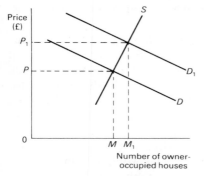

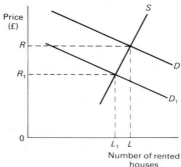

Similarly, in our earlier examples of interests, a relative increase in the demand for the insurance company's 'with-profits' policies would result in it having a greater preference for FHs compared with FGRs. This would be reflected in a change in the slope of its indifference curves (they would become more horizontal), and the new equilibrium position would be at a relatively higher FH price.

Increases or decreases in demand result mainly from changes in:

(a) *Expectations of future yields* resulting from, for example, a change in the price of the final product (where land is a factor of production), a possible switch in government policy (e.g. towards rent control or more restrictive planning), or expected changes in the rate of inflation;

(b) *Taxation*, e.g. tax concessions to owner-occupiers but not to renters, favourable treatment of charities (where relief from income tax leads them to favour high-yield rather than growth assets);

(c) *Income or tastes*, so that a resource or interest becomes more desirable for personal reasons, e.g. more leisure increases the demand for golf courses and fishing facilities;

(d) *Institutional factors*, e.g. the costs of transferring assets may be altered, or funds become more difficult to obtain in an imperfect capital market.

(3) *To induce supply to adjust to changes in demand*

Changes in supply take time, and it is usual to distinguish between the short and the long periods. Since these are discussed in Chapter 4, we shall ignore them for the time being.

The supply of interests in real property can change by:

(a) *Developing real property*, either by the adaptation of existing buildings or by constructing new buildings. Thus, in Figure 3.2(b) as demand switches from rented to owner-occupied houses, the price falls to OR, and supply contracts from OL to OL_1, LL_1 being sold for owner-occupation (expanding supply there by MM_1). Eventually, new equilibrium prices are established, OP_1 in the owner-occupied market and OR_1 in the rented market.

(b) *Changing existing interests*, with no physical alteration in the property. For example, assume that, initially, freeholds are selling at £20,000, whereas similar ninety-nine-year leases are making £16,000 and their FGRs are just over £400. An increase in the demand for freeholds drives up their price to £24,000. Dealers could now buy FGRs and leaseholds separately, marry the two, and make a profit upon sale of the single freehold. As a result, the prices of FGRs and leaseholds (through the increased demand) would rise, and that of freeholds (through the increased supply) would fall. This would continue until a new set of equilibrium prices had been established, say freeholds £22,000, leaseholds £17,000 and FGRs £500. On the other hand, an increase in the demand for leaseholds and FGRs could lead to the division of freeholds.

These amalgamations and separation of interests are continually taking place in all sections of the real property market in response to people's preferences. A property developer, for instance, has often to marry the FGRs and the shop leases on a given site in order to secure the freehold for development. Similarly, an agricultural estate may be formed out of many separate farms. Or a shooting syndicate may purchase or rent the shooting rights from a number of adjacent small farms in order to combine them into a viable shoot. On the other hand, interests may be separated. A property developer may have originally intended to retain the whole of the freehold interest in a development. But a rise in demand, resulting in a higher price for freehold investments, may induce him to sell a part share to an institution, reinvesting the proceeds in a new development.

Of course, such changes take time to complete, and are subject to the imperfections of the real property market. Moreover, it assumes that all interests are divisible and that there is a perfect capital market. Neither is true. Office blocks come in large 'lumps' (though the emergence of property bonds and property unit trusts has helped to overcome this difficulty). Imperfections of the capital market may prevent a full response to preferences regarding interests. Thus a building society may not give a mortgage on a long-lease flat in the centre of a town, the would-be purchaser thereby being forced to go to a modern semi-detached freehold house in the suburbs (see p. 212), or a speculative builder may be short of capital, thereby forcing him to lease the land instead of buying outright.

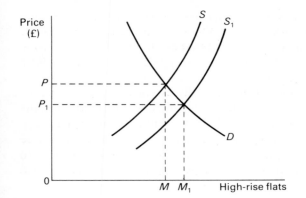

FIGURE 3.3

The effect of a change in the conditions of supply on price

(4) *To indicate changes in the conditions upon which land resources can be supplied*

Improved techniques in constructing high-rise buildings, for example, may make flats cheaper compared with low-rise houses and flats. Thus in Figure 3.3 the supply curve moves from *S* to *S*₁. This is signalled in the market by a fall in the price of high-rise flats from *OP* to *OP*₁.

(5) *To induce demand to respond to changes in the conditions of supply*

As a result of the fall in the price of high-rise flats, demand for them expands from *OM* to *OM*₁ (see Figure 3.3). Demand for low-rise houses therefore decreases from *D* to *D*₁ (see Figure 3.4) with an actual fall of *MM*₁. These changes simply illustrate the fact that prices of substitutes move in the same direction.

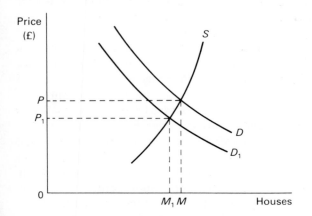

FIGURE 3.4

The response of demand to changes in the conditions of supply

(6) *To 'reward' the owners of land resources*

Rewarding the owners of land resources is a by-product of the market. Such rewards are of two main kinds.

First, there is the return on capital invested. When a person looks for a certain return without risk (e.g. FGRs) then the return corresponds closely with the opportunity cost – what that capital could have earned in the best alternative (e.g. government stock). There is therefore little 'profit' element in such return.

But the yield from a land resource usually extends far into the future. Being a fixed factor the reward on it will depend upon demand. Thus the return is largely in the nature of 'economic rent'. It can be high, e.g. people who own land banks before an increase in demand, or it may be negative, e.g. builders who have bought land banks before a slump. In short, the return, 'supernormal profit', arises because of the risk attached to any fixed factor.

Conclusion

The function of the real property market is to establish a pattern of prices and rents so that, given sufficient time (the long period), land resources are allocated according to their most profitable ('highest and best') use relative to other land resources. This occurs because competition in the market induces owners to switch resources to the use which yields the highest net return. For example, agricultural land is used for housing, a house is divided into flats or changed to offices, and, in time, sites are cleared for redevelopment.

Of course, efficiency of the market economy may be impaired because the conditions stipulated in Chapter 1 do not hold. Thus imperfect knowledge can lead to different forms of pricing – a process of trial and error (as with houses), auction (where a quick sale is sought), or tender (where a property has special features which may appeal to a particular user).

But, given competitive conditions, the creation of different interests in real property is the response to differences in individual preferences. While we have illustrated the argument in terms of the main forms of interest, we must recognise that there are a wide variety of interests meeting individual preferences, e.g. through restrictive covenants. When looked at in this way, we have to acknowledge how well the market performs its task, allowing just a small change in price to reflect individual preferences. In contrast, the state is likely to be rigid, e.g. council-house tenants may not be able to keep a dog or paint the front door to the colour of their own choice even if willing to pay slightly more rent. This leads us to ask, too, how land is to be allocated if taken over by local authorities.

FURTHER READING

R. Barlowe, *Land Resource Economics* (Englewood Cliffs, N.J.: Prentice-Hall, 1958) ch. 12.

J. Harvey, *Modern Economics*, 3rd edn (London: Macmillan, 1977) chs 3–5.

W. Lean and B. Goodall, *Aspects of Land Economics* (London: Estates Gazette, 1966) chs 3, 4.

M. Newell, *An Introduction to the Economics of Urban Land Use* (London: Estates Gazette, 1977) ch. 1.

4

The Pricing of Land and Land Resources

I LAND AS A WHOLE

Undeveloped land, or 'pure' land, refers solely to natural resources and space. Thus land as a *whole*, i.e. the earth's land surface, can be regarded as being fixed in supply. Increasing such land by reclamation from the sea involves so much investment of capital that it is more appropriate to view it as an addition to capital goods rather than to land.

This idea of land as a whole being fixed in supply has been important in past discussions of cost and value. With man-made commodities, including capital goods, price is a function of demand and supply and, in so far as supply is influenced by cost of production, price itself is influenced by cost. But since land as a whole is a fixed supply provided by Nature, the earnings of 'pure' land are determined solely by demand.

Thus in Figure 4.1 *POMN* represents the earnings of land when demand is D, and P_1 *OML* when demand is D_1. In fact, however small the earnings, the total supply of land is still the same. We can say, therefore, that its opportunity cost is zero. Hence all the earnings of land as a whole are an excess over opportunity cost. They represent *economic rent*, that part of the earnings of a factor which results from it having some element of fixity of supply (in economic terms, supply is not perfectly elastic).

Certain points should be noted as regards this general statement:

(1) To say that the earnings of land are a surplus over opportunity cost does not mean that payments do not have to be made for land. Price still performs the vital function of rationing scarce supply among *competing* uses. This is necessary to ensure that, in each location, land is put to its highest and best use according to the preferences of consumers and society.

(2) It follows from (1) that the supply of land can never be regarded as fixed from the *viewpoint of any one use* (unless it can only be used in one way). Additional supplies can always be bid from other uses if the proposed new use has a higher value than the existing use.

(3) Except in the purely technical sense of space, additional supplies of land can always be created in response to additional demand by a more

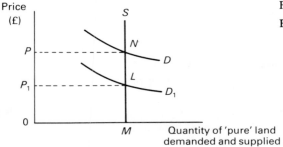

FIGURE 4.1

Economic rent

intensive use of existing land. Points (2) and (3), therefore, should lead us to challenge such loose statements as 'such and such an area is suffering from a land shortage'. What this really means is that some land users (usually the complainants) cannot afford to bid land away from its existing use, e.g. agriculture, to the use they prefer, e.g. houses.

(4) The fact that the earnings of land as a whole are entirely demand-determined is important from the point of view of taxation – land will still be there no matter how high the tax. In other words, a tax on pure land has no disincentive effect on the supply of land. Economic rent can be taxed away entirely. This is the basis of taxes on land, e.g. petroleum revenue tax, development land tax (see Chapter 13).

But two important points should be noted:

(a) Unless all forms of land use are taxed equally, the pattern of land use will be distorted. Whether such distortion is good or bad on balance can only be decided by: (i) a comparison with the inevitable distortions produced by alternative taxes; (ii) its connection with spillover benefits and costs; (iii) one's political views.

(b) Costs of production include normal profit – what is necessary to keep the entrepreneur in the current line of production. But the size of normal profit may be blurred, and taxes may overlap super-normal profit and fall on normal profit. Thus, as first mooted, the petroleum revenue tax was too high, and oil-drilling companies threatened to withdraw from further operations since it cut into the normal profit required to cover the risk involved. The government therefore had to modify its proposals.

II   THE COMMERCIAL RENT OF LAND

Commercial rent is simply a periodic payment for the hire of land. Normally, there is competition for land between the different potential users. The rent of land, therefore, as with other factors of production, is determined, in the absence of any government interference with free-market forces, by the interaction of demand and supply.

Demand

Let us assume that:

(a)   the land under discussion is homogeneous;
(b)   buyers are only interested in maximising private utility or money returns;
(c)   conditions of demand and supply do not change, e.g. as regards sources of raw materials, transport facilities, public utilities, building technology;
(d)   a long-period situation prevails in that firms can vary the quantities of all factors employed; and
(e)   the output at which profits are maximised is known.

Here we are concerned with *occupation* demand, either as a consumer good or as factor of production (see p. 22). We will concentrate on the latter.

In order to maximise profit the equilibrium output must be produced at the minimum possible cost. The demand for land as a factor of production is a *derived demand* – it is wanted for the contribution it can make to a final product. Moreover, it has to be combined with other factors, labour and capital, to produce the goods that are wanted. Thus the quantity of land a firm demands depends upon: (i) its productivity; (ii) its price relative to other factors; and (iii) the price of the final product.

In determining the demand curve for land, therefore, three main problems have to be answered: (1) How does a change in the price of land relative to other factors affect the demand for land? (2) How will a change in the productivity of land in a particular use affect demand? (3) How will a change in the price of the product affect the demand for land in that use?

The isoquant technique can be applied to solving these problems. In Figure 4.2 EP_{10} and EP_{20} are isoquant curves showing all the different combinations of land and capital which will yield outputs of 10 and 20 units of accommodation respectively. According to the profit-maximising output (which we will assume to be EP_{20}), there will be a minimum given outlay on factors of production. Spent wholly on land it would buy OL units; spent wholly on capital it would buy OC units. The slope of the budget line CL indicates the relative prices of land and capital.

The cost-minimising factor combination for the EP_{20} level of output is OM land plus OP capital. Any other combination would yield less than 20 units of accommodation (that is, it would fall below EP_{20}). At A the marginal rate of technical substitution of land for capital equals

$$\frac{\text{Price of land}}{\text{Price of capital}}$$

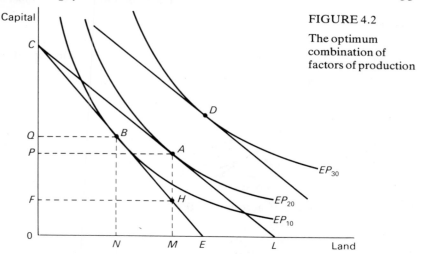

FIGURE 4.2

The optimum
combination of
factors of production

If the profit-maximising output had been EP_{30}, a larger money outlay would have been required, but, given the same land and capital prices, the slope of the outlay curve would remain unchanged. Here the cost-minimising point would be D.

It should be noted that:

(1) If the price of land were to rise so that the same money outlay as before now buys only OE land, it will produce a new budget line CE and a new cost-minimising combination of ON land plus OQ capital. Thus the rise in the price of land has had two effects: (i) more capital is now combined with less land than before; (ii) because less land can be bought with the given outlay, the level of output has been reduced from 20 units to 10 units of accommodation.

(2) An increase in the productivity of land will produce a new isoquant for 20 units, as shown by the dashed line (see Figure 4.3). The same output (20 units) can now be produced for a smaller minimum outlay – the budget line is nearer the origin – by increasing land from OM to OS and by decreasing capital from OP to OR.

(3) The smooth continuity of the isoquant curve denotes that factors are infinitely divisible; as regards land, this means that the homogeneous plots are infinitely small. Moreover, our analysis assumes that the quantity of land can be adjusted. Suppose, however, that when the price of land rises from CL to CE (Figure 4.2) the quantity of land remained at OM. This would produce a new equilibrium position of H (only HM capital could be afforded on the given budget), with a product of something less

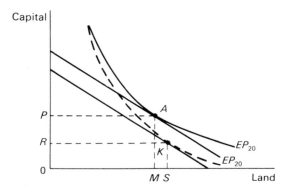

FIGURE 4.3

The effect on the demand for land of an increase in its productivity

than EP_{10} (say 8 units of accommodation) because land is having to be employed too extensively.

(4) Suppose, through an increase in demand, that the price of the standard unit of accommodation rose. The new profit-maximising output would now be larger than EP_{20}, say EP_{30}. At this output more capital and more land would be demanded even at the same relative prices.

We can sum up by saying that a fall in the price of a factor (in this case land) will lead to an extension of demand (the demand curve slopes downwards), while an increase in its productivity or an increase in the price of the product will lead to an increase in demand for the factor (the demand curve moves to the right). The sum of the demand for land of the individual firms will give the industry's demand for land.

The equilibrium market price

As the price for land in a particular use rises, it will be surrendered by less profitable uses. In short, the higher the price, more will usually be supplied; there is an upward-sloping supply curve (see Figure 4.4).

The interaction of demand and supply will give an equilibrium market rent OR for this type of land. Competition will have ensured that at this rent it goes to the highest and best use.

It should be noted that what we have analysed is the determination of the rent of land where there is a homogeneous supply. Non-homogeneous land will now be considered, and in Chapter 6 we examine the price which has to be paid for a *single fixed plot* for development purposes.

Non-homogeneous land and economic rent

In practice, land varies in quality. Thus *agricultural land* differs in fertility, climate, altitude, topography and accessibility to the market.

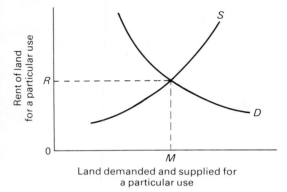

FIGURE 4.4

The determination of the commercial rent of land

Farmers compete for land, being able to offer the difference between the yield from the product less the other costs of production (including normal profit). It is useful to analyse the components of this commercial rent.

Consider a piece of land which produces $2\frac{1}{2}$ tonnes of wheat per acre. There will be less fertile land, but, we will assume, such land will still be used for growing wheat provided it yields $1\frac{1}{2}$ tonnes per acre. This latter land just earns its *transfer cost* – it is said to be marginal as regards wheat-growing. In contrast, the $2\frac{1}{2}$-tonne land yields 1 tonne per acre above the marginal land; this 1 tonne is an *economic rent* resulting from its greater fertility.

The same argument applies to **urban land**. Different characteristics, e.g. accessibility, the physical condition of the site and institutional restrictions (development plans and covenants), give rise to differential rents. Shops in Oxford Street and offices in the City of London all earn a high *economic* rent as a result of the high *commercial* rents which they command. Economic rent accrues to any factor which is fixed in supply, and is determined by demand. Thus if the demand for shops in a district increases, an existing shop let on a lease earns a *profit rent* until the next rent review. This profit rent is economic rent, and can be capitalised in the form of a premium if the lease is sold. Similarly, an owner-occupier who has a house near a city centre obtains a windfall gain (economic rent) should the price of such houses rise as the result of increased demand through higher transport costs.

III THE PRICING OF LAND RESOURCES

Whereas land refers to natural resources, land resources can be defined as 'the total natural and manmade resources over which possession of the earth's surface gives control' (Barlowe, 1958). That is, land resources are

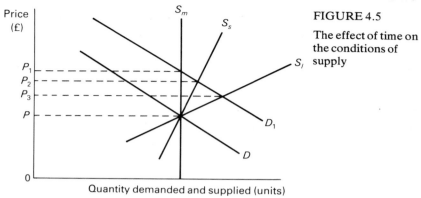

FIGURE 4.5

The effect of time on the conditions of supply

equal to the natural content of land plus any improvements attaching to or incorporated in the land. Indeed, when we talk about a transaction in land, we are usually referring to land resources. In agriculture, for instance, land would include the farmhouse and buildings, the fences and water supply, while a freehold residence is the land plus all the fixtures on the land – the house, conservatory, fishponds, swimming pool, fences, and so on.

In what follows, our study will be largely confined to land resources. What is important from an economic point of view is that while land as a whole has a fixed unalterable supply, capital can be applied to it according to the cost of capital and the expected return.

Supply, price and the time period

Price in the market is determined by demand and supply. In economic analysis it is usual to allow for the fact that changes in supply take time by dividing time into three main periods (see Figure 4.5).

In the 'momentary' period an adjustment of supply is confined to drawing on stocks (S_m). In the 'short period' supply can be altered by engaging more variable factors (S_s). Eventually, however, supply can be increased by adding to fixed capital, thus combining the factors of production in their best proportions (the 'long period', S_l). Thus if demand increases from D to D_1, the price of the product changes from OP to OP_1, OP_2 or OP_3 (corresponding respectively to the above periods).

The relative size of stocks and flows

While not incorrect, the general analysis of the formation of price over time suffers from two main weaknesses when applied to individual goods:

(1) *The time taken to achieve the long-period situation varies considerably.* The full response of supply to a rise in the price of eggs will take about 6 months, for beef $2\frac{1}{2}$ years, and for rubber about 7 years.

With buildings it can be much longer. The various interests in a site required for redevelopment have to be amalgamated (usually by acquiring leases), planning permission has to be obtained and any compulsory purchase orders subjected to time-consuming procedures. This means that, when applying the usual time-period analysis to land resources, we have to recognise that for a considerable period of time we are virtually dealing with a fixed stock. Thus changes in demand will tend to be more significant than changes in supply in determining market price.

(2) *No allowance is made for the size of stocks of existing goods relative to flows of new goods coming on to the market.* With most goods we do not have to pay much attention to this. Because their life is relatively short, existing goods (the stock) have to be replaced frequently by new supplies (the flow over a period). This is true even of consumer durable goods, such as washing-machines, refrigerators and motor-cars.

Take cars, for example. Other things being equal, any increase in the demand for cars will, in a free market, push up the price. Extra imports may help to meet this additional demand. But if manufacturers consider that the higher price is likely to be permanent, they will eventually add to plant so that the supply of cars coming on to the market increases. This flow of new supplies will be significant relative to the supply coming on to the market from existing *stocks*, and will thus be a main determinant, with demand, of price.

But the position is somewhat different with certain goods, e.g. ships, aircraft, and land resources. Because such goods are so durable, stocks of them accumulate over time. As a result, new flows on to the market (additions, say, per annum) are small or insignificant in comparison with the supply to the market coming from existing stocks. As a result, *new* supply has relatively little influence on price; for all practical purposes, supply from old stock dominates the market.

Two qualifications, however, should be made. First, it is the turnover of old stock which is really significant (see p. 38). Second, over the years accumulated flows affect the size of stocks, and have their effect in this way. But the possibility of this is very limited in developed city centres.

Price is therefore largely determined by demand; new supplies follow this price rather than have much influence in determining it. The position is summarised in Figure 4.6 overleaf.

It is worth noting that it is this distinction between the relative size of stocks and flows which is at the heart of the difference between Keynes's theory of the rate of interest and the Classical economists' explanation (see p. 54). For the present we can illustrate from the housing market.

An illustration from housing

Since buildings have a long life, the stock of owner-occupied housing units in the United Kingdom is approximately 11.5 million. The turnover

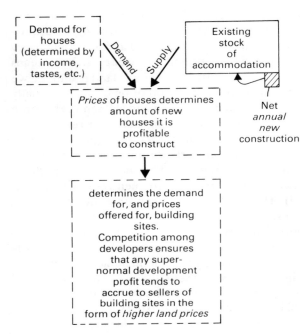

FIGURE 4.6

The dominance of the stock of real property on its price

of this stock (about 5 per cent) is large relative to the flow of *additional* units being produced each year, about 100,000. Indeed, in areas (like Greater London) which are surrounded by a green belt, practically every house coming on to the market is from the existing, and almost fixed, stock of houses.

In such a situation demand determines the price of houses. For example, let us assume an increase in the demand for living accommodation. In the short run existing dwellings are used more intensively, e.g. by a decrease or disappearance of the number of vacant dwellings, an increase in sub-tenancies, a doubling up of families, an increase in the number of persons per room. Eventually, this will cause the prices of owner-occupied houses and rents of existing accommodation to rise.

But since the flow of new houses on to the market is insufficient to affect significantly the supply, this higher price of existing houses will represent the price of *all houses* in the market. Any newly built house which comes on to the market will be sold at the higher price. In other words, the price of new houses is determined by the price at which existing houses sell.

The price paid for land for new housing is thus the residual between what the new house will sell at (determined by the demand for old houses) and what it costs to build, including normal profit. Take, for instance, a builder bidding for a spare site in London on which to erect a house.

Suppose similar old houses are selling for £30,000, and that he estimates that it will cost him £20,000 (including his normal profit) to build. He can therefore afford to bid £10,000 for the land, and indeed will have to if he is to secure it in competition with other builders.

Because houses take time to build, this is a situation which exists in all localities in the short period. Where building land is available, however, the high price offered for existing and, therefore, new houses will encourage builders to erect new houses, and this will continue so long as the cost of new houses is less than the price of old houses. Over time the flow of these new houses on to the market will be sufficient to influence the stock of houses, and the price of old houses will tend to fall. This is most noticeable in districts where the supply of building plots is plentiful, e.g. New Towns, over-flow towns (Swindon, Ashford, etc.) and the fringe land of certain towns where planning permissions have been freely given to permit expansion. In the long period, therefore, these new flows affect the price of old houses, and when the prices of old and new houses coincide the cost of building new houses does affect the price. But it may take a very long time before this situation happens and, where cities are surrounded by green belts which cannot be built on, the price of houses will tend to be dominated by demand.

Corollaries of the above analysis

(1) *Current construction costs are not relevant in determining prices and rents of real property*

Such costs include the price of land, building materials and labour costs, and the cost of builders' borrowing, e.g. on overdrafts.

As regards the price of land, it is sometimes stated, for example, that the high cost of land is responsible for high house prices, thus limiting home ownership. Our analysis gives scant support to this view. An increase in demand for houses causes the price of old houses to rise. This enables builders to bid more for land – up to the difference between what they can sell a new house for (the price of similar existing houses) and the cost of building (including normal profit). Thus, in our example, if the price of houses rose to £50,000 and building costs remained unchanged, £30,000 could now be paid for the land.

Of course, to the individual builder, the price of land is a cost; as with building components, he has to pay the going competitive market rate to obtain it. But the 'individual' view that land prices should be controlled because they are 'bad' puts the cart before the horse. What we have done is to examine the underlying factors – the demand for houses – which determine the price of land from the point of view of builders as a whole.

Empirical support of the above analysis is contained in the *Digest of Building Land Prices 1974* (published by *Estates Gazette* and the House

Builders' Federation). In 1972 the average price paid for land on housing estates was £25,000 an acre. In the last quarter of 1973 it had fallen to £21,000, and builders who had acquired land banks at 1972 prices were showing a loss. The reasons for the fall in land prices were the fall in house prices and the rise in costs. The *Digest* comments that current conditions make it clear 'that land prices are determined by house prices rather than the other way round' – an example of the inductive method of establishing hypotheses as opposed to our deductive method.

Three other points should be noted:

(a) It is the builder's super-normal profit which represents the maximum he can bid for land. Unless this is sufficient to attract land from its next-best use, e.g. agriculture, he cannot build.

(b) Since the price of land is determined by the demand for housing, controlling its price artificially would not result in house prices falling. Instead, the surplus return would simply go to somebody other than the landowner, e.g. the first purchaser or local authorities who acquire land compulsorily at existing use values. Furthermore, it would upset the allocative function performed by market prices, ensuring that scarce land is used for its highest and best use. Artificially low prices, maintained by some form of price control, would lead to a 'wasteful' demand for land in less profitable uses (see pp. 276–7).

(c) As the price of houses rises, land costs form a greater proportion of that price. Thus, in our earlier example, when the house sold for £30,000, the land cost formed one-third of that price; when the house rose to £50,000 through increased demand, the land cost rose to three-fifths.

Similarly, we have to ask whether a rise in *the cost of building materials and labour* will put up the price of houses in the short period. The answer is that, where building land is earning an economic rent (that is, its price is above its 'transfer' or next-best use), a rise in building costs has no effect on the current price of houses. Since the supply of houses comes mainly from existing stock, their price in the market is determined by demand. A rise in building costs therefore simply means that the builder has a smaller margin to bid for the land. Thus, in our original example, had building costs risen by £2,000, his maximum bid for land would have been only £8,000.

Price changes in 1974 support this argument (see Table 4.1). Whereas average construction costs rose by approximately 18 per cent, the price of new dwellings rose by only 6 per cent, and the price of housing land fell. On the other hand, in 1979 the price of new dwellings rose by 32 per cent but the price of housing land rose by 52 per cent.

The effect of a rise in the *rate of interest* must be considered from the viewpoint of both the builder and the house purchaser. On the supply

TABLE 4.1

Index of house prices, land prices and construction costs, 1969–79
(1970 = 100)

	Average price of new dwellings in which building society mortgages were approved, UK	Private-sector housing land at constant average density, England and Wales	Average construction cost in tenders approved for local authorities, England and Wales
1969	94	91	—
1970	100	100	100
1971	113	113	—
1972	114	190	—
1973	206	295	181
1974	219	293	213
1975	239	203	235
1976	259	204	248
1977	285	214	279
1978	330	244	322
1979	437	371	371

Source: *Housing and Construction Statistics.*

side, the builder has to pay more for his overdraft, but this will affect only what he can bid for the land, not the house price. It is on the demand side that the rise in the rate of interest has the major effect – the higher cost of borrowing on mortgages leads to a decrease in demand, and thus the price of houses will tend to fall! Thus the rise in the building society mortgage rate from 9 per cent to 12 per cent in 1973 and the scarcity of building society loans led to a decrease in demand which brought the boom in house prices of the previous two years to an end.

(2)   *A tax may be imposed on the economic rent of land resources*
Since, in practice, the short period tends to be very long, the government can impose a tax on land resources up to the level of economic rent they earn since this will make no difference to their supply. It should be noted, however, that land resources include capital. If the tax should be so large as to overlap on the transfer earnings of capital or on normal profit, further building will not take place. This was probably the situation in 1974 when uncertainty regarding the 1973 development gains tax brought property development virtually to an end, and this was prolonged by the falling off in the demand for property.

(3)   *Developers can be required to cover some of the social costs of projects*
A different type of 'tax' may be imposed. So long as it does not cut into normal profit, a local authority can, as a condition of planning permission,

require developers to include in their schemes either houses (although these are less profitable than offices) or improvements to the infrastructure, e.g. sewers. The first is largely on political-social grounds; the second can be regarded as covering some of the social costs of the scheme.

(4)   *An increase in transport costs will increase economic rents at the city centre*

Increased transport costs will make houses on the periphery of a city a poorer substitute for houses at the centre. This will diminish the extent to which the increase in new flows of houses can be significant compared with the existing stock. Thus the difference in economic rent between the centre and the periphery will increase as house and therefore land prices rise at the centre, and will tend to persist.

FURTHER READING

R. Barlowe, *Land Resource Economics* (Englewood Cliffs, N.J.: Prentice-Hall, 1958) ch. 6.

J. Harvey, *Modern Economics*, 3rd edn (London: Macmillan, 1977) ch. 18.

J. Harvey and M. K. Johnson, *Introduction to Macro-economics* (London: Macmillan, 1971) ch. 10.

M. Newell, *An Introduction to the Economics of Urban Land Use* (London: Estates Gazette, 1977) ch. 15.

5

Investment in Real Property

While real property can be demanded primarily for occupation purposes (see p. 22), it can also be held as an asset for storing wealth over time. It is in this sense that we use the term 'investment' in what follows.

The broad objectives of investment are to preserve or enhance the real value of the asset and to receive a flow of income over time. We therefore begin by describing in outline the extent to which different interests in real property fulfil these objectives, and the priorities of the main investing groups.

I INVESTMENT CHARACTERISTICS OF DIFFERENT INTERESTS IN REAL PROPERTY

As we saw in the previous chapter, different interests in real property really represent different bundles of rights. However, they can be classified according to their broad *investment* characteristics as follows:

(1) *Freeholds*
The holder of a freehold, whether occupier or investor, takes the full financial risk of ownership. If rents increase, e.g. through inflation, he gains, whether he is an owner-occupier or an insurance company regarding the property as an investment. A freehold is therefore equivalent to the ordinary share in a company: it is an 'equity' interest.

Freeholds are usually let on a lease, the owner receiving a periodic rent and reversion at the end of the lease. But to obtain the full equity interest there must be frequent rent reviews; otherwise it resembles more closely a leasehold interest.

Freehold investments usually involve some management, e.g. collecting the rent and ensuring that the tenant observes his repairing and insuring obligations and other terms of the lease. Indeed, the lessor may be responsible for some maintenance. All these costs have to be deducted from the rent received to obtain the net income.

Like ordinary shares, freeholds differ in yield. The yield depends upon: (i) the purchase price; (ii) the current rent; (iii) the prospect of future rent rises as a result of increased demand for the type of property or of inflation; (iv) the frequency of rent reviews; (v) the type and condition of the property; (vi) the strength of the occupier's covenant; (vii) management costs; (viii) estimates of future changes in government policy, e.g. as regards rent freezes, depreciation allowances; and (ix) development possibilities.

As with ordinary shares, there is a reverse yield gap with freeholds – for first-class properties the yield is less than the current yield of long-dated government securities (see p. 61). This implies that purchasers of freeholds are expecting the difference to be made up by future increases in rent and thus in the capital value.

Yields on prime properties, e.g. city-centre shops (4 per cent) and first-class offices (6 per cent), are low. This is because the demand for such interests by institutional investors is keen, and they have the funds necessary for expensive acquisitions. On the other hand, private persons have to consider the less expensive secondary properties. Nor can they overcome the difficulty by borrowing, since insurance companies and merchant banks are reluctant to lend against secondary property. The result is that such properties are sold on a much higher yield – 10 to 16 per cent. Indeed, since the collapse of the property market in 1974, there has tended to be a dichotomy between the prime and secondary markets, the former being active in response to institutional demand, the latter remaining sluggish.

In practice, yields differ slightly on the different types of freehold property. Thus prime shops have a lower yield than offices, while the latter's yield tends to be less than that on industrial and residential properties. We can explain this by considering the characteristics of the main types of property.

(a) *Shops*. With shops, location is all-important in determining yield. Generally speaking the best High Street positions are occupied by the multiples, their values being enhanced by complementarity with one another. The main reasons for the low yield on prime shops are:

(i)   the supply of such sites is limited by purely spatial considerations;

(ii)   multiples, the fastest-growing outlet of the retail trade, are willing to pay high rents for these sites;

(iii) the goods sold have a high income elasticity of demand, thereby ensuring growth in turnover; and

(iv)   the institutions seek such investments because occupiers have excellent covenants and the rental rate of growth has been the highest for all types of urban development.

Even a short distance from the prime shopping location rents fall off considerably. Moreover, potential rent growth is not nearly so good. Hence yields on secondary shops are in the region of 10 per cent.

(b) *Offices.* The low yield on office blocks is mainly the result of the preference for them by institutional investors. Increasing demand for office accommodation, especially when it is modern and air-conditioned, has increased the prospects of rising rents, provided there are periodic rent reviews. Moreover, a large block can often be let to a single tenant responsible for repairs, thereby reducing management costs.

(c) *Industrial factories and warehouses.* Until recently industrial premises have been less popular as investments than other types of property. The reasons are:

  (i)   rents tend to be affected more by economic depression;
  (ii) many factories are built for a special purpose, and if they have to be relet difficulty may be experienced in finding a similar tenant, or, alternatively, expense is incurred in adaptation;
  (iii) changes in techniques of production and handling goods can make the factory obsolete, e.g. greater height may be required for fork-lift stacking in a warehouse; and
  (iv) the intensive use of industrial premises leads to more rapid depreciation than with other properties, though tax reliefs give some compensation.

The result is that the current yield on industrial premises is 7–12 per cent. Nevertheless, there are indications that newly built factories are becoming more popular as investments. Such premises are of simple construction, on the ground floor only, have large clear spaces, roof lighting and office accommodation attached, and are easily adapted to different uses. Furthermore, they can be written off as depreciation for tax purposes, and may carry special tax allowances. Surveys by Percy Bilton, industrial property developers, show that whereas office rents in the Greater London area rose 231 per cent from 1966 to 1976 industrial rents increased by 292 per cent.

(d) *Residential.* For a number of reasons residential property usually shows the highest yield:

  (i)   rent control has meant that rent increases have lagged well behind the rate of inflation;
  (ii) costs of management, e.g. through frequent rent collection from many different tenants, tend to be relatively high; and
  (iii) the cost of repairs, for which the landlord is usually responsible, tend to be heavy, partly because many properties are old, and partly because of inflation.

However, yields on this type of property may be kept down by the long-term possibilities of obtaining vacant possession and government relaxation of rent control.

(e) *Rural estates.* In Britain the two main types of tenure for farms are tenant farming and owner-occupation.

Where a rural estate is let for farming, the landowner (investor) usually provides fixed capital (e.g. buildings, roads and drainage), while the tenant provides movable capital (e.g. implements, livestock, fertilisers) and labour. But there are no rigid rules. With complete freedom of contract the arrangement reached would be the one that maximised the joint earnings of the two parties. In practice, ignorance, inertia and even obstinacy of one party may reduce free bargaining.

Tenant farming, once predominant, has declined markedly since 1945, and today accounts for less than 50 per cent of all holdings in England and Wales. The Agricultural Holdings Act 1948 made it difficult to end a tenancy. and the right of succession was extended to relatives working on the farm by the Agriculture (Miscellaneous Provisions) Act 1976. While a revision of rentals is possible every three years, they remain somewhat below the free-market level. Investors' income is therefore low, and many farms have gone to owner-occupiers.

Even so, most institutions hold some farmland in their investment portfolios since it has proved an excellent hedge against inflation. In addition, rich individuals and farming and investment companies all retain investments in agricultural land. Between 1956 and 1979 first-class agricultural land increased in price twentyfold from £100 to £2,000 an acre. This capital appreciation has been the result of buoyant demand brought about by:

   (i)   rising prices of agricultural products;
   (ii)   the appreciation in the value of additional sources of income, e.g. woodlands, mineral workings, sporting rights, which now form part of the total investment value of an estate;
  (iii)   the prospect of possible urban development, though this is of less importance with the coming of development land tax;
  (iv)   owners who have sold land for development at very high prices have reinvested the proceeds in farmland to take advantage of the 'roll-over' concession for capital gains tax;
   (v)   when Britain joined the EEC British farmland was cheap compared with prices in other EEC countries;
  (vi)   a lower rate of capital transfer tax for working farmers, and, in 1976, for investors in farmland;
  (vii)   the social standing which land ownership gives in a rural community, and the satisfaction of walking round a rural estate compared with a block of offices; and
 (viii)   a new demand for agricultural estates from farming and investment companies, insurance companies, pension funds, property bonds and trusts, all of whom may farm directly through a manager.

All the factors mentioned in Chapter 2 which differentiate real property investments from other investments are accentuated in the rural estate market: (i) not only is each estate unique in its size and position, but it differs in topography and fixed capital; (ii) the rural estate market is highly localised; and (iii) many estates change hands by private treaty and therefore at undisclosed prices, with demand being influenced by non-economic factors, such as family considerations. Thus the rural estate market tends to be imperfect.

Nor is there any exact analogy between rural estates and stocks and shares as investments. The landlord does not receive a share in the profits, but, rather, obtains a rent which is more akin to the interest on debentures. If agriculture is prosperous, he may be able to secure an increase in rent; if depressed, he may allow the rent to accumulate or grant a rebate. Basically he is concerned with capital security rather than income.

(2) *Leaseholds*

A freeholder has either to occupy the premises himself or rent them out to somebody else. The usual practice is to grant a lease for a fixed number of years in return for a capital sum (a 'premium'), or a rent, or a combination of both. These leases have value and can be exchanged in the market.

At the end of the given period the property reverts to the freeholder. Then the value of the lease to the lessee is zero. This means that if the purchaser of a lease is to maintain his capital intact, a part of the income has to be set aside to replace his capital. Such amortisation has to come out of income after tax has been paid. As a result, yields on leaseholds tend to be higher than yields on comparable freeholds. Thus, because they pay no tax on income, pension funds and charities find leaseholds advantageous (see p. 50).

(3) *Freehold ground rents*

Freehold ground rents (FGRs) refer to the annual payments received on long leases. Originally they were mostly charged on land leased for development, but they are now received for flats sold on long leases. Since they are small relative to the full value of the developed site upon which they are secured, FGRs are almost as gilt-edged as government securities. But, being less liquid, they have a somewhat higher yield. Indeed, if some management is involved, as with FGRs on flats, the current yield is around 20 per cent.

Because of inflation, the recent tendency for freeholders granting long leases is to require revision of the ground rent at the end of stipulated periods.

When reversion is less than fifty years, FGRs increasingly assume
equity characteristics. The reversionary value will tend to rise according
to the likely income on reversion, the security of the current ground rent,
and the current rate of interest. The price of a FGR will also tend to be
higher if it has a special value to a particular person, e.g. the current lessee
of the property or a property developer who wishes to assemble land for
future development.

(4) *Mortgages*

Mortgages are long-term money loans secured on real property, with
interest payments being prior charges. Thus the risk of non-payment of
capital or of interest is small. Unlike leaseholds, capital is repaid, and so
no sinking fund is necessary. In effect, therefore, mortgages are similar to
debentures or government bonds, and their yields tend to move together.

II   INVESTORS IN REAL PROPERTY

Investment in real property is carried out by private persons, private
trusts and the institutions – insurance companies, pension funds,
charities, property companies, property bond funds and property unit
trusts. To some extent each has different objectives, and so their preferences differ.

(1)   *Private persons*

Anybody who purchases a property rather than renting is an investor.
The satisfaction or return received should at least equal what could be
obtained if, instead, premises were rented and the money invested
elsewhere. For example, a person may rent rather than buy a shop either
through lack of capital or because he considers the money can be more
profitably employed in carrying stock, etc.

Owner-occupiers, e.g. shop-owners, farmers and householders, are
holding wealth in the form of real property. They enjoy a full equity
interest – income or satisfaction from the use of their property, and
normally a hedge against inflation.

Other private persons investing in real property usually only have
limited funds. Thus their direct investment tends to be restricted to
dwellings and secondary shops. Indirectly, however, they can invest in
prime shops and offices by buying property bonds or shares in property
companies.

(2)   *Insurance companies*

By and large, life-insurance companies try to match assets to future
liabilities, and this largely determines the spread of their portfolios as

between short- and long-term fixed-interest investments and equity holdings.

The post-war trend of insurance companies' asset holdings has been away from fixed-interest securities towards ordinary shares and property (see Table 5.1). In order to give endowment and life-insurance policies an 'inflation-hedge', companies introduced 'with-profits' policies. As a result, they increased their holding of property, chiefly in first-class office blocks. Most property is acquired by direct purchase, but because of a shortage of the right type of property many institutions now participate directly in development, usually in conjunction with development companies, property companies and construction firms.

TABLE 5.1

Changes in the distribution of assets of insurance companies and superannuation funds, 1968–78

	Assets (% of total)			
	Insurance companies		Superannuation funds	
	1968	*1978*	*1968*	*1978*
Short-term assets	1.4	6.0	1.7	4.3
Government securities	26.9	27.0	20.4	21.8
Ordinary shares	22.4	28.0	53.2	44.2
Preference shares and debentures	19.2	5.7	12.5	9.0
Loans and mortgages	15.8	6.9	4.0	1.6
Land, property and ground rents	10.3	19.7	6.0	17.1
Other assets	4.0	6.7	2.2	2.0
TOTAL	100.0	100.0	100.0	100.0

Source: *Financial Statistics.*

For various reasons insurance companies find it advantageous to own properties directly rather than through shares in property companies:

(a)   direct investment in property gives the company more control than an investment in property company shares;

(b)   a substantial holding of the shares of a property company (necessary to exercise some control) may be more difficult to dispose of than a first-class building;

(c)   the prices of buildings have tended to be less volatile than the prices of property company shares, an important consideration for insurance companies facing tighter regulations regarding solvency margins;

(d)   the high gearing of a property company is of little advantage to an insurance company which always holds part of its assets in fixed money terms; and

(e)   holding shares in a property company represents an inefficient way to invest in property since 52 per cent corporation tax is deducted from profits attributable to dividend, whereas the insurance company pays a lower tax rate on life income.

Insurance companies still hold a part of their assets in mortgages on property as an alternative to fixed-interest-bearing stock. Mortgages are also given on residential property, with these tending to grow whenever building societies' lending is restricted. Here the main attraction of mortgage lending is the endowment insurance business which it brings (see p. 209).

(3)   Pension funds
Pension funds now compete strongly with insurance companies and property companies for first-class properties. Not only does property's inflation-hedge help to retain the real value of the accumulated pension funds but tax advantages make the high yield of leaseholds attractive.

The smaller pension funds invest in property indirectly through *pension fund property unit trusts*, where the trust deed limits membership to pension funds and charities which enjoy tax exemption. Such trusts afford the advantages of property investment without management problems. The larger funds, however, prefer to purchase and manage their own properties. The disadvantage of holding shares in property companies is even greater for pension funds than for insurance companies since pension funds do not pay tax on income or capital gains.

(4)   Charities and trusts
Charities and trusts are concerned not only with income (from which periodic distributions are made) but also with retaining the real value of the trust funds. Thus they cannot invest entirely in high-yielding securities the tax implications of which are especially beneficial but have to maintain a part of their portfolio in equities and property. Thus the Church Commissioners, who pay clergy stipends from investment income, must endeavour to preserve the real value of that income. They therefore hold equity interests including property and farmland.

Unlike most institutional investors, charities receive little 'new' money for investment each year. They are therefore constantly reviewing their existing portfolios to see what possible adjustments could best serve their beneficiaries, both present and future.

(5)   *Property companies*

Property investment and development companies have grown considerably since 1945, largely reflecting the boom in urban redevelopment which lasted until 1972. Most tend to be highly geared, their capital consisting of a high proportion of loans to ordinary shares. Properties owned provide the security against borrowing, while interest charges are covered by regular rents. High gearing is beneficial to the few ordinary shareholders when profits are good, while it is easier for them to retain control.

The larger companies tend to specialise in office blocks or prime shop property, and a few (e.g. Slough Estates) in industrial property. Residential property is confined mainly to smaller companies, many of which engage in 'break-up' operations, selling houses and flats to sitting tenants or, when vacant possession is obtained, to owner-occupiers.

Nevertheless, it is doubtful whether the present structure of property companies can survive. As already pointed out, their tax rate on rental income and capital gains is higher than for many institutions. The tendency is therefore for institutions to invest directly in property. Moreover, in order to acquire the first-class property which is in such short supply, the institutions could purchase property companies, wind them up and then manage their properties directly.

It therefore seems that the only property companies with a long-term future are:

(a)   those concerned mainly with property development and which sell completed developments;
(b)   combined construction/property companies, which counteract a downturn in demand for construction work by initiating their own projects; and
(c)   those which are unattractive to the institutions because their portfolios consist mainly of secondary properties or because they are existing precariously on short-term or foreign borrowings.

(6)   *Property bond funds*

The person wishing to invest in property is faced with the snag of having insufficient funds to buy prime property, the kind which has shown the greatest capital growth. A comparatively recent innovation, the *property bond fund*, partly succeeds in overcoming this difficulty. Subscribers buy a number of units in a property bond fund (e.g. Abbey Life Property Fund, Hambro Property, City of Westminster Property) which invests money in first-class property. Thus Abbey Life, the largest of the property funds, has over £200 million invested in offices, shops and industrial property in the major cities of Britain, and also in Belgium, Holland, France and

West Germany. Agricultural estates are also held. In this way the holder of property bonds has a wide spread in first-class property, with the value of the bonds varying directly with the value of the property held.

In conjunction with their agents, these funds take an active interest in the management of their properties. These are revalued at fixed intervals, often monthly. To make the bonds more attractive and to secure tax advantages, they are usually linked to life assurance.

(7)   *Property unit trusts*

A similar principle operates with those unit trusts which specialise in property (e.g. Ebor Property Share, Slater–Walker Property Share). But in order to avoid management commitments, such unit trusts use their funds to buy shares in property companies or in companies such as hotels which are concerned with property.

(8)   *Building societies*

Building societies can be regarded as institutional investors since they are the most important source of loans for house purchase. Their activities are analysed in Chapter 12.

As we shall see, demand for property as an investment asset has a considerable effect on its capital value and, through this, influences the supply of different types of property. Two initial questions have to be dealt with. First, what determines the over-all level of yield on investment assets in general? Second, what determines the level of yield on the different types of real property assets? Having answered these questions, we can examine the influence of investment demand on the functioning of the market.

III   CHANGES IN THE YIELD ON INVESTMENT ASSETS IN GENERAL

At different times all asset yields move in the same direction; it seems that the 'bench-mark' upon which they are based rises or falls. The question we have to answer, therefore, is: How is this bench-mark determined?

Alternative ways of holding assets

People can hold wealth in many different forms – money, bonds, debentures, shares, land, houses, paintings or antiques. All except money yield either a flow of income or direct satisfaction.

On the other hand, only money is perfectly liquid: that is, it can be changed into some other form without delay, cost or possible capital loss.

FIGURE 5.1

Alternative forms of holding assets

Money	Building society deposits	Treasury Bills	Debentures and mortgage loans secured on real property	Irredeemable bonds and freehold ground rents with distant reversions	FGRs with early reversions	Shares in companies	Freeholds

The yield forgone by holding money is thus the opportunity cost of being perfectly liquid.

Questions of risk apart, a person will arrange his 'portfolio' of assets according to the emphasis he puts on liquidity as opposed to yield. If he wants complete liquidity, he will hold money; if he prefers some return, he holds other assets. There is a whole spectrum of assets to choose from. Figure 5.1 shows some examples.

In order to eliminate complications arising because assets differ in liquidity and risk, it is assumed that the only asset other than money is undated, fixed-interest government bonds. This gives us a model in which there are only two kinds of asset in which wealth may be held – money and bonds (see Figure 5.2).

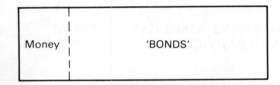

FIGURE 5.2

Holding wealth as an alternative between money and 'bonds'

The determination of the price of 'bonds'

Let us assume that, at any time, there is a given stock of money and a given stock of bonds available for holding as assets. This stock of money will equal the total supply of money (cash and bank money) in the economy less the amount demanded by persons and businesses for normal buying and selling operations.

Now the price of bonds, as with other commodities, is expressed in terms of money. And, in our simple asset market, equilibrium will occur where, given the stock of money and of bonds and the preferences of the public for holding one or the other, a money price of bonds is established at which the public is willing to hold just the amount of bonds and money available. At any other price there would be no equilibrium. If, for example, the bond market price were below the equilibrium price, demand would exceed supply. In other words, there would still be some people preferring to hold money rather than bonds. As they switched, the price of bonds would rise until nobody wished to switch further. This would be the equilibrium price.

It should be noted that the equilibrium price of bonds can be viewed as the equilibrium rate of interest (yield) on bonds since the two are directly and inversely related. A 5 per cent bond (i.e. one paying annual interest of £5 per £100 nominal value) will in fact be yielding a return of 10 per cent if its price on the market falls to £50. Conversely, should the price rise to £125, the bond rate of interest would fall to 4 per cent.

This simple model explains the determination of the rate of interest, the 'bench-mark' for yields on the whole spectrum of assets. It should be noted that it is a 'stock' rather than a 'flow' theory. The justification for this is that neither the stock of money nor the stock of bonds is subject to great variations except over considerable periods of time. The supply of money is controlled by the government; the flow of bonds (new issues by borrowers) is small compared with the existing stock of old bonds. Current borrowing will therefore have little effect on the 'bench-mark' rate of interest. It is therefore the supply from the existing stock of bonds, together with demand, which determines the price of bonds at any one time. The price at which new issues are offered is determined by the current price at which old bonds are being traded. The situation is parallel to that of the housing market (see pp. 37–9).

IV   THE YIELD ON DIFFERENT ASSETS AND ON REAL PROPERTY ASSETS IN PARTICULAR

The structure of interest rates and asset prices

We can now relax the assumption of a single income-bearing asset, bonds. In real life, wealth can be held in a range of assets differing in lender's risk, income yield and liquidity.

Lender's risk may relate to income or capital. A very short-term investment (say, in a Treasury Bill with only a few weeks to repayment) will be almost completely riskless so far as capital is concerned but will provide no guarantee that the money repaid can be reinvested to obtain the same income yield, since short-term rates of interest may have fallen in the meantime. In short, such an asset would be capital-certain but income-uncertain. On the other hand, a long-term investment yielding a fixed money return (e.g. a FGR) is income-certain but capital-uncertain, since its market value will fall if interest rates generally should rise. Other assets such as shares in speculative mining concerns or in companies concerned with speculative development (e.g. hotels along the North African coast) may be both income-uncertain and capital-uncertain.

Given stocks of such varied assets (including money), what will be the condition of equilibrium? Depending on: (i) the expected income yield; (ii) the degree of risk as regards income and capital; (iii) liquidity (ease and cost of marketing); and (iv) the asset preferences of the general public with respect to (i), (ii) and (iii), the answer is suggested in our simple money and bonds model. There will be some equilibrium pattern of asset prices and associated yields such that, after taking into account dealing costs, nobody feels he can gain by switching between assets. With any other pattern some switching will be profitable and prices will change until there is equilibrium.

Real property assets can be slotted into this asset structure. Like the investor in stocks and shares, investors in real property will examine an estate or interest for the possibility of growth of income, capital gain, income risk or capital risk. The relative prices of property interests will also be affected by marketability and transfer costs. As we have seen, different interests vary in their appeal to different investors. Thus, other things being equal, a high marginal rate income-taxpayer will be attracted more by prospective capital gains (e.g. on agricultural land) than by income (e.g. on FGRs) since capital gains carry a lower rate of tax. On the other hand, a charity, not subject to income tax, will put less emphasis on the prospect of capital gains.

Thus a more realistic model of an asset market would be:

> Money (M)
> Treasury Bills (T)
> Debentures or bonds with a fixed repayment date (D)
> Irredeemable bonds (B)
> Ordinary shares (S)
> Mortgage loans secured on real property (Mo)
> Leasehold investments (L)
> Freeholds (FH)
> Freehold ground rents (FGR)

Depending on (i) income yield, capital risk and liquidity characteristics, (ii) the relative stocks of each asset, and (iii) people's asset preferences, an equilibrium pattern of asset prices will emerge.

Deductions from the model

We can deduce a number of propositions from this model:

(1) Since money is included in the asset pattern, any change in the economy's total supply of money, unaccompanied by a compensatory change in the transactions demand for money, will alter M. It will thus have a disequilibrating effect on the existing pattern of asset prices.

Suppose the monetary authorities were to increase the over-all supply of money in the economy by open-market operations. If they buy Treasury Bills, M increases and T decreases; if they buy bonds, M increases and B decreases. In both cases the pattern of asset prices and yields is affected. Thus if the monetary authorities buy Treasury Bills, their yield will fall, and consequent switching operations will reduce all short-term rates. The prices of longer-term assets are also likely to be affected, though the speed and extent of the change will depend on market expectations. If the fall in short-term rates is expected to be reversed in the near future, there will be little profit in switching to long-term securities. In these circumstances prices of short-term assets may rise considerably without inducing much change in long-term asset prices. On the other hand, if the change in short-term rates is regarded as a shift by the monetary authorities towards a permanent lower level of short-term rates, switching operations will be more pronounced, and long-term asset prices will rise in sympathy.

Thus expectations, and uncertainty with regard to them, blur the edge of any formal analysis of the asset market – which is why personal success in the capital market depends as much on flair as on the application of scientific principles. Consider freehold investments as an example. To an investor, a freehold investment has two main aspects – the rent income and a 'growth' element depending on prospects of future increases in rent and capital value. Should monetary policy cause short-term interest rates to rise, the yield factor alone would dictate some switching out of freehold investments, bringing yields into line. But such selling is unlikely if expectations of growth are strong. Such expectations may be due to inflation, and if people think that the monetary authorities' raising of short-term rates is unlikely to be effective in controlling inflation, the prices of freeholds could be pushed up: that is, freehold yields may fall even though short-term rates are rising.

(2) The equilibrium pattern of prices will be affected by people's expectations of income from the various assets and their estimate of future capital appreciation. Thus when the Indians sold Manhattan, New York, to the white settlers in 1626 for $24 it was for them a profitable investment switch having regard to income and capital appreciation. On the latest estimates the site values of Manhattan Island are today worth $12 billion. But if the Indians had invested the $24 in an investment yielding 6 per cent per annum, and had allowed the income to accumulate over the past 350 years, that investment would now be worth $17 billion.

Similarly, an institution investing in a freehold showing a current yield of 6 per cent with five-year rent reviews must anticipate a compound growth in rent of 8.35 per cent per annum over twenty years to match a current return of 13.65 per cent on undated $2\frac{1}{2}$ per cent Consols.

People's attitude to risk will also affect the pattern of asset prices. Thus prices in a market dominated by widows and orphans seeking income-certain investments (e.g. government stock) will be different from one dominated by speculative investors primarily interested in capital gains (e.g. shares in oil-prospecting companies).

(3) It is unrealistic, indeed misleading, to separate investments in real property from other investments. Although real property assets may incur extra costs of acquisition and management, they are not a homogeneous group of assets different from other assets in the market. Thus investors seeking income stability and certainty will regard FGRs and bonds as good substitutes for each other, while investors looking for capital-growth prospects will see more affinity between shares and freeholds than between shares and debentures. In other words, it is more informative to regroup our assets as follows:

$$[M \quad T \quad \textbf{Mo}] \qquad [D \quad \textbf{L}] \qquad [B \quad \textbf{FGR}] \qquad [S \quad \textbf{FH}]$$

where the bracketed groups each contain close substitutes, and the *real property assets* (in bold type) are interspersed in the portfolio pattern.

In real life the above assets would vary considerably even within particular categories, leaseholds, for instance, having different maturity times.

(4) Because all assets are, in varying degrees, substitutes for one another, a change at any point affects the equilibrium pattern and will result in switching until equilibrium is restored.

The extent of the change will vary according to the degree of substitution, close substitutes experiencing a greater movement than poor substitutes. For example, a switch from irredeemable government bonds to ordinary shares offering prospects of capital gain will not only lead to a fall in the price of bonds but also the price of, say, FGRs with distant reversions. Similarly, the rise in the price of ordinary shares will be extended to freeholds since these, too, are likely to be affected by factors making for capital growth.

The prices of intermediate assets will move in sympathy according to their substitutability, on the one hand for government bonds, and on the other for ordinary shares. Eventually a new equilibrium pattern of asset prices will be established where there are no opportunities for profitable switching. Of course, this consistency does not imply equality of interest yields and prices. Differing risks, investors' asset preferences and cost of switching will all be reflected in the final equilibrium pattern of prices and yields.

The complete investment decision

So far we have looked at interests in property as investments competing with other types of assets. But having decided on his broad strategy, an investor has to consider the detailed attributes of *similar* investment assets. Thus those who have decided to invest in ordinary shares must weigh up the respective merits of different companies. Furthermore, they must also suit their particular requirements, by choosing between high-yielding shares and those offering likely capital appreciation. Similarly, if freeholds are preferred, a choice has to be made between the different properties being offered on the market.

Thus portfolio management consists not only of switching between different types of investment in general but also between particular investments within the same class.

The role of flows on to the asset market

After a disequilibrating event equilibrium in our 'stock' model of an asset market was restored solely by switching operations. This was justified because the size of the stock of old securities dominates any new flows.

In practice, however, we must recognise that flows are continually coming on to the market in the form of new borrowing (which necessitates the issue and sale of new financial assets). This has two effects. First, flows tend to reinforce the switching of *existing* assets to restore an equilibrium pattern. This is because any additional supply of new financial claims through borrowing will tend to come from those sectors currently favoured by investors. Second, over a very long period of time, flows on to the market have a cumulative effect on the size of the stock, and thus affect the yield in the long term.

The effect of imperfections in the asset market

In a perfect asset market:

(a)   there would be complete knowledge of prices and opportunities prevailing in every part of the market;

(b)   there would be no barriers, such as dealing costs or day-to-day management obligations, to hamper switching operations or the form new flows (borrowing) should take;

(c)   assets would be so divisible that they could be bought by many buyers each having a small amount of funds; and

(d)   investors would act solely on the basis of financial gain.

Given these conditions, the asset market would be a single market in which an equilibrium pattern of prices and yields would be established reflecting the size of the stock of different types of asset relative to investors' preferences.

In practice, perfection is not realised. Thus the denominations in which Treasury Bills are issued mean that they can only be purchased by the institutions. In addition, there are the costs of purchasing and selling assets, e.g. stamp duty, broker's commission, transfer stamp, etc.

With real property assets imperfections of the market are even greater (see Chapter 2). As a result, the prices of many real property assets, e.g. freeholds and leaseholds, may respond only very sluggishly to a change in another part of the asset market. Above all, certain characteristics of real property present barriers to investors in moving from stock market assets. Thus, although Table 5.2 below shows a correlation over time between yields on real property and other assets, those of the former tend to be higher than those of the latter. For instance, FGRs show a higher yield than long-term government bonds, while the yield of multiple shops is higher than that of ordinary shares except when the stock market is disturbed by special events or when the rate of inflation is high.

The main characteristics of real property interests which make for these higher yields are:

(1) They are *less liquid*, as there is no central market comparable with the Stock Exchange.
(2) They are *less homogeneous*, so that the services of a valuer and solicitor are required, and transactions take time to complete while the title to the property is investigated.
(3) They are often *not divisible* into small and uniform units, thereby excluding direct purchase by the small investor.
(4) Most interests *require management*, a function outside the experience and time of many investors. To pay for the services of an agent, a higher yield is required.
(5) Real estate is subject to specific legislation (e.g. rent controls, planning requirements) which may increase transactions costs and uncertainty regarding expected income.

V ASSET YIELDS OVER TIME: AN EMPIRICAL STUDY

The model

The previous section has developed a model explaining how yields on property assets are determined over time. While it emphasises short-term variations, it can also deal with long-term secular changes in yields.

As regards *short-run* yields, it is basically a stock theory. The main influence on the over-all yield of assets is changes in the demand for money. Thus an increased desire to be liquid will result in the yields on all assets rising, including property yields. Suppose the initial impact is on undated government bonds: an increase in the demand for money will lead to a fall in the price of bonds and thus a rise in their yield. Bonds will now be cheap relative to property interests, particularly FGRs, thus giving a relatively higher yield. The holders of property interests will thus tend to switch into bonds. As this occurs, the price of bonds will rise and the prices of property interests will fall until a new equilibrium set of relative prices is established such that nobody wishes to switch any further.

Two refinements, however, should be noted. First, because of the imperfections of the property market, there may be a time lag before property yields are brought into line with the rest of the market. Second, since the total value of property interests is small relative to stock market investments, it is changes in demand for the latter which is likely to dominate the asset market. Only in abnormal circumstances, e.g. 1973–4, is the property market likely to initiate changes in yields.

Once the over-all trend of asset yields has been established, variations in the yields between assets can be explained by differences in the demand for the different types of asset (see p. 55) and the relative supply situation. For example, the low yields on prime shops and offices is the result of the high demand of institutions coupled with their relatively limited supply.

In the *long run* the yield on an asset will be affected from the supply side through the accumulation of flows over time. If the price of equities is relatively high (yields low), selling shares will represent the cheapest way for firms to raise capital for expansion. If this continues over a considerable time, the accumulation of these flows will have a significant influence on the stock of equities, so that, other things being equal, their price falls (yield rises).

Investment yields 1929–77

The long-run trend over the past fifty years was for yields on assets to fall until 1949, and thereafter to rise (see Table 5.2).

The interwar period was dominated by the depression. Because government stock offered certainty of yield compared with equities and most property interests, its yield was consistently lower. Furthermore, under Chancellor Dalton's 'cheap-money' policy (1945–9), the money supply was increased and, with no change in liquidity preference, the price of government bonds rose, Consols, for instance, yielding only around 3 per cent.

However, in 1949 Dalton's policy broke down. Investors considered that the high price (low yield) of Consols could not be maintained. As they began to sell, their expectations were self-justified. Yields rose, and in 1951 Bank Rate (now Minimum Lending Rate) was raised. The year 1949 therefore represents the watershed; since then there has been an upward trend in asset yields.

Initially, however, the yield on fixed-money-interest-bearing assets (including FGRs) was still low in comparison with equities and freeholds. Earnings on ordinary shares and property were rising with the general increase in prosperity and the gradual dismantling of controls. Historically, too, yields on equities had always tended to be higher than the yields on government stock because of the greater risks involved. This risk factor dominated until 1959. Thereafter the yield on ordinary shares, and eventually on freeholds, became lower than the yield on Consols. We have the phenomenon of the 'reverse yield gap', a situation produced by inflation.

Inflation and the pattern of asset yields

Inflation dominates the yield on assets from 1960 onwards. First, it affects relative yields, people requiring high yields on 'money' bonds to allow for a fall in the value of money. Even so, the high rate of inflation in 1974 and 1975 meant that, in fact, a negative real rate was received. In contrast, over a long period, equity interests do offer some hedge against inflation. At first, ordinary shares were favoured, but investors, particularly the institutions, saw the advantages of prime property. By 1972 the yield on offices was little more than that on equities, and on agricultural land it was lower. It should be noted, however, that the figures shown in Table 5.2 apply only to prime properties, those favoured by institutions. The shortage of these properties tended to force down the yield considerably in comparison with other properties, though, as substitutes, these too experienced some fall in yields. Second, inflation led to restrictive government measures to protect the balance of payments. Rates of interest rose; earnings on shares and property looked less rosy. In such circumstances yields on assets generally rise.

Political crises, too, tend to produce short-term rises in yields. Not only do they create uncertainty about future earnings, especially as government measures usually involve increased taxation, but people generally seek to be more liquid. Asset prices therefore fall. The movement is accentuated if previously a speculative position had been built up.

This is illustrated by the events of 1971–4. In 1971–2 the Heath government, intent on growth, increased the money supply. This made spending easier, the effect being felt on the asset, house and consumer-durable markets. Asset yields fell, as did the real rate of interest.

But inflationary pressure forced the government to take counter-measures, including a freeze on business rents in November 1972, and this sparked off a liquidity crisis in the property market. When the oil crisis in late 1973 gave a further twist to inflation, pessimism spread to the Stock Exchange. In both markets people had invested in expectation of continually rising prices, and this speculative position led to larger falls than would otherwise have occurred.

While asset prices have since recovered, the world economy is still

TABLE 5.2
The Allsop schedule of investment yields from 1930

					Real estate					
Year	*UK ordinary shares (%)*	*Minimum Lending Rate (MLR) (%)*	*Average yield 2½% Consols (%)*	*Building society rate (%)*	*Prime shops (%)*	*Secondary shops (%)*	*Prime offices (%)*	*Industrial (%)*	*Residential (%)*	*Ground rents 99 years lease (%)*
World economic crisis										
1930	7	4½/3	4½	4/5	*Analysis of auction sales show that 80–90% of properties submitted were 'Brought in' or 'no bid'. No real market.*					
1931	7½	2½/6	4½	5½						
1932	8	5/2	4	4/5						
1933	5½	2	3½	4/5	6½	8	7		7/8	4
1934	4½	2	3	4/5	5½	6/7	7		7	4
1935	4½	2	2¼	4/4½	4/5	6	6		6/7	4
1936	4½	2	3	4½	5	7/8	7/8		6/7	4
1937	5	2	3½	5	5½	7	6½		8	4
Minor recession										
1938	6	2	3½	5	6/6½	8	7/7½		9	4½
Munich										
1939	6½	4/3	3¾	5½	*Second World War: no real market – lack of records* (1939–1947)					
1940	6	2	3½							
1941	5½	2	3¼							
1942	4½	2	3							
1943	4¼	2	3							
1944	4¼	2	3							
1945	4¼	2	3							
1946	4	2	2½							
1947	4½	2	2¾	4	5½	7	6		6½	4/5
1948	4	2	3¼	4	5	6			6	4/5
1949	4½	2	3½	4	5	6	6		6	4/5

Sterling devaluation										
1950	5½	2	4½	4½	5½	6½	6½		7½	4/5
1951	6	2½	4	4	5¼	6	6½		7½	4/5
1952	5½	4	4¼	4½	5½	6	6½		7½	
1953	7¼	3½	4	4½	5½	6	6½		7½	
1954	7	3	3¾	5	5½	6	7		7½	4/5
Korean war										
1955	6¼	3½/4½	4½	5½	5½	6	7		8	4/5
1956	6¼	5½	4¾	5½	5½	7			8	4/5
1957	7	5/7	5	6	5½	7	7½		8	4/5
1958	7	5½/4	5	6	5½	7	7½		8	4/5
1959	7	6/4½	5	6½	6	8	7½	10	8	4/5
Rent reviews commenced										
1960	5	5/6/7	5¼	6	5½	7	7	10	8	4/5
1961	4¾	7/6	6¼	6½	5½	7	7	10	8	4/5
1962	5½	6/4½	6¼	6	5½	7	6	10	7½	5
1963	5¾	4	6	6	5½	7	6	10	7	5
1964	5	5/7	5½	6¾	5½	7	6/7	10	7	6
1965	5¼	7/6	6	6¾	6	7/8	6/7	9	6½	8
1966	6	6/7	6½	7	6	7	6½	9	6½	10
1967	6½	6½/5½/8	6¾	7½	6½	7½	6½	9	6½	12
Sterling devaluation										
1968	5¾	8/7	8	8½	7	7½	7	9	6½	12
1969	4½	8	9	8½	7	7/8	6½	8/9½	6	12
1970	5	8/7	9	8	7½	8	7½	9	6	12
1971	5¾	7/4½	9	8½	6½/7	7	6½/7	8½	6	12
1972	4	4½/7½	11	10	6	6/7	4½/5½	7½	6	12
1973	4½	8½/13	14	9/12	5/5½	8/10	4/5	7½	7	12/14
Oil crisis and serious inflation										
1974	10	12½/12	17	11/12	7/8	12/15	7/8	10	9	15
1975	6.74	10.5	14.8	11/12	6/6½	9	6/6½	9	10	15
1976	6.10	9/15	14.23	10½/13	5½/6	8	6/6½	8½/9	10	18/20
UK oil – on stream										
1977	5.71	14¼/5/7	12.56	9/12	4½/5	7½/8	5½/6	7/8	8	15
1978	5.62	7/6½/12½	11.92	8½/11.94	4/4½	6½/7	4½/5½	6½/7½	8	15
1979 (to 30 November)	5.71	12½/12/14/17	11.34	11.94 (15% from 1 December)	3½/4	6/6½	4½	6½/7	7/8	15

Source: *Allsop & Co.*

under the influence of the rising price of oil. This has produced general deflation of incomes, while at the same time making it more difficult to bring inflation under control.

VI   THE EFFECT ON THE REAL PROPERTY MARKET OF THE DEMAND FOR LAND RESOURCES AS AN INVESTMENT

Occupation and investment demand

We have said that real property interests are wanted for:

(1) *Occupation*, because they yield utility or profit.

(2) *Investment*, i.e. as a means of holding assets. Here property interests will be compared with other forms of asset as regards liquidity, yield, interest risk and capital risk, management costs, and safety in retaining their value in real terms (that is, as an inflation-hedge). Demand and supply in the asset market will generally produce equilibrium prices and yields for all these different assets. There will thus be a given 'acceptable yield' for each different kind of property interest which, in its turn, will be partly dependent on the yields of comparable stock market assets. This means that investment demand may have a considerable effect on the price of land resources.

The price of gold

We can illustrate by examining the price of gold. Gold is demanded for two main purposes: (i) for use in industry; (ii) as a store of wealth. In the first case it is a factor of production, and the demand is similar to the occupation demand for property. In the second, it is wanted partly as a medium of exchange, but mainly as a hedge against inflation. Without the demand as a store of wealth, the price of gold would be much less than $650 per fine oz. (in 1980).

Changes in the demand for gold as a store of wealth are the main cause of fluctuations in its price. But price changes influence output. Should, for instance, its price rise, e.g. through world inflation, it will stimulate the production of gold, diverting resources from elsewhere.

Land resources

A similar situation exists with land resources. They are wanted: (i) for occupation, i.e. for their use in production; (ii) as a store of wealth, yielding an income and providing an inflation-hedge. Therefore, like gold, the price of a land resource is not determined wholly by its yield in its occupation use but is also affected by the demand for it as an asset. This demand will depend heavily upon the price of substitute assets in the 'asset market'.

As an example of such a substitute asset, let us take a blue-chip ordinary share, such as Unilever. Such a share has (i) actual current earnings, (ii) prospective earnings, and (iii) an inflation-hedge based largely on (ii). People bid in the market for it largely in accordance with how they view its attributes compared with other assets, e.g. gilt-edged stock and alternative blue-chip shares. Now, while the size of the earnings on a Unilever share is relevant, the important point is that such earnings are capitalised at the rate of yield which is acceptable on a Unilever share *compared with other types of asset*. If earnings double, but 'acceptable yield' remains unchanged, the price of the share will double; if earnings remain unchanged, but 'acceptable yield' is halved, the price of the share will likewise double.

And the same applies to land resources. Office blocks are wanted by investors, chiefly institutional ones. Their current earnings are capitalised at a rate reflecting their future earnings and their inflation-hedge *compared with alternative assets*. Their capitalisation rate may enhance their value considerably *irrespective of actual earnings*, i.e. irrespective of the demand for occupation purposes.

Take the Centre Point office block as an example. Here two factors served to increase its value to at least £45 million in 1972:

(a) earnings potential increased as rents rose because of occupation demand for offices; and

(b) acceptable yield on prime office blocks fell from 6 per cent to 4 per cent (note also that some of this investment demand is speculative, thereby driving up the price and lowering the yield).

Suppose Centre Point cost £15 million to build (included normal profit) and that potential current earnings were £900,000 a year. Therefore, if the going rate at which office blocks are capitalised is 6 per cent, its capital value would be the same as its cost, £15 million.

If now the rent doubles to £1,800,000, the capital value of Centre Point will increase to £30 million.

Now assume that, with this higher rent, the acceptable yield on office blocks falls from 6 per cent to 4 per cent. The capital value of Centre Point will now be £1,800,000 times 25, i.e. £45 million.

The effects of changes in the capitalisation rate

Such changes in the rate at which earnings are capitalised has important effects on the real property market.

First, it influences the relative supply of the different types of property. The resources of the construction industry are diverted into office-building rather than into properties, e.g. rented flats, which are capitalised at a lower rate, say a ten years' purchase.

Second, it increases the cost to the public sector of its own construction, e.g. roads, schools, hospitals, since resources have to be bid away from producing high-priced offices. For this reason, in times of rising property prices, there tends to be a proportionate falling off in gross fixed capital formation in the public sector.

Third, it can have adverse effects on the working owner-farmer. Suppose a farmer owns 500 acres which he bought by means of a loan for £100,000, i.e. £200 an acre, some five years previously. If the rate of interest which he has to pay is 15 per cent, he must make at least £30 an acre per year (after all other costs and normal profit have been covered) to justify his capital outlay.

Now suppose that the Church Commissioners decide to invest in land. They buy 3,000 acres which they let at £30 an acre, the going rate. But it is the yield which they are prepared to accept on this investment which is of vital importance. Suppose this is 5 per cent. Other institutions in the market will accept a similar yield, and competition forces the price up from £600,000 (originally £200 an acre) to £1,800,000 (that is, £600 an acre).

This has important results for the working owner-farmer:

(a)   He has a windfall capital gain – though this is of doubtful value unless, with his family, he is retiring from farming.

(b)   It raises the amount of capital transfer tax upon gift or death and, although he enjoys alleviating provisions, it still makes it virtually impossible to transfer a farm intact to a member of his own family.

(c)   As a result of (b), there is a tendency towards fragmentation of agricultural estates.

(d)   Because the capital outlay is prohibitive, tenant farmers are unlikely ever to become owners of large farms. This may partly account for the fact that, unlike the position in 1965–72, small farms of 100 acres were fetching more per acre in 1979 than larger farms, the shortage of capital having increased competition for the small farming unit.

(e)   Farms are increasingly owned by institutions since the working farmer cannot compete with them in the market.

FURTHER READING

P. Ambrose and B. Colenutt, *The Property Machine* (Harmondsworth: Penguin, 1975).

N. Enever, *The Valuation of Property Investments* (London: Estates Gazette, 1977) chs 2–6, 11, 13.

J. Harvey and M. K. Johnson, *Introduction to Macro-economics* (London: Macmillan, 1971) ch. 10.

J. Ratcliffe, *Introduction to Urban Land Administration* (London: Estates Gazette, 1978) chs 3, 4.

6

The Development Process

I THE NATURE OF DEVELOPMENT

Why development takes place

Over time the demand for land resources changes, brought about by changes in the size and composition of the population, the relative incomes of different groups, attitudes towards accommodation, the rate of growth of economic activity, methods of transport and the techniques of production and distribution. On the supply side, existing buildings wear out or become less suitable to present uses, and the costs of constructing new buildings or adapting old buildings change. Development is the response to such changes.

It should be noted that the development process may itself be dynamic, one development generating development elsewhere. Thus a house-owner who gives his property a 'face-lift' may stimulate his neighbours to do likewise. As a result, demand increases for nearby houses which can be improved, and eventually a whole neighbourhood may be upgraded, as happened in Islington and Pimlico. Similarly, a comprehensive replacement of large houses by blocks of flats can lead to the redevelopment of a shopping centre in order to serve the needs of the increased population.

Forms of development

Changes in the demand for and supply of land resources produce changes in the prices of the interests concerned. As we saw in Chapter 3, one response of the real property market may be a simple amalgamation or separation of interests involving no addition of capital. This is not development in the usual sense of the term.

Generally changes in demand and supply require structural change, which may take different forms:

(1) *Modification of the existing building*, existing buildings being improved or converted if it is estimated that the capitalised value of the additional returns will exceed the cost of alterations. Thus we have offices being refurbished, shop-fronts modernised, the lay-out of shops adapted to self-service, and houses being converted into flats, flatlets or even offices.

(2) *Redevelopment*, where supply changes by demolishing existing houses, offices and shops, and rebuilding occurs, usually to greater density.

(3) *New development*, taking the form of outward expansion on undeveloped land, e.g. houses. Usually this outward movement is the result of what is happening in the centre of a town: houses and factories cannot afford the high rents offered by shops and offices, traffic congestion becomes intolerable, people prefer the garden space of a suburban house, or industrialists want all their factory space to be at ground-floor level.

These types of development usually require planning consent for change of use or construction work. As a rough yardstick, therefore, development covers those projects which entail planning consent. Minor additions of capital, e.g. converting an apartment from an unfurnished to a furnished letting, are thus excluded and, in any case, are not development in the usual sense of the term. But within this definition development ranges from the private house-owner who wishes to add a garage or bedroom to the major commercial developer or local authority rebuilding a city centre.

The importance of development in the UK economy

While the figures in Table 6.1 include depreciation, they nevertheless indicate the relative importance of development in the UK economy for 1979.

TABLE 6.1

The importance of development in the United Kingdom, 1979

(a) Gross National Product		£163,936m
(b) Gross Fixed Capital Formation		£33,646m
(c) Gross Fixed Capital Formation in land and buildings		
Private sector	£9,346m	
Public sector	£6,768m	£16,114m
(d) (c) as a percentage of (b)		48%
(e) (c) as a percentage of (a)		10%

Source: *National Income and Expenditure* Blue Book (London: HMSO, 1980).

Development in the private and public sectors

In the *private sector* development is carried out by (i) occupiers, or (ii) specialist developers, property companies (e.g. Hammersons) or construction firms (e.g. Wimpey) working through the price system.

The advantage to the occupier of initiating his own development is that he obtains a building which is tailor-made to his individual requirements.

An adapted building is unlikely to be so satisfactory and, moreover, can prove relatively expensive where the cost of fitting out a building is almost equal to the cost of the basic structure, as in the case of Marks & Spencer. But development involves know-how and highly specialised skills not usually found in the main business of the occupier, and only a few firms are large enough to have their own property division responsible for development. Most occupiers wishing to develop their own property, therefore, compromise by employing a specialist developer, e.g. Bovis. They submit a specification of their requirements for a building, and the developer endeavours to meet these on previously agreed terms.

Irrespective of whether the development is carried out by the occupier or a specialist developer, the same basic decisions and calculations have to be made, for (given competition) each has to pay the full opportunity cost in order to secure a site.

Public-sector development accounted in 1979 for 42 per cent of total development, but the percentage varies from year to year. While some public development decisions, for instance in the nationalised industries, may be based on market prices, most are taken on a mixture of political, social and economic grounds. Public development therefore tends to fluctuate both with the politics of the government in power and also the economic climate, being increased when expansion of the economy is desired and decreased when it is necessary to apply the brakes. For example, local authority house-building tends to increase under Labour governments, while school-building and road construction are used as part of the economic regulator.

Our analysis will deal mainly with problems of urban development, though the same principles apply elsewhere. In Chapters 6 to 9 we concentrate on commercial development in the private sector, analysing in particular how it functions within the price system. Chapter 10 is concerned with public development decisions.

II PROBLEMS OF THE DEVELOPER

Functions of the developer

The commercial developer may be defined as 'an entrepreneur who provides the organisation and capital required to make buildings availa-ble in anticipation of the requirements of the market in return for profit' (Bowley, *The British Building Industry*, 1966). This definition emphas-ises that the developer is essentially an 'entrepreneur' accepting the unshedable risks of producing for an uncertain demand. When his forecasts prove correct, he makes supernormal profit. Unfortunately, this often generates an emotive response, with the developer being accused of exploiting shortages (e.g. of building land and houses) and making excessive windfall gains at the expense of the community. Scant regard is given to the other side of the coin: when economic conditions turn sour, e.g. in 1974, losses replace profits.

Consideration of the developer's chief functions reveal not only his major problems but also the risks involved.

(1) *He recognises the potential for development*
In essence this means: (i) estimating future demand for alternative uses of existing land resources, and (ii) calculating the cost of building for new uses. From among these different uses he must choose the scheme which will produce the maximum net return subject to the constraints involved, e.g. the availability of finance, building restrictions, planning, etc.

Here the developer bears the uncertainty of the scheme. On the demand side he may have overestimated returns on the new use: economic conditions may lead to a fall in incomes, a new out-of-town hypermarket may adversely affect the profitability of city-centre shops, taxation on the development may be increased. On the supply side the cost of finance may rise or construction costs escalate owing to un-foreseen site conditions, inflation, or delays in the grant of planning permission or in the process of construction.

(2) *He assembles the site*
This involves acquiring the proprietary rights over the land for the construction of buildings. The different interests have to be bought as they become available and held until the whole site has been assembled. In the meantime there is the risk of a fall in potential profitability, e.g. the government may restrict office development or construction costs may escalate. Moreover, there may be difficulties in acquiring certain interests which exploit the monopoly power inherent in owning a site essential to the scheme. As we shall see (Chapter 9), this may involve collaborating on a partnership basis with the local authority – but with some loss of profit to the developer.

Here it is essential to note that, because assembling the site and the actual construction process takes time, the developer is involved in costs additional to those incurred in the acquisition of the existing land and building, clearing the site and rebuilding to a new use. These additional costs may be described as *ripening costs* and *waiting costs.*

Ripening costs are defined as the costs incurred in holding land in anticipation of future development or redevelopment. Where the future development is certain and widely known, ripening costs are simply the interest on the capital tied up less any return earned from the existing use in the meantime. However, a developer may be willing to buy land in anticipation of a more profitable use, e.g. through the grant of planning permission. Typical examples are land on the fringes of towns or along transport routes where the price includes a degree of 'hope' value. Here the price paid is in excess of the current use price. Ripening costs are then the interest on the capital tied up (less any return earned from existing use) plus the amount paid for the land in excess of its current-use value. In this context ripening costs are, in the main, purely speculative – a gamble on a change in the law or on its application, e.g. as regards planning permission.

Waiting costs, on the other hand, are incurred even when the land already has planning permission, simply because construction takes time. Such costs are defined as those necessary to span the period between the start of the construction process and the actual receipt of revenue from the development. They would thus cover items such as architects' fees and interest on capital used for stage payments, or, if the developer's own capital is used, what it would have earned if invested elsewhere.

(3)   *He obtains the necessary planning permission*

Initially the developer will study the statutory regional structure plan and the substantive local plan, noting the views of the local authority in formulating the latter. He will then be able to assess whether the use he proposes is likely to prove acceptable. Contact will then be made with the Chief Planning Officer so that an initial opinion can be given on the outline scheme, especially as regards its density, lay-out, design and materials. The local authority may, however, impose special conditions, e.g. additional housing within an office complex or the construction of roads and sewers at the developer's expense. Such a risk of reduced profitability is inherent in any development. Indeed, as we see in Chapter 9, with large schemes some form of partnership with the local authority may be advisable.

(4)   *He arranges finance for the development*

Since the development does not produce revenue until it is complete, finance is required for the whole of the development process (see Chapter 8).

It should be noted that, because the capital market is imperfect, a shortage of finance may mean that the highest and best development may not be achieved. For instance, the cash-flow position of a speculative builder may force him to build houses rather than a more profitable block of flats simply because houses can be sold as they are finished, whereas with flats the whole block has to be completed before any sales are possible.

(5)   *He gets the scheme built*

Here again there is a risk of incurring costs in excess of those budgeted for through delay or modification of the original design after construction has begun. Some check on costs can be achieved by consulting with the quantity surveyor at all stages of construction.

(6)   *He arranges the first letting or sale of the development*

The developer may retain the whole or part of the development. Retention of the best developments provides asset backing for future borrowing and a steady rental income. On the other hand, it means that the developer has to manage the property, one of the functions of a property company. In practice, the decision as to whether a property is retained may hinge on the availability of finance. For instance, a speculative builder of houses or flats usually sells to repay outstanding loans, while an insurance company may only lend for a commercial development on condition that upon completion it receives a part or even the whole of the freehold interest.

Once the construction process has started, the development becomes a fixed asset. As such, its price will be demand-determined. When the development is offered for letting or sale, therefore, the developer's estimate of demand is put to the test, and the result can be a profit – or a loss.

In recent years there has been a tendency for each of the above functions to be performed by a team of specialists consisting of an architect, quantity surveyor, letting agent, etc. At their head is a project manager or co-ordinator (who may be the developer himself). Indeed, nowadays insurance companies and property bond funds may not only supply the finance for development but will fulfil the uncertainty-bearing role of the developer by directly employing such a team to find, evolve and carry out development schemes.

The rationale of development

Development is necessary to ensure the efficient use of land resources. In the main the life of a building ends not because the structure is physically worn out but for *economic* reasons. Sometimes operating costs exceed revenue and, because there is no alternative use, the structure is abandoned, e.g. Cornish tin mines. More usually the site can be used more profitably. As we shall see, the developer who can put a site to its most profitable use can make the highest bid for it. Thus, given a competitive price system, land resources are used to their greatest efficiency. However, it is important to note that the developer's bid is based solely on his private benefits and costs. Externalities may justify government interference in the development process.

The decisions of the developer

The question which the developer asks is: Will the value of a replacement building exceed both the value of the present building and the cost of rebuilding? If so, the old building will be demolished and a new one built.

Development therefore poses largely the same problems facing any firm contemplating investment in fixed capital. We simplify by confining our discussion to the specialist developer and by assuming that his objective is to maximise profit.

This objective involves a number of decisions, all of which present difficulties. They can best be considered under the following headings:

(a)   choosing between development projects;
(b)   estimating demand for a particular development;
(c)   deciding on the quality of the building and its initial cost as opposed to future maintenance costs;
(d)   calculating how intensively the site shall be developed;
(e)   estimating how much can be bid for the site;
(f)   obtaining finance; and
(g)   deciding whether to develop in partnership with a local authority.

The first five decisions are examined in this chapter, and the last two in Chapters 8 and 9 respectively.

III   CHOOSING BETWEEN DEVELOPMENT PROJECTS

Comparing capital costs and net revenue over time

In a development project we have: (i) the initial capital cost of providing the development; (ii) subsequent periodic costs, e.g. on maintenance; and (iii) periodic gross yields, e.g. annual rents received. We define net annual revenue (NAR) as gross annual yield less annual costs – that is, (iii) minus (ii). In order to simplify we deal with NAR.

Where, as usually happens, capital funds are limited or where only one development is possible on a given site, projects are said to be 'mutually exclusive'. It is essential, therefore, whether in the private or public sector, to choose the most profitable development of those available. This choice involves problems because: (i) benefits received and costs incurred at different points of time are not directly comparable; (ii) the future is uncertain; (iii) benefits and costs, particularly in public investment, may be difficult to measure quantitatively. Here we concentrate on the difficulties arising from (i) and (ii). Chapter 10 deals with (iii).

Differences in development projects

Capital projects differ as regards: (i) initial cost; (ii) phasing of capital expenditure; (iii) size of expected yields; (iv) timing of future yields; (v) certainty of yields; and (vi) estimated life and terminal value (if any). Table 6.2 illustrates. All four projects are assumed to have the same initial cost and no terminal value. They differ as regards (iii), (iv) and (vi), and we shall concentrate on these differences. NARs are assumed to be net of tax and to accrue at the end of each period.

TABLE 6.2
Differences in capital projects

Project	Initial capital cost (£000)	NAR (£000)			Terminal value
		Year 1	Year 2	Year 3	
A	100	50	50	50	Nil
B	100	100	10	—	Nil
C	100	—	50	120	Nil
D	100	100	50	—	Nil

Methods of evaluation

Projects can be evaluated by different methods which vary in complexity. The simpler ones are, as we shall see, only preferred where special considerations apply.

(1) *Comparative cost*

Here a straight comparison is made between the initial capital costs of projects, and these may be the determining factor when funds are limited. Otherwise it suffers from the obvious weakness that it fails to take into account the size and timing of NARs, all projects in Table 6.2, for example, being rated equally.

(2) *Cut-off period*

This method chooses a period by which the initial cost must be recouped. If, in our example, this period were two years, all projects except C would be acceptable, preference being given to D on account of its higher total yield. The difficulty is that project C is rejected solely because returns accrue late in its life irrespective of whether it is a desirable project. Nevertheless, using a cut-off period to choose D could be justified where: (i) project D hinges on an innovation which cannot be protected by patent and is likely to be copied by other firms within two years; (ii) political uncertainty necessitates recouping the initial cost within two years.

(3) *Pay-back period*

Here investment options are ranked according to how long income yields take to recoup the initial outlay. In our example, both *B* and *D* achieve pay-back in year 1. This method can be justified where uncertainty, either as regards future cash returns or obsolescence of equipment, is marked, for then a possible quick exit must be borne in mind. But it fails to take account of: (i) differences in the timing of yields earned before the pay-back date; (ii) yields earned after the pay-back date. On the latter count, for instance, *D* is obviously superior to *B*.

(4) *Average rate of return*

This can be calculated in various ways:

(a) Adding the *NAR*s, dividing by the years of the project's life, and expressing this average as a percentage of the initial cost. With *D* this would be

$$\frac{150}{2} \times \frac{100}{100} = 75 \text{ per cent}$$

(b) Obtaining a *net* average rate of return by adding the *NAR*s, deducting the initial capital outlay, dividing by the number of years, and expressing this net average yield as a percentage of the initial outlay. Thus taking project *D* as an example, we would have

$$\frac{150 - 100}{2} \times \frac{100}{100} = 25 \text{ per cent}$$

The average rate of return method has two main disadvantages. First, it depends upon the number of years chosen. Thus, if in year 3, *D* had had a *NAR* of 20, it would cease to rank above *C* even though its over-all profitability had increased! As a result, the method produces a bias in favour of short-term investments having high yields. Second, it ignores the pattern of yields, higher earlier *NAR*s being treated the same as low later ones.

The major criticism of the above methods is that they fail to take into account both the number and the timing of yields. Other things being equal, the greater the number of *NAR*s, the more profitable the investment. Similarly, early *NAR*s have the advantage that they can be reinvested profitably or used to reduce borrowing. Both the number and timing of yields are allowed for by the *net present value* and the *internal rate of return* methods described below.

(5) *Net present value*

Here the future *NAR*s of the investment are discounted at a target rate of interest (see pp. 150–4) to give their present value. The net present value (NPV) of the project equals the sum of these discounted *NAR*s minus the capital cost of the project. For example, if we take 8 per cent as the discount rate, the present values of the *NAR*s of project *A* are

$$\frac{50}{1.08} + \frac{50}{(1.08)^2} + \frac{50}{(1.08)^3} = 128.9$$

Thus the net present value is 28.9.

In general, if we regard costs as negative benefits

$$\text{NPV} = \sum_{t=0}^{t=n} \frac{B_t}{(1+i)^t}$$

where *B* is net benefit (*NAR*), *i* is the target rate of discount and *t* the life of the project in years. A project is profitable where NPV > 0.

It should be noted that:

(a) The discounted NPV of a particular investment depends upon the rate of discount used: the higher the rate of discount, the lower will be the discounted NPV.

(b) Where projects differ in their patterns of *NAR*s, the ranking of projects can depend upon the rate of discount chosen. For example, comparing projects *C* and *D* for rates of discount of 8 per cent and 20 per cent gives the information contained in Table 6.3.

TABLE 6.3
NPV at rates of discount of 8% and 20%

	8%	20%
C	38.1	4.2
D	35.5	28.0

This can be shown diagrammatically by plotting the NPV of each project at different rates of discount (see Figure 6.1). At a discount rate of less than *r* the NPV of *C* is greater than *D*'s; at a discount rate greater than *r*, the NPV of *C* is less than *D*'s. The reason is that *NAR*s for *C* are realised later in the project's life, and the higher rate of discount penalises

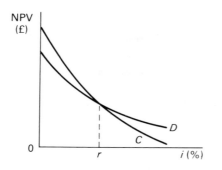

FIGURE 6.1

Relationships of NPV
and the rate of
discount for projects
having different net
annual revenue
patterns

later benefits more heavily. Alternatively, we can explain the situation by considering the rate of interest at which earlier *NAR*s can be reinvested to provide a sinking fund to cover the cost of the project. Since project *D* has earlier *NAR*s, raising the rate of interest at which these can be reinvested means that eventually they outweigh *C*'s larger, but later, *NAR*s.

(6) Yield – the internal rate of return (IRR)

Here projects are ranked according to the rate of discount which needs to be applied to all future *NAR*s to achieve a present value of the capital cost of the project or, if this is deducted, a NPV = 0. More generally

$$\sum_{t=0}^{t=n} \frac{B_t}{(1+r)^t} = 0$$

where *B* equals net benefits (*NAR*s) and *r* equals the IRR.

For example, with project *D* we have

$$\frac{100}{1+r} + \frac{50}{(1+r)^2} = 0$$

Here *r*, the IRR, equals 37 per cent. It is found either by solving the equation for *r* or by a process of trial and error, using valuation tables to see which rate of discount will make the PV of 100 for one year plus the PV of 50 for two years equal to 100.

The advantages of the IRR method are:

(a) No rate of discount has to be specified (as with NPV), since *r* is thrown up by expected *NAR*s.
(b) It conforms with the more usual business practice of comparing rates in order to assess profitability. All projects are profitable if their IRRs are greater than a target borrowing rate of interest. But if

projects are mutually exclusive, they have to be ranked, and this can be done according to their IRR.

(c) It is easier to take account of the risk element than the NPV method since the margin between the IRR and the target borrowing rate of interest will indicate whether there is sufficient to cover risk.

Nevertheless, the IRR method presents difficulties.

First, if the life of the project has *n* years, the IRR has *n* roots, and more than one of these may be positive. Which one do we choose?

Second, where a choice has to be made between different projects, the IRR ranking may differ from the NPV's.

IRR discriminates against later-benefit projects when NPV is calculated at a low rate of discount. This is because the IRR always makes the NPV $= 0$, and must therefore be greater than a rate of discount which produces a positive NPV. In the above example, the IRR ranks D (37 per cent) above C (22 per cent), and this ranking is confirmed by the NPV method, with D (28.0) above C (4.2) when the rate of discount chosen is 20 per cent (see Table 6.3). There is thus no difference between the two methods – because the 20 per cent rate of discount is fairly close to the IRR.

However, a discrepancy arises when the rate of discount is only 8 per cent, for now the NPV of C (38.1) ranks it above D (35.5). To guard against such a discrepancy when using the IRR method, the correct procedure would be to compare the *incremental* yields of C and D, i.e. their different cash flows. D has a NAR of 100 in year 1, whereas C has a NAR of 120 in year 3. That is, with C an effective outlay (income forgone) of 100 yields 120 in two years' time. This is equivalent to a yield of $9\frac{1}{2}$ per cent, whereas D's initial 100 can only earn the market rate of 8 per cent when reinvested. Thus C is preferable to D.

The IRR also discriminates against higher-cost capital projects. For example, consider two projects X and Y both having a life of ten years (see Table 6.4). By the IRR method X is preferable to Y; whereas, judged by NPVs, Y is preferable to X. The correct procedure would be to obtain the IRR on a hypothetical additional project representing the difference in capital cost of Y over X ($= £100$m.). This additional project

TABLE 6.4
IRR and differences in the initial cost of projects

	Initial cost (£m.)	NAR	IRR	NPV at 8%
X	100	20	15	3.4
Y	200	36	12	4.2

would have annual benefit flows of £1.6m., giving an IRR of 9 per cent, which is above the 8 per cent discount rate which the £100m. could earn elsewhere.

The conclusion is that we should test projects by both NPV and IRR methods to ensure that they do not differ. In general, the NPV method is safer. In effect it chooses the market rate of interest at which to invest early benefits, whereas the IRR assumes that early benefits can be reinvested at the rate of return on the project, a somewhat higher (and more doubtful) figure. A further advantage is that the NPV can incorporate future changes in the interest rate at which to discount *NAR*s.

IV ALLOWING FOR RISK AND UNCERTAINTY

So far we have treated expected future benefits and costs as if they will actually occur. In practice, however, they are not certain, and in assessing projects allowance has therefore to be made for the risk of forecasts being wrong. How can this allowance be made?

In economics it is usual to distinguish between *risks* and *uncertainty*. With the former there is a known probability distribution. With uncertainty (which arises, for instance, through a change in consumers' demand or a change in technology), the 'law of large numbers' does not apply. However, many of the methods described below, with the notable exception of the application of probability distribution, apply equally to both risk and uncertainty.

Most methods in general use for allowing for risk can best be described as 'rule of thumb'.

(1) For very risky projects, a *cut-off period*, e.g. three or four years, can be adopted (see p. 75).

(2) A *risk premium* can be added to the discount rate when calculating present values. That is,

$$NPV = \sum_{t=0}^{t=n} \frac{B_t}{(1+i+p)^t}$$

where p is the risk premium. Not only is this method simple, but it also penalises distant returns, where uncertainty is considered to be greater, more heavily. However, this presents difficulties because:

(a)   it is unlikely that risks are so orderly as to be constant in each year;
(b)   the risk premium penalises projects where benefits are mainly received late in life; and

(c) the investment decision-maker has no guide as to how large the premium should be.

(3) A *percentage addition* to costs or a *percentage reduction* in benefits can be made where these are uncertain. In practice, however, this method really provides only for over-optimism, and there are risks apart from this.

More systematic ways of allowing for risk are:

(4) Applying the mean of the *probability distribution* for the different risks involved, e.g. the probability of a building project exceeding the stipulated completion date. The difficulty here is that while two distributions can have the same mean, they may differ significantly in their dispersions.

(5) Making a *sensitivity analysis*. For example, where there is doubt over the exact rate of discount which should be applied to future *NAR*s, they can be discounted at different rates in order to show how a change in the rate would affect the viability of the project. The method can be applied to other variables, e.g. the future rate of inflation. It is thus possible to obtain the NPV for the combination of values giving the best possible outcome and also for the worst possible outcome. The trouble is that the range between the two is usually so wide that it provides little guidance for the decision-maker.

(6) For uncertainty, *rule of choice* can be formulated for different degrees of certainty, and that rule is chosen according to whether the planner is optimistic and can afford to take risks, or whether he is pessimistic and cannot take a chance on possible bankruptcy. In the former case the rule would allow him to maximise the possible return, while with the latter he would seek the best possible minimum return.

For example, Table 6.5 gives possible outcomes at different degrees of optimism for two different projects, *A* and *B*. Thus the most optimistic outcome for *A* is 14 and the most pessimistic is 4, whereas for *B* the most optimistic is 17 and the most pessimistic 2. It is likely that a large firm (e.g.

TABLE 6.5
Uncertainty and the returns on projects

	Possible NPVs (£m.)		
Project	Optimism ← Best	Medium	→ Pessimism Worst
A	14	7	4
B	17	8	2

Wimpey) having many projects or capital reserves can afford to be optimistic. It therefore adopts a policy of 'maximax' by choosing project *B*. On the other hand, a small firm with fewer projects and less capital reserves would have to take a more cautious view. If a NPV of £4m. is necessary to cover building costs, it must choose project *A* since the worst possible outcome of *B* could lead to bankruptcy.

While 'games theory', of which the above is an example, may provide no definite solution to the problem (as for the large firm above), it does allow the developer to consider uncertainty possibilities in a logical form.

V   ESTIMATING DEMAND

The NPV of a development indicates to the developer the likely value of the completed project. Since the NPV depends upon the stream of future *NAR*s, demand for the type of building and its operating costs both now and in the future have to be estimated.

The problem of estimating demand for a small, single development differs somewhat from that of a city-centre project. We can illustrate by concentrating on shops in particular.

Single development

With a single development, a guide to the likely selling price can be obtained from current market information on similar buildings. If, for instance, enquiries from estate agents reveal that, in the same shopping area, a prime shop unit sells with vacant possession for £50,000, the developer has a yardstick for his own unit since the known sale price has been arrived at in the market with the buyer and seller taking into account present and estimated *NAR*s. Similarly, if the market rent is £10 a square foot, this will reflect the current *NAR*.

The developer will have to adjust this selling price or rent for his own particular project by allowing for differences in location, nearness to multiples, complementarity with similar shops, occupation rates (if a specialist shop) and such features as lay-out, storage facilities and staff accommodation. Some consideration would also have to be given to the potential supply of similar developments; this involves examining the register for outstanding planning consents and applications currently under consideration. Some allowance may also have to be made for how quickly the type of shop sells or lets, and whether the lay-out would be easily adaptable to future changes in demand (e.g. towards those goods having a high income-elasticity of demand as the prosperity of the locality increases) or to new techniques of retailing.

City-centre projects

Typically shopping areas have developed along High Streets on a shop-by-shop basis. But post-war New Town projects, comprehensive redevelopment of city centres and suburban growth of the more prosperous towns have necessitated planning in advance the size and lay-out of shopping areas.

The size of the *shopping space* must be related to the over-all demand for shopping facilities. The latter is usually expressed in terms of the total value of retail turnover. From turnover in existing shopping centres, a floor-space ratio (FSR) for each particular type of shop can be obtained, using the formula

$$FSR = \frac{\text{Units of floor space}}{\text{Turnover in current prices}}$$

This known FSR can then be applied to the forecast retail sales of the new shopping centre: floor space required = FSR × forecast retail sales. Since each type of retail shop will have a different FSR (jewellery, for example, with its low physical turnover will have a higher FSR than groceries), the total floor space requirement will be an aggregate of the floor space requirements of all shops in the shopping area calculated according to their individual FSR.

This crude application of central-place theory has two main weaknesses. First, the 'units of floor space' in the formula will itself be dependent on shop rents. If these are high, increased turnover may be met by more intensive use of existing floor space rather than by adding to it. Second, the method ignores the power of a new shopping centre to attract customers from a rival centre.

Reilly's law of retail gravitation covers this latter problem. The law is based on empirical studies of shopping habits in the USA in the 1920s. W. J. Reilly (1931, 2nd edn 1953) concluded that, as a general rule, two cities will attract retail spending from the area between them in direct proportion to the size of the city's population and in inverse proportion to the square of the distance to the city from any particular point in the area between. Thus a city of 180,000 population located three miles from the intermediate area will attract twenty times as much trade from it as a rival city of 49,000 located seven miles away. In numerical terms we have

$$\frac{180,000}{9} : \frac{49,000}{49}$$

We can apply the theory to derive the retail catchment area of a city.

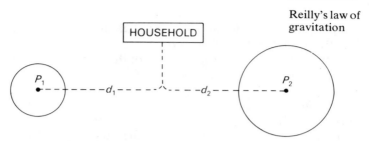

FIGURE 6.2

Reilly's law of
gravitation

Supposing we have a smaller town of population P_1 and a larger town of population P_2, there would be some point between them where a household would be indifferent whether it shopped in town 1 or town 2 (see Figure 6.2). According to Reilly's law, the location of such a point is determined by the formula

$$\frac{P_1}{(d_1)^2} = \frac{P_2}{(d_2)^2}, \text{ i.e. } \frac{\sqrt{P_1}}{d_1} = \frac{\sqrt{P_2}}{d_2}$$

But $d_1 + d_2 = D$, the distance between the two cities. Substituting,

$$d_2 \sqrt{P_1} = D\sqrt{P_2} - d_2\sqrt{P_2}$$

Dividing through by P_2 we have

$$d_2 \frac{\sqrt{P_1}}{\sqrt{P_2}} + 1 = D$$

giving

$$d_2 = \frac{\sqrt{P_1}}{\sqrt{P_2}} + 1$$

Thus d_2 locates the watershed of city P_2 as regards its 'pulling power' relative to P_1, and is defined once we know D, P_1 and P_2.

This crude formulation illustrates the basic technique. With refinements it has provided the framework for the evaluation of many shopping developments in Britain. Thus, since the attractive power of a city rests on spending power rather than just its population size, consideration has to be given to the composition of the population (e.g. by age group and working proportion), its earning capacity (e.g. whether they are skilled workers), government subsidy policy within the district and the spending habits of different income groups. Ease of transport between the inter-mediate area and the centre is also important.

The main weakness of Reilly's law, however, is that it is a static formula. Some allowance must be made for future population growth. More important, it fails to allow for the fact that a new large shopping centre may generate its own growth. For example, specialist shops enhance the reputation of such a centre (e.g. Croydon) which thus grows over time relative to smaller centres (e.g. Wimbledon).

Not only the size but also the *lay-out of a new shopping centre* must be planned carefully. With a single-shop development, the subsequent provision of a municipal car-park nearby or the opening of a supermarket or a Marks & Spencer store next door would increase revenue-earning capacity. Both are external economies since neither can be planned for by the developer. In contrast, with a comprehensive city-centre develop-ment, such externalities are under the developer's control. That is, externalities can be 'internalised', and the developer's plans must take account of them in order to maximise the value of the total area.

As regards the shopping area, this means relating it to public transport and car-parks, and then siting shops in order to secure complemen-tarities, i.e. 'special accessibility'. Such 'merchandising' involves planning the size, shape and location of shops to maximise the value of aggregate turnover, which in turn should maximise rentals. The developer is likely to start from the key retail outlet, such as the department store or supermarket, perhaps granting favourable rental terms. Secondary mag-nets, such as banks and the post office, are then located, and multiples positioned between them. The object is to avoid having dead spots that can result from too high a concentration in one area, but instead to generate movement of shoppers around the whole centre. The remaining space is then allocated to the specialist shops, such as jewellery, shoes, cameras and clothing, having regard to their complementarity prefer-ences. Thus food stores prefer to be located together, with the specialist shops, such as delicatessen and patisserie, being close to the supermarket. Other trades, such as stationers, hairdressers, florists, restaurants and toy shops, are less demanding, but they add colour and variety to the centre and so have to be carefully located in order to secure the over-all objective.

Since different types of shop have different requirements as regards window space (Dixon's cameras prefer corner shops), show space (furni-ture), customer-circulating space (clothiers) and storage space (ironmon-gers), merchandising demands detailed planning in advance, especially if provision is made for flexibility to meet future changes in requirements.

VI   OPTIMUM CONSTRUCTION OUTLAY

Revenues are determined not only by the use to which a site is put but also by the capital outlay on the building erected. Thus important economic decisions have to be made on the construction outlay:

(1)   What refinements should be incorporated in the building?
(2)   To what extent should higher initial capital costs be incurred in order to save future maintenance costs?
(3)   How intensively should the site be developed?

As we shall see, the answers to these questions all hinge on the principle of equating marginal revenue and marginal cost. More specifically, any addition to construction outlay must be at least covered by the addition to NPV from the resulting higher net revenues. We discuss the first two questions in this section; the third, and most important, in section VII.

The quality of refinements

When deciding on refinements, e.g. lifts and air-conditioning in offices, the basic question is: How much will such refinements add to revenue? If the enhanced NPV exceeds the cost of installation, such refinements should be incorporated. Since the revenue from additional refinements will depend largely on the demand for them, expectations will be important.

Capital costs as opposed to maintenance costs

For most buildings there will be some possibility of trading off higher initial construction costs against reduced maintenance costs. Here again the same marginal principle applies.

If higher initial building costs lead to lower future maintenance costs, annual *net* revenues will be greater than for a building costing less. We therefore have to choose that combination of construction costs and discounted *net* revenues which will yield the highest NPV. Here the rate of interest and expectations of future wage-rate levels would be major determinants. A high rate of interest penalises projects whose returns are received further in the future, such as a building with high initial capital costs but lower maintenance costs. Thus a high rate of interest operates in favour of a low-capital/high-maintenance building. On the other hand, maintenance costs tend to be labour-intensive, and if wage rates are expected to increase more than other factor rewards it would give an advantage to the dearer, low-maintenance-cost building.

Finally, other factors may be decisive. For instance, the imperfections of the capital market may impose a limit on available funds, so that a cheaper building has to be erected, while the height may be controlled by building and planning restrictions.

VII THE INTENSITY OF SITE USE

Buildings as the addition of capital to land

As well as determining the highest and best use of a site, the developer has to decide how intensively it shall be developed. If, for instance, the most profitable use of a large suburban site is for housing, to what density shall the houses be built? Or, if an office block is to be built in a city centre, how many storeys upwards, given no government restrictions, shall it go? In economic terms, how much capital shall be combined with the site?

Although the two decisions, most profitable use and capital-intensity of development, are arrived at simultaneously, we shall simplify the analysis by assuming that the highest and best use has already been determined, confining the immediate discussion to capital spending on the actual building.

Combining capital with a fixed supply of land

Since we are dealing with a particular site, we can regard land as a fixed factor. To simplify the explanation, we shall assume that the project has a life of one year and that all returns are received at the end of the first year. (The obvious example of this in practice would be where a non-renewable one-year lease is held on a vacant site.)

The problem now resolves itself into the familiar one of applying units of a variable factor, which we shall term 'capital', to a fixed factor, land. It is assumed that:

(1) All costs of developing the site – material and labour costs, ripening and waiting costs, legal fees and normal profits – are capital costs.

(2) The capital unit may be an unspecified physical amalgam of materials and labour with the return and cost likewise unspecified (see Figure 6.3(a)). Alternatively, we can be more precise, defining the capital unit as £100-worth of capital factors, with the cost of this unit for the year thus being £100 + the going rate of interest (see Figure 6.3(b)).

(3) There is perfect competition in both the capital and product markets. Thus all the capital the developer requires can be obtained at a given price, and the product sells at a given price per unit. The latter means that the marginal physical product curve can be regarded as the marginal revenue product curve since *MRP* equals *MPP* times the price

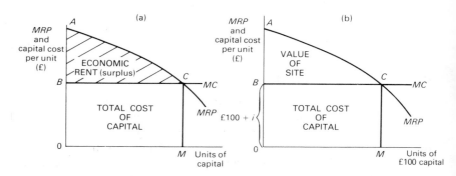

FIGURE 6.3

Applying capital to a fixed site

per product unit whatever the output. The *MRP* is *net*, operating costs having been deducted.

(4) A site is being developed for offices, with one suite of offices occupying one storey. It is assumed that the height of the office suite makes no difference to the rent, and so, following from (3), each suite lets at the same rent.

(5) There are no government controls on height.

As extra units of capital are applied to the fixed site, the law of diminishing returns eventually comes into operation, and the *MPP* of capital falls. This is because building upwards incurs extra costs, e.g. a more expensive substructure is necessary, labour costs per unit rise with height, and lifts and fire escapes have to be provided. Thus the return on given additions to capital eventually decreases, giving a downward-sloping *MRP* curve (see Figure 6.3).

Development of the site will take place up to the point where marginal revenue equals marginal cost: that is, to where the *MRP* of a unit of capital equals the cost of a unit of capital (*OB* in Figures 6.3(a) and 6.3(b)). The building reaches its optimum height, i.e. the development is complete, when *OM* units of capital have been applied to the site.

VIII   THE AMOUNT WHICH CAN BE PAID FOR THE SITE

In Figure 6.3 total proceeds of the development will be *AOMC*, and the total capital cost *BOMC*. In practice, the developer will have plans of the optimum building to be constructed, and he can obtain preliminary cost estimates based on these plans. In addition, he will have to cover waiting and ripening costs, extra costs arising from the operation of escape

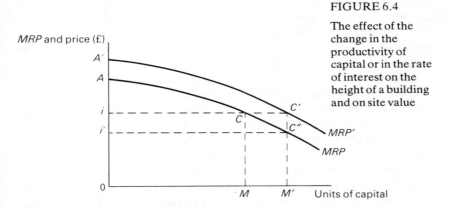

FIGURE 6.4

The effect of the
change in the
productivity of
capital or in the rate
of interest on the
height of a building
and on site value

clauses before the building is completed, overheads and normal profit. All costs will be included in *BOMC*. Thus the maximum which he can pay for the land is the residual, *ABC*, the shaded area.

Corollaries

Certain corollaries follow from our assumptions and analysis:

(1) If offices were the only or the highest and best use to which the site could be put, *ABC* would represent the demand price for the site. Thus if the site were 1,000 square metres in size, its demand price would be £*ABC*/1,000 per square metre. *Competition among developers would ensure that this price was in fact bid.*

(2) Suppose, however, there were alternative uses (e.g. a departmental store) with greater productivity. This would be shown by the higher *MRP'* curve (Figure 6.4) giving a larger residual surplus. Such a de-veloper could therefore bid more for this site. Thus competition ensures that the site goes to that use which is capable of producing the largest residual surplus: that is, *it goes to its highest and best use.*

(3) Competition also ensures that the site is developed upwards to the point where $MR = MC$, for this allows for the maximum size of *ABC*, the bid for the site. Thus, not only does the site go to its most profitable use, but the type of building upon it is the one which secures the highest possible yield from the site – having regard to the cost of alternative sites (see below).

(4) A *higher building* and a *higher site price* will result either from a rise in the *MRP* of capital or from a fall in the rate of interest.

A rise in the marginal revenue productivity of capital from *MRP* to *MRP'* (Figure 6.4) could occur through: (i) an increase in the marginal *physical* product as a result of improved techniques (e.g. self-service selling) or increased productivity of the construction industry; (ii) higher revenue, e.g. from increased prices of the existing product supplied by the building or from a new higher and best use as the demand for another good increases or planning permission is granted. The height of the building increases from OM to OM'.

A fall in the rate of interest from Oi to Oi' would, with the MRP curve, similarly increase the height of the building from OM to OM'.

Similarly, the *price of the site* will rise from AiC to $A'iC'$ when MRP rises to MRP' or from AiC to $Ai'C''$ when the rate of interest falls to Oi'.

(5) From the viewpoint of the individual developer, land is a cost; he has to pay the competitive market price in order to obtain it. His argument therefore runs as follows: 'The higher the price of land, the more I have to economise in its use. Thus a site has to be used more intensively by applying more capital per square metre. High land prices have caused high buildings.'

Now while this may be quite true from the viewpoint of the individual, our analysis of the *land market as a whole* turns the argument on its head: (i) where demand is high, the use capacity of land is high; (ii) this means that a highly intensive use of land is profitable; and (iii) because high building is profitable, land values are likely to be high.

Relaxation of the one-year-life-project assumption

We can now relax our assumption that the project has a life of only one year. Provided that we assume that the price of capital and the price of the product do not change over time, the above solution holds, for yields can be discounted back to their present value according to the year in which they are obtained and then added together. The area $AOMC$ in Figure 6.4 will now represent the value of the aggregated discounted yields throughout the estimated life of the project.

The extensive use of land

By building higher, the developer is in effect saving on the cost of land. But diminishing returns mean that the cost of obtaining a given addition to revenue increases. Thus the developer will only build an extra storey so long as this is cheaper than acquiring extra land. In other words, there is a 'margin of building' in terms both of intensive use (adding an extra floor) and of extensive use (adding extra land).

Suppose the demand for office suites in a district increased. A developer could respond either by adding a storey to a building or by building a ground-floor suite on undeveloped land. The alternative adopted would be that which cost less to produce a given addition to revenue. In practice, competition for land for different uses will ensure

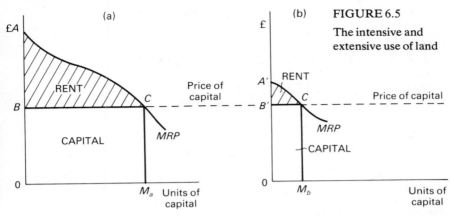

FIGURE 6.5

The intensive and extensive use of land

that, in the long run, development everywhere will be pushed to the point where the marginal return to capital is equal to the marginal cost of capital for every site. Thus in Figure 6.5, plots of land of the same size are developed for (a) the city-centre site by the addition of capital OM_a, and for (b) the suburban site by the addition of OM_b. In the first case the rent is ABC, and in the second $A'B'C'$.

FURTHER READING

J. Harvey, *Modern Economics*, 3rd edn (London: Macmillan, 1977) chs 10, 11, 18.

C. J. Hawkins and D. W. Pearce, *Capital Investment Appraisal* (London: Macmillan, 1971).

Mainly for Students, 'Merchandising', *Estates Gazette*, vol. 239, 4 September 1976, p. 740.

E. J. Mishan, *Elements of Cost Benefit Analysis* (London: Allen & Unwin, 1971) part IV.

M. Newell, *An Introduction to the Economics of Urban Land Use* (London: Estates Gazette, 1977) chs 2, 3, 5, 11.

J. Ratcliffe, *Urban Estates Management* (London: Estates Gazette, 1979) chs 7–12.

W. J. Reilly, *The Law of Retail Gravitation*, 2nd edn (New York: Pilsbury, 1953).

M. Roberts, *An Introduction to Town Planning Techniques* (London: Hutchinson, 1974).

L. Smith, 'The Assessment of Shopping Needs', *Chartered Surveyor*, January 1964.

K. E. Way, 'Viability in Property Development', *Estates Gazette*, vol. 239, 4 September 1976, p. 705.

7

The Timing and Rate of Redevelopment

I THE TIMING OF REDEVELOPMENT

When does redevelopment take place?

Where land is already developed by having a building on it, fixed capital is embodied in the land. Such capital has no cost in the short period; as a result, redevelopment to a new use, which requires expenditure of further capital, usually occurs only after a considerable period of time. In this chapter we consider redevelopment in the context of the time dimension.

In general terms redevelopment takes place when the present value of the expected flow of future net returns from the existing use of the land resources becomes less than the capital value of the cleared site. We have therefore to calculate the present value of the site in its current use and compare this with the value of the cleared site. Our method of arriving at both values follows the present value method described in the previous chapter. In our analysis it is assumed that over the period under consideration there is no change in the value of money.

The present value of the site in its current use

It must be emphasised that we are seeking to establish a *capital* value. Since this depends on the *net* returns expected to be earned in future years, such returns must first be estimated and discounted to the present and then aggregated in order to arrive at the present capital value.

(1) *The expected net annual returns from current use*

The net annual return (NAR) during any given year of the life of a project is the difference between the gross annual return (such as the rental received) and the operating costs (including repairs and maintenance). Since we are dealing with the future, both the gross annual return (GAR) and the operating costs are estimates. These estimates are shown diagrammatically in Figure 7.1.

As the years go by GAR is likely to decrease because: (i) where there were super-normal profits accruing to the initial development, they will encourage similar developments, and this will lower future returns, e.g.

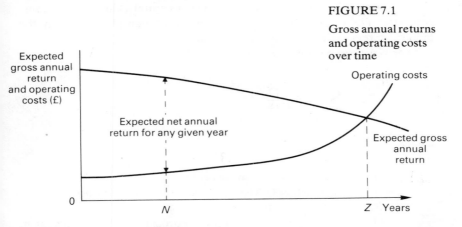

FIGURE 7.1

Gross annual returns and operating costs over time

from rents; and (ii) expectations are subject to greater uncertainty and risk the further one looks ahead. Offsetting these, complementary developments may come along, thereby raising rents.

In contrast, operating costs rise as the years go by because: (i) the structure deteriorates physically; and (ii) the older the building, the less adaptable it is to new technical requirements, e.g. office lay-out, conversion to self-service (for instance, compare a Spar supermarket with a purpose-built Tesco), parking facilities for car-shopping, and so on. This would apply even if the building is let on a full repairing and insuring lease, for higher repair bills would reduce the rent which could be obtained.

(2) Discounting and aggregating NARs to obtain present capital value

The *NARs* for the whole of the future life of the building have to be discounted to the present and then aggregated in order to obtain the present value of the land resource in its current use (see Figure 7.2).

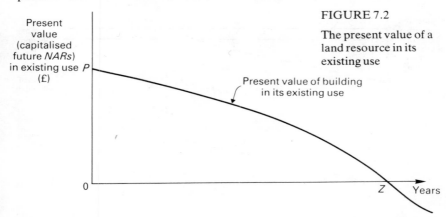

FIGURE 7.2

The present value of a land resource in its existing use

In Figures 7.1 and 7.2 *NAR* and present capital value both become zero after *OZ* years. If no redevelopment has taken place by then, the land resources are left derelict, e.g. Cornish tin mines.

The above can be summarised as

$$P = \sum_{t=i}^{n} \frac{R_i - O_i}{(1 + r)^i}$$

where

P = value of property in current use
n = period when *GAR*s can be earned in current use
R_i = *GAR*s from i to year n
O_i = operating costs, excluding depreciation, from i to year n, and
r = rate of discount

The value of the cleared site

The value of the cleared site is equal to the present value of the alternative highest and best use *less* the cost of clearing the site and rebuilding to the new highest and best use (see Figure 7.3).

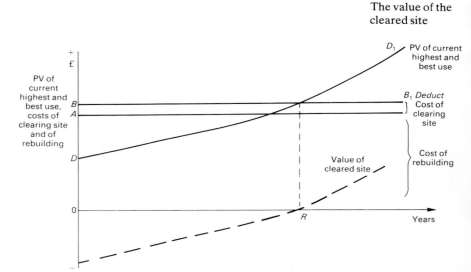

FIGURE 7.3

The value of the cleared site

(1)   *The present value of the alternative highest and best use*

This is obtained by the procedure used for calculating the present value of the current use: (i) the future *NAR*s in the best alternative use are calculated; and (ii) these *NAR*s are discounted to the present and aggregated to give a capital present value, DD_1 in Figure 7.3.

It will be observed in Figures 7.2 and 7.3 that in year 0, when the existing building was constructed, the present value in the current use (*OP*) was greater than the present value in the new alternative highest and best use (*OD*). It was for this reason that the land went to its current use. From then on, however, the value of the alternative use (DD_1) rises. This occurs for two main reasons. First, changes in the conditions of demand and supply (discussed later) mean that a new building will produce, as regards both use and lay-out, a greater *NAR*. Thus an existing cinema may be replaced by a supermarket, while an old office building may give way to one that is centrally heated and air-conditioned and has the structure and space suitable for modern office equipment. Second, any new building would probably have a longer time horizon than the old building (which has already run a part of its life) so that there would be more future *NAR*s to be aggregated.

(2)   *Deductions of the cost of bringing the site to its alternative use*

From the present value of the best alternative use at any one time, we have to deduct:

(a)   the cost of demolishing and clearing the site (*AB* in Figure 7.3); and
(b)   the total costs of rebuilding for the new use, including ripening costs and normal profit (*OA*).

For simplicity, we have assumed that costs (a) and (b) both remain constant over time. *OB* represents the sum of (a) and (b).

The value of the cleared site is thus the difference between DD_1 and BB_1 in any given year. Up to year *R* it is negative. In year *O* the value of the best alternative use would be only just below that of the chosen current use. Then, however, each was competing for a cleared site. Once a site has been allocated to a given use and has had a building erected upon it, any new use has the additional handicap of demolishing and rebuilding. In Figure 7.3 this handicap is not overcome until year *R*; from then onwards the value of the cleared site is positive.

Using the previous notation, and using *R′* and *O′* to refer to the best alternative use, and where

C = the value of the cleared site
D = the cost of demolition and clearing the site
B = the cost of rebuilding to the new highest and best use

we have:

$$C = \sum_{t=0}^{n} \frac{R'_i - O'_i}{(1 + r)^i} - D - B$$

(3) *Redevelopment of the site*

By combining Figures 7.2 and 7.3 in Figure 7.4, we can show when redevelopment takes place. From year T the value of the cleared site exceeds the present value of the building in its current use. Thus redevelopment takes place in year T, when $C = P$.

It should be noted that in year T the building is still *technically* efficient, for it can earn a NAR until year Z. However, in year T it becomes *economically* inefficient because resources can be switched to a new use having a greater value. Thus we can define the economic life of a building as that period over which it earns net annual returns and where replacement is not a viable economic alternative.

Application of the model

The diagrammatic model can be used to analyse all redevelopment situations. By way of illustration we will examine: (i) the rate of redevelopment; (ii) the 'twilight zone' of towns and cities; and (iii) the problem of preserving historic buildings.

II THE RATE OF REDEVELOPMENT

Method of approach

The rate of redevelopment will depend upon changes which occur over time in the relationship between:

(1)   the capital value of the existing use of the land resources;
(2)   the capital value of the best alternative use; and
(3)   the cost of rebuilding.

It will be accelerated if (2) increases relative to (1), or if the cost of rebuilding falls. It will be retarded if opposite changes occur. What we have to consider, therefore, are the factors affecting (1), (2) and (3).

Capital value depends upon expected future NARs and the rate at which they are discounted to the present. The latter will be common to both existing and alternative uses. We can thus concentrate on the NARs

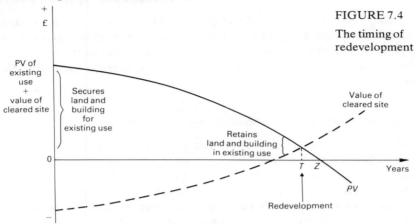

FIGURE 7.4

The timing of redevelopment

of each, the difference between *GAR (rentals)* and *operating costs*. The first is concerned largely with changes on the demand side, the second with changes on the supply side.

Changes on the demand side affecting GAR

Let us assume that the current use of a site in the city centre is large residential houses and that the best alternative use is offices.

A change in the *demand for large city-centre houses* can arise through changes in: (i) tastes (e.g. a switch in preferences towards flats or smaller suburban houses); (ii) real income (e.g. people tend to move out of intensively occupied city houses as their income increases); (iii) the distribution of income (e.g. higher taxation of the rich forces them to vacate expensive city-centre houses); (iv) the price of substitutes (e.g. cheaper suburban houses); (v) transport costs or facilities (e.g. fare rises or the building of a motorway or underground railway); (vi) borrowing opportunities (e.g. building societies' conditions for mortgages); (vii) complementary activities (e.g. new schools or golf courses in the suburbs); (viii) government policy (e.g. the extension of security of tenure to furnished lettings may prolong residential use, while the introduction of capital value rating which shifts the rate burden towards expensive houses, or making planning permission to convert large houses to flats conditional upon the provision of off-street parking, would tend to shorten it).

Similarly, the *GAR* of offices, the alternative use, would be affected by changes in both occupation and investment demand. Thus a rise in *occupation demand* for professional services or for offices in city-centre positions would increase *GAR*, while government dispersal policy would tend to decrease it. But since *GAR* depends largely on *expected* future rentals, *investment demand* would increase the capital value if such rentals were expected to keep step with a continuing high rate of inflation. Put in an alternative form, the current yield on offices would be capitalised at a lower rate for investment purposes, thereby increasing the capital value of offices.

Changes on the supply side affecting operating costs

Basically the same considerations apply to both houses and offices, but we shall illustrate for the former. With houses, operating costs may change because: (i) maintenance costs and repairs change, e.g. builders' charges may rise, or repairs may be curtailed (as, for instance, in the twilight zones of towns); (ii) technical improvements may allow conversions to a more intensive use, e.g. flatlets may become economically viable as a result of cheaper partitioning and the development of compact units incorporating a sink, refrigerator and electric cooking facilities; and (iii) government policy may alter, e.g. improvement grants will reduce conversion costs, whereas more stringent fire-precaution regulations will increase them.

The effect on the rate of redevelopment of a change in the rate of interest

A change in the rate of interest is unlikely to have equivalent effects on both the present and alternative use.

First, at any given time a part of the physical life of a building has passed. Thus the years of future yields are fewer, and so is its present capitalised value. In contrast, the next-best-use building has not yet begun its life, so that there are more yields to be capitalised. This means that a rise in the rate of interest will favour the present use since it applies to fewer future yields. In other words, it will reduce the value of the next-best use more than that of the current use.

Second, a higher rate of interest will increase ripening and waiting costs, thus decreasing the present capital value of the next-best use.

Figure 7.5 illustrates how, for the above reasons, a rise in the rate of interest brings about changes in the position of the capital-value curves of the present and next-best uses. The net result of a rise in the rate of interest is to retard redevelopment from year T to year S; a fall in the rate of interest would tend to accelerate it.

Third, in addition to a rise in the rate of interest, the imperfection of the capital market may mean that certain forms of development may encounter additional penalties. Thus house purchasers tend to rely more on borrowed funds than insurance, industrial and property companies. For instance, insurance companies have a net inflow of premium income, while larger firms can usually borrow temporarily from a bank when the

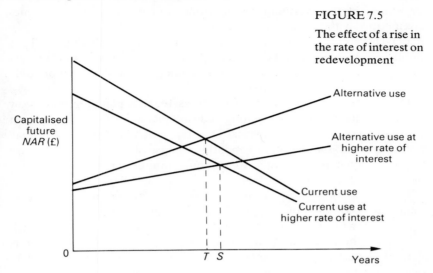

FIGURE 7.5

The effect of a rise in the rate of interest on redevelopment

rate of interest seems high, funding the loan later when the long-term rate has fallen. In contrast, house purchasers will find that a higher rate of interest will reduce the maximum loan available through the application of the building societies' income/repayment ratio (see Chapter 12).

Building costs

Redevelopment will be accelerated by a fall in real building costs because this will increase the value of the cleared site. Such a fall may occur through: (i) improved technology, e.g. in the building of high-rise office blocks or modular construction; and (ii) an increase in the construction industry's productivity (see Chapter 11).

Similarly, redevelopment will be retarded by an increase in building costs.

Relaxation of the assumptions of a perfect market and perfect competition

Conditions in the real world may affect the pace of redevelopment:

(1) Imperfect knowledge, immobility of factors, or just inertia, may mean that it takes time for profitable redevelopment to get under way.

(2) Imperfections of the capital market may affect the type of development. For instance, houses may be built instead of a block of flats because selling the former on completion gives the developer an earlier cash flow.

(3) Legal restrictions, e.g. a covenant prohibiting the building of a particular type of shop, may prevent a particular highest and best

development, thus postponing redevelopment until another use becomes competitive with the current use.

(4) There may not be perfect competition in the supply of sites. Thus publicly owned land is not commonly offered for sale, while some owners of sites essential to the complete development exercise their monopoly powers in the price they demand.

(5) Government policy, particularly as regards planning, may slow down development by preventing redevelopment to the existing most profitable use. Thus an Industrial Development Certificate (IDC) may not be granted. On the other hand, the exercise of compulsory purchase powers may make it easier to combine interests and so accelerate development, e.g. for slum clearance.

Other examples of government policy affecting the rate of development are taxation policy (e.g. residential and commercial buildings cannot be written off as depreciation), improvement grants (which encourage the modernisation of owner-occupied or rented, older, residential properties), the Leasehold Reform Act 1967 (which, by enabling owner-occupiers to purchase the freeholds of their leasehold interests, made it virtually impossible to retain estates intact for future comprehensive redevelopment), and the Development Land Tax 1976 (which, by exempting most refurbishment, led developers to concentrate on the improvement of existing properties rather than on renewal by re-building).

III   THE 'TWILIGHT' ZONE OF TOWNS AND CITIES

In the twilight (or transition) zone of towns and cities existing buildings (small factories, shops and, particularly, houses) have a run-down appearance, and residences are over-crowded.

With residential accommodation GAR is maintained by more intensive use, houses, for example, being let in individual rooms or converted to a students' hostel. On the other hand, operating costs, chiefly repairs, are reduced to a bare minimum. Thus in Figure 7.6 redevelopment in the existing use (1) would normally take place in year T. However, conversion to a more intensive use (2) in year S increases future NARs and thus the capital value, so that redevelopment is postponed to year Y.

As regards commercial and industrial sites, operating costs are similarly minimised, especially towards the end of leases. Technological change often makes buildings too small or structurally unsuitable for their original use. Thus, as leases fall due, buildings are either left empty until a complete area can be redeveloped or let on very short leases often in a new use, e.g. car repairs. Alternatively, the building is demolished and the site used temporarily as a parking lot or a scrap-iron yard.

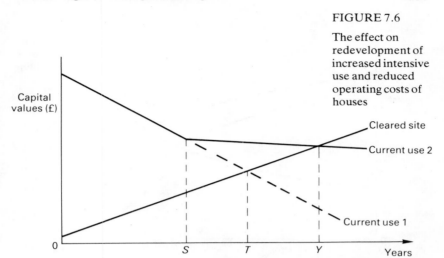

FIGURE 7.6

The effect on redevelopment of increased intensive use and reduced operating costs of houses

Eventually redevelopment takes place, either through the operation of the price system, e.g. as with the Victoria Street development, or through public authorities, e.g. slum clearance (see Chapter 9).

IV   THE PRESERVATION OF HISTORIC BUILDINGS

Conservation is necessary to secure the optimum use of resources over time. As regards land resources, it is concerned with green belts, National Parks, public bridle ways and footpaths, parks and common land, nature reserves, National Trust property and buildings of special architectural or historic interest. Here we use our diagrammatic model to examine the problem of preserving historic buildings, but much of the analysis is applicable to the other subjects.

Possible weaknesses of the market solution

If left to market forces, the demolition of a historic building would take place in year T in Figure 7.7. On what grounds may *economics* justify interference with this market solution? The case rests largely on the fact that, with a historic building, assumptions implicit in our model have to be qualified:

(1) The estimate of GARs, from which is derived the present value of the historic building, may ignore 'option demand'. Where decisions are irreversible (as with the destruction of a historic building), many people would pay something just to postpone such a decision. The difficulty lies

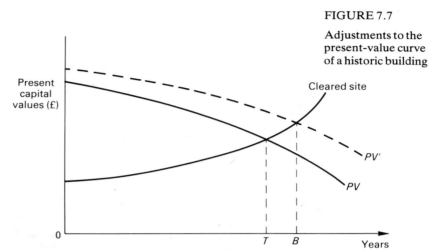

FIGURE 7.7

Adjustments to the
present-value curve
of a historic building

in quantifying such 'option demand', but its existence is evident in the fact that many people subscribe voluntarily to, say, the National Trust and the World Wildlife Fund. The rest enjoy the option as 'free riders', but their demand should also be included. Such higher GARs would give a higher present-value curve, e.g. PV' in Figure 7.7.

(2) There is no unique rate for discounting future NARs in order to obtain present value (see p. 152). Furthermore, because the rate of social time preference is lower than that of private time preference (see p. 153), a present value derived from the lower rate of discount appropriate to the *social* time preference would be higher than one based on a rate of discount which merely reflected *private* time preference. Thus the present-value curve for a historic building should be higher, e.g. PV' in Figure 7.7.

(3) NARs only measure private assessments of benefits and costs. Thus external benefits, such as the pleasure which the view of a historic building gives to passers-by, are ignored. Again this would produce a higher present-value curve, e.g. PV' in Figure 7.7. In this case, as with the first two, the life of the building would be prolonged by TB years.

(4) Knowledge is not perfect, especially when we are dealing with the future. Thus a decision to demolish a building may be based on a defective assessment of the future conditions of demand and supply. This is not serious when we are dealing with flows, such as the services provided by offices, since new offices can always be built if demand increases in the future. But demolishing a historic building diminishes a stock which cannot be replaced. The situation is illustrated in Figure 7.8.

In period *t* the historic building has a low value, OH. On the other hand, an office block would command price OP. Over time, however, the value

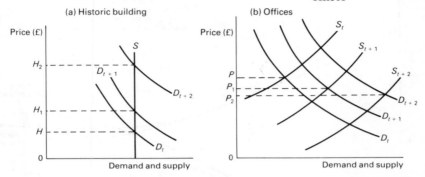

FIGURE 7.8

Changes in the future relative prices of historic buildings and offices

of the historic building increases relative to that of offices. This is because, with higher incomes and more leisure, people take a greater interest in historic buildings. Increased demand means that in, say, period $t + 2$, the price of the historic building has risen to OH_2. On the other hand, the demand for offices is not likely to increase so quickly, income-elasticity of demand being lower. Moreover, with technological improvements in construction, the supply curve shifts to the right over time. As a result, in period $t + 2$ the price of offices falls to OP_2.

The situation is transferred to Figure 7.9. We can assume that the price of the office block in period t gives a cleared site value of FD, so that demolition of the historic building and redevelopment of the site as offices has become a viable economic proposition. Eventually, however, the value of the historic building starts to rise, while the rate of increase in the value of the cleared site declines. Indeed, if demolition in year D could be prevented, by year E the present value of the historic building once again exceeds the value of the cleared site.

Government policy for preserving historic buildings

The above analysis suggests that the government must interfere with the free operation of the price system in order to preserve historic buildings. Such interference can take a variety of forms.

First, the building could be brought under public ownership. Such a policy would usually be followed where the cost of excluding 'free riders' would be prohibitive, e.g. Hadrian's Wall. Equally important, it would allow welfare to be maximised, e.g. Apsley House, Hyde Park Corner, which houses the Wellington museum. Maximum welfare requires that

FIGURE 7.9

Methods of
preserving a historic
building

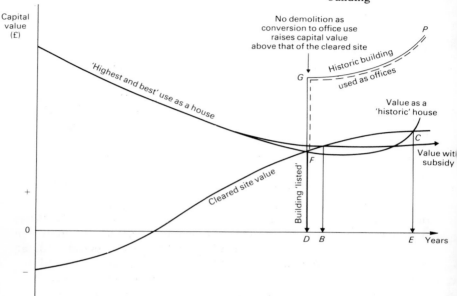

output should be pushed to the point where marginal cost equals marginal benefit. Thus where marginal cost is zero, admission to the historic building would be free, fixed costs being met from the proceeds of taxation. Finally, public ownership would automatically allow external benefits to be internalised.

Second, the historic building could be left in private ownership but a subsidy given through repair grants or capital transfer tax concessions on the grounds of the external benefits enjoyed. Such a subsidy would increase *NAR*s, and so raise the present value. However, there are difficulties. Many external benefits cannot be quantified (see p. 143), while shortage of funds would mean that the subsidy would be insufficient to raise the present-value curve permanently above the cleared-site curve so that demolition is only postponed to year *B*, unless other action is taken.

Third, any building of special architectural or historic interest may be 'listed'. This means that it cannot be altered or demolished without the consent of the Secretary of State for the Environment. While this gives protection against positive acts of demolition, it may not cover destruction by the neglect of the owner. Such neglect occurs because high maintenance costs result in negative *NAR*s. Even though in such circumstances the local authority may appropriate the building, there is reluctance to do so since the cost of maintenance now falls on limited public funds. Thus, in practice, 'listing' may only be a 'stop-gap' measure, bridging the years between D and E (see Figure 7.9) until increased NARs raise the value of the historic building above that of the cleared site. More frequently, 'listing' simply imposes a prohibition on demolition until an alternative policy can be formulated.

Fourth, giving permission for the building to be adapted to a more profitable use provides such a policy. Thus stables may be converted into a dwelling, and houses into offices. This has the effect of increasing NARs and thus raising the present-value curve so that it is above the cleared-site curve. This change of use is shown as taking place in year D and the new present value is depicted by the line FGP in Figure 7.9.

In consenting to a change of use of a historic building the objective of the authorities must be to retain as many of the original features as possible. Thus some flexibility is necessary as regards building regulations, for example as regards height of rooms, window space and even fire precautions. As in Figure 7.9, the distinctive character of the converted building may produce increasing rentals over time, e.g. for prestige reasons, so that (as well as the building being preserved) there is no charge on public funds.

FURTHER READING

B. Goodall, *The Economics of Urban Areas* (Oxford: Pergamon Press, 1972) ch. 8.

8

Finance for Development

I GENERAL CONSIDERATIONS

Principle of financing real property development

Development needs finance: (i) to cover the development period; and (ii) to purchase the finished development and hold it as an investment. The former is usually referred to as a 'short-term' or 'bridging' loan, and the latter as a 'long-term' or 'funded' loan. There are thus usually three main participants: (a) the *borrower*, i.e. the developer (who may also be the long-term holder of the equity interest); (b) the *provider of short-term finance*, e.g. a joint-stock or merchant bank; and (c) the *lender of long-term finance*, usually an institution such as an insurance company or pension fund.

The method of raising finance, whether short- or long-term, is based on the principle of creating an interest in the real property. The owner can use the property simply as security for a bank loan (which can be regarded as a short-term mortgage). Alternatively, he can sell a definite interest. For instance, the owner of the 'fee simple absolute' of a particular property may lack the capital necessary to develop. He might obtain this against a rent charge. Or the owner-occupier of a shop or farm may wish to raise additional working capital. He could do this by 'sale and leaseback' (see p. 114). On the other hand, the creation of an interest enables the lender to obtain an income from real property without having to occupy the property himself.

The essential point to note is that, for the person creating the rent charge or selling and leasing back his property, the form chosen represents, *other things being equal*, the most preferred way of raising capital. Similarly for the lender: the particular interest created, a rent charge or leaseback, represents the best way of using capital.

Market imperfections

However, 'other things being equal' assumes that in the market: (i) there are a number of competitive lenders; and (ii) there is always a 'price' represented by the rate of interest at which a would-be borrower can obtain funds as an alternative to selling an interest.

In practice, these conditions do not hold. First, the borrower may be faced with a monopoly lender, as occurs, for instance, with the small developer who has to rely mainly on a bank. Thus a speculative builder might find that the conditions of a loan are the same from all banks, being limited to one year only. As a result, he has to watch his cash-flow position carefully. This may even force him to build houses, which can be sold as they are completed, rather than a block of flats.

Second, property often consists of 'large lumps', an office block costing, say, £20 million to build and a city-centre redevelopment considerably more. In such cases finance is usually secured by negotiation between principals, and the precise terms will reflect their relative strengths in bilateral bargaining.

Third, government policy may influence the terms of a loan. For example, if the government restricts lending by joint-stock banks, a loan may have to be arranged through an insurance company, which can stipulate a part-equity interest. Similarly, 'rent freezes' can result in the drying up of certain sources of finance, e.g. from pension funds, since the money market may temporarily offer a better return. Above all, taxation affects property finance. Corporation tax, capital gains tax and development land tax leave smaller profits for ploughing back into future developments. Exemption from income tax means that leaseholds have advantages to certain lenders, such as charitable trusts, while capital gains tax may discourage 'sale and leasebacks'.

Thus the main effects of these market imperfections are:

(a)   Interests may be created which would not have been had the market offered alternative sources of finance. Thus a sale and leaseback may be preferred to a mortgage simply because it provides finance to the full value of a property as opposed to only two-thirds.
(b)   Particular conditions can be imposed by the lender as an alternative to raising the rate of interest. As we shall see when discussing building societies (Chapter 12), this can have far-reaching effects on real property.
(c)   Since funds cannot always be obtained when needed or on terms which suit the borrower, finance plays an important role in the timing, quantity and type of development undertaken.

The response to market imperfections

A study of property development since 1945 reveals no hard-and-fast ways by which capital is raised. Rather, it demonstrates the ingenuity of developers in obtaining funds as conditions have changed in the capital market, usually as a result of changes in government policy. Thus until 1954, when capital expenditure above £10,000 had to obtain the sanction of the Capital Issues Committee, developers worked in conjunction with insurance companies who were not subject to this limitation. Similarly, in the 1960s when the 'Big Four' banks were required to limit their lending to property developers, the latter turned to merchant banks, foreign banks and even finance companies who had previously specialised in hire purchase.

Sources of capital also alter as the requirements of lenders change. This may be due to a change in policy, e.g. insurance companies sought equity interests with the introduction of 'with-profits' policies. On the other hand, it may simply be the result of an adjustment in an institution's portfolio of assets. Thus, as a hedge against inflation, a pension fund may increase its lending for property development in return for a part-share in the freehold interest.

What follows, therefore, is simply a survey of the different arrangements which have been made in practice, largely in response to market imperfections, to raise both short-term and long-term finance.

II   SHORT-TERM FINANCE

The requirements of the borrower and lender

Every developer needs *short-term* finance for the development period in order to purchase land, meet ripening and waiting costs and pay the building contractor and professional consultants. The period usually extends from one to three years, but for comprehensive developments it can be much longer. With the latter, the developer may rely on rolling over short-term loans; more usually, long-term finance from the institutions will be required from the start.

Since, from the lender's point of view, there is limited security in an incomplete building, short-term finance can be quite expensive, though naturally the price will vary with the borrower's financial status. Consequently, the *borrower* will try to start building as soon as possible after the site has been acquired and get the building completed quickly. He is then able to realise his profits, either by selling the development, or, should he wish to hold it as an investment, by arranging long-term finance.

The *lender*, on the other hand, is concerned with the security, liquidity, 'opportunity cost' and inflation-hedge of his capital. Thus his loan terms will depend upon the following.

(1)   *The financial standing of the borrower*
Here the well-established property company carrying out a development is at an advantage. Not only do its existing property holdings provide collateral but net revenue from them may cover interest payments on the new loan.

In contrast, the small developer, such as a house-builder, can only offer limited security. Consequently, the lender hedges against risk by: (i) limiting the loan to only a proportion (60–80 per cent) of the land and building costs; (ii) staggering the loan by stage payments based on the architect's certificate; and (iii) evaluating the market conditions for the sale of the finished project.

(2) *The current market conditions for the sale of the project*

Repayment of the original loan usually rests on the sale of the finished development. Because market conditions may change, the lender usually limits the loan to two years. Where the development takes longer, and particularly with housing-estate development, the project is often divided into phases, with the loan being reviewed on the completion of each phase.

(3) *The current market rate of interest*

Since the borrower of development finance is competing in the money market at large, the interest rate he pays will be influenced by general market conditions. Short-term rates tend to fluctuate more than long-term rates and are closely related to Minimum Lending Rate.

(4) *The degree of inflation-hedge which can be offered*

Where the lender is a merchant bank, one condition of the loan may be participation in the equity of the development company – otherwise the benefit of rising rents during the construction period will accrue exclusively to the developer.

As we shall see, institutions providing finance may also impose conditions when they prefer interests having an inflation-hedge.

Sources of short-term finance

In many respects short-term development finance can be likened to the working capital of industry, for such capital covers the production period until the finished good is sold. Thus the sources of short-term finance for development tend to be similar to those for businesses in general.

Short-term finance is obtained mainly from the banks – the joint-stock 'Big Four' banks, long-established merchant banks (e.g. Hambros, Rothschild) and the UK subsidiaries of foreign banks. Until 1974 finance could also be obtained from finance houses (e.g. United Dominions Trust, First National Finance Corporation) and the 'fringe banks', which, like Twentieth Century Banking and London & County Securities, accepted short-term deposits which were reinvested in property development. However, with the collapse in the property boom, these withdrew from the property finance market (see pp. 117–20).

Joint-stock banks lend up to about two-thirds of the value of a development, either by granting overdraft facilities or by providing a term loan. While the overdraft is cheaper, it can be ended should government policy put pressure on the bank's liquidity, e.g. by a call for special deposits. Thus a term loan gives the developer greater security. Even so, it is usually limited to two years and, although the expectation is that it will be rolled over, it is by no means certain. The impact of government monetary policy is still primarily on the joint-stock banks, which may, for instance, be instructed to cut back on their lending to developers. Moreover, the rate of interest charged can fluctuate as government measures influence rates in the money market.

A developer may therefore prefer to raise short-term finance through a *merchant bank* because the interest rate charged, though a little higher, may be fixed for the whole period of the loan, usually about two years. This allows him to forecast his development costs more accurately. Moreover, a merchant bank may lend up to four-fifths of the value of the development.

Normally all banks structure the loan to the nature of the project. Thus a loan for an industrial warehouse development would be for a shorter period than for an office block since the former usually takes less time to complete. However, the bank's main concern is for the security of the loan and its repayment on time. First, it restricts its lending to (at the most) four-fifths of the value of the project. Second, it considers the financial background of the developing company, such as its gearing, cash flow (e.g. rents from property owned or sales of developments completed) and links with long-term sources of finance. Third, it requires the developer to have proved management ability.

Since the collapse of the property market in 1973, banks have followed cautious policies. Valuations are more conservative, there is a greater desire to see pre-lettings, and more emphasis is placed on the developer's ability to cover interest payments from his own cash flow. Moreover, having burned their fingers severely, many banks, such as the First National Finance Corporation and United Dominions Trust, have withdrawn from further property finance.

Major developments

For a major development, e.g. urban renewal, a shopping centre or a large office block, short-term finance on a two-year basis presents difficulties. Such projects therefore require long-term finance from the institutions or government from the very commencement of the development.

Similarly, when a development company is building for an occupying institution, the latter may provide long-term finance from the start (see p. 70).

Repaying short-term finance

The developer can realise the profit from a project either by selling it during construction or upon completion, or by holding it as an investment.

Suppose the development is a block of offices with a capital cost of £4 million. A merchant bank makes the developer a short-term loan of £3 million, leaving him to find £1 million from his own resources. While the building is still under construction, the developer finds a tenant at a net rental of £500,000 a year, which, on a ten-year purchase basis, gives a capitalised value of £5 million. At this stage the developer can fund his short-term loan and recover his own outlay by selling the project to an institutional investor on an initial payment with the balance being paid as the development proceeds.

However, it is likely that a successful development company will wish to retain some of its better developments, particularly as these provide collateral and income against future borrowing. To do this, it needs long-term capital.

III   LONG-TERM FINANCE

Finance through equity capital

Finance can be divided broadly into *equity capital* and *loans*. Equity capital is obtained by ploughing back profits or by selling shares. Except for well-established and fairly large companies the former is unlikely to provide sufficient capital to purchase developments of high value. It is interesting to note, however, that Percy Bilton Ltd was able to use $8 million from rental income in 1976 for further development. On the other hand, raising capital by the sale of shares is really open only to a public company, and usually a minimum of £500,000 must be raised to make an issue by public offer an economic proposition. While this sum may be no obstacle to a successful developer, equity financing has two main disadvantages.

First, the cost of this type of finance depends largely upon the current popularity of property-company shares on the Stock Exchange. If such shares are wanted, e.g. because they are regarded as an excellent inflation-hedge, they will sell on a low-yield basis relative to fixed-interest-bearing bonds: that is, there is a reverse yield gap. New capital from the sale of shares can therefore be obtained on favourable terms, giving owners of existing shares a capital gain. Thus a number of expanding property companies came to the market in 1970–2 (such as Fairview Estates, Royco and Joviel), a proportion of their equity already being held by merchant banks as a condition for making loans. On the other hand, if property shares are in disfavour, e.g. as after 1973, they have to be sold on a high-yield basis. In such circumstances few companies would seek to raise capital by selling shares even through a rights issue.

Second, property companies prefer to be highly geared. Holding first-class property entails little risk since rents are regular, fairly certain and, with inflation, likely to rise. It is thus possible to raise finance by borrowing; increasing the equity merely lowers earnings per share.

Yet while a straight loan in money terms is preferred by a property company, the imperfections of the capital market may restrict its choice. For instance, because of continuing inflation, many institutions may lend only on some form of equity-loan basis, for example by linking the yield to a rent charge. What follows, therefore, is simply a survey of the various possibilities of raising long-term finance, the availability of each changing from time to time.

Methods of raising long-term finance

Since long-term finance is secured on completed buildings, capital is much safer. Moreover, the margin between interest payable and rental income provides an indication of the security of the loan. Thus long-term finance is usually available on easier terms than short-term development finance, and is tied closely to the current yield on long-term government securities.

(1)   *Mortgages*

Ideally a developer would prefer to obtain a straight loan from an insurance company, pension fund or trust against a mortgage on the completed development. The rate of interest paid will depend upon the current level of interest rates in general, the estimated risk and the degree of inflation in the economy. At one time it was usual for the capital to be repaid at the end of the mortgage period; nowadays, in order to protect themselves against inflation and rising interest rates, lending institutions tend to require periodic repayments of the loan which can then be reinvested.

The difficulty for the developer is that he may not have a sufficient cash flow to cover the interest charge plus the capital repayments, especially as the latter are not chargeable to income for taxation purposes. Thus whether a mortgage loan is feasible depends upon (i) the timing of future revenues with respect to outgoings, and (ii) how the lender requires repayment of capital. Figures 8.1 and 8.2 illustrate two possibilities.

In Figure 8.1 the developer's flow of revenue is quite adequate for servicing the loan, and this in spite of the fact that the lender requires repayment of the capital by equal amounts during each year of the loan.

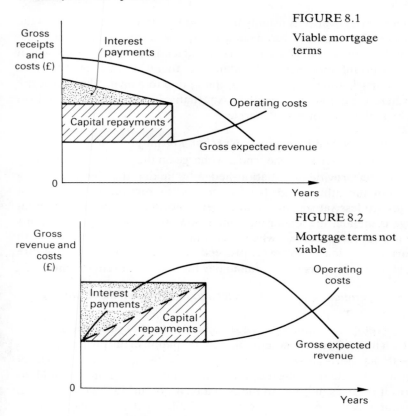

FIGURE 8.1

Viable mortgage terms

FIGURE 8.2

Mortgage terms not viable

In Figure 8.2 the borrower has negotiated more favourable terms. With equal yearly sums to cover both interest and capital repayments, the latter is smaller at the beginning of the loan. In spite of this, however, the developer's cash flow is insufficient to service this total yearly sum simply because gross revenue is small in the earlier years of the project, though they are expected to increase over time, either through increased demand for this type of development or through inflation.

In practice, the deficiency in cash flow may be substantial. If, therefore, the developer does not already have income from other property to cover the shortfall, he has to rethink his financing along one of the following lines. These alternatives avoid early capital repayment, providing the full sum for a longer period usually because they offer the lender some form of inflation-hedge.

(2) *Mortgage debenture*

Here an advance is made against the security of a particular property but the lender has in addition a general charge against the assets of the company. An advance is usually limited to two-thirds of the value of the *completed* development, but capital repayment is not required until the end of the loan period. While such a straight loan may suit the borrower, it provides no inflation-hedge. Lenders may therefore add some form of equity-participation condition, e.g. the option to convert the debenture into share capital at a future date. Alternatively, the return on the loan may be in the form of a rent charge.

(3)   *Long-term finance against a rent charge on the property*

Here the developer gives the lender a charge on the rents of the property and this can provide an inflation-hedge by linking the charge to rising rents. On the other hand, legal remedies for recovering unpaid rent charges are less satisfactory than under a mortgage or lease. If the rent charge is unpaid, the lender may enter into possession and collect rents until the debt is recovered, when the property reverts to the owner. With a mortgage or lease, however, proceedings can be taken for forfeiture should the tenant persistently fail to pay his interest or rent on time.

(4)   *Co-operation between the developing company and the occupying institution*

If the developing company has a successful record of property develop-ment, an institution may accept fuller participation in the project, provid-ing both the short- and long-term finance. The institution acquires a legal interest in the site from the developer and grants him a licence to build. In return, it receives interest on the sum advanced during the construction period and, when complete, occupies the building at a rent calculated on an agreed percentage of the total cost of development.

In methods (1)–(4) the developer normally retains the freehold, while the lender incorporates some form of inflation-hedge. Alternatively, the lender can own the freehold, i.e. the equity interest, as follows:

(5)   *Sale and leaseback*

This method really dates from the post-war situation when development over £10,000 needed approval by the Capital Issues Committee. How-ever, this restriction did not apply to insurance companies (who had funds from premiums to invest) provided the use of the property was retained.

The essence of a sale and leaseback is that the freehold is sold in advance to an institution on condition that it leases back the completed development to the developer/property company for a stipulated period. The property company finds its own tenants. The principle has been extended to cover shops, offices, factories, flats, and even car-parks and telephone exchanges.

Shops and offices, however, tend to be preferred. With prime shops, site value represents a large part of the total value of the shop, and the prospect of appreciation in site value offsets possible depreciation in the value of the building. Impetus to shop leaseback transactions was also given by the increase of multiple-shop trading, for the retail companies concerned preferred expansionary policies to holding low-yielding safe freeholds represented by their own shops. Offices have the advantage of not depreciating so quickly as factory buildings.

For the institution, the sale and leaseback transaction has attractive features:

(a) Periodic rent reviews give a hedge against inflation.
(b) A leaseback secured against first-class shop property provides a valuable reversion when the lease ends. Although a distant reversion may not affect the current capital value, institutions can look well ahead.
(c) Freeholds and long leaseholds are a more permanent form of investment than mortgages, which may be ended at short notice. Insurance companies' commitments may be forty years ahead, and the companies seek to match assets accordingly.
(d) Ownership of property may offer greater income security than other equity investment since rent is a prior charge against a company.
(e) By dealing directly with one developer/property company (the lessee), an institution can have a stake in property without carrying the encumbrances of management of buildings in multi-occupation.
(f) Because of the large funds which insurance companies have to invest daily, a large sale and leaseback transaction, say of £2 million, is less trouble, both now and in the future, than investing £200,000 in ten different holdings.
(g) A geographical spread of investment, for example through a chain of multiple shops distributed in the major towns in Britain, reduces the risk to the investor from such factors as local unemployment.

From the developer's point of view, the creation of a sale and leaseback may represent the only source of capital. But it has disadvantages. While initially the difference between the mortgage borrowing rate and the rent payable under a leaseback is likely to be small, rent revisions may widen the gap since rents have tended to increase faster than mortgage interest rates. Moreover, while a mortgage may be terminated, a leaseback is irreversible. Lastly, in periods of inflation the sale of a freehold on leaseback condition still involves loss of capital gains. Leasebacks have been favoured, therefore, only where the dominant consideration has been the ability to raise finance up to the full value of the property.

It is appropriate to mention here that sale and leasebacks have also been used by owners of shops and farms to raise working capital. If, for instance, a company can earn 20 per cent on capital employed in its trading activities, but holds a large proportion of capital in the form of premises, it may be able to sell these at a rent equal, say, to 10 per cent of the capital realised. Other things being equal, this would be a profitable course to adopt. But other things may not be equal. First, inflation could result in future rent increases and capital appreciation of the building. If the capital required could be raised by other means at about the same rate, a dynamic company might prefer to form its own property-holding company, bringing with it also the advantages of diversification of activities. Second, taxation of capital gains tends to make leasebacks unprofitable, for the vendor becomes subject to immediate payment of tax, thus depriving him of capital.

(6)   *Joint company*
The developing company and the lending institution can form a joint company, shares being held in agreed proportions. Indeed, even the landowner, including local authorities, may have shares (see p. 127).

One advantage to the institution of a joint company is the acquisition of modern developments which are in short supply. Moreover, it obtains a secure return on the finance advanced, together with an inflation-hedge through its equity interest in the development.

On the other hand, under the Finance Act 1965 only interest payments are a deductible item in assessing a company's liability for corporation tax, so that dividends on ordinary and preference shares are reduced by corporation tax, even though such shares were held by non-taxpaying institutions such as charities.

(7)   *Direct development by institutions*
Because of the tax disadvantages of the joint company, many institutions turned after 1965 to carrying out developments themselves using consul-tants. Later government anti-inflation policy made this course even more desirable. Until 1979 as a shareholder in a joint company, an institution was limited to annual dividend increases of 10 per cent under the Price Code whereas there was no restriction on rent increases.

(8)   *Specialist finance corporations*
Specialist corporations, set up under the auspices of the Bank of England and the joint-stock banks, exist for certain purposes. They include the Film Finance Corporation and the Agricultural Mortgage Corporation, from which farmers can borrow for farm and building extensions.

More important is Finance for Industry, which consists of the Industrial and Commercial Finance Corporation, which lends up to £500,000, and the Finance Corporation for Industry, which lends larger amounts. Both are concerned with industrial and commercial expansion rather than property development, but certain developments, e.g. hotels, may be granted a loan.

(9) *Government sources*

Apart from the private-sector sources of finance described above, government funds are also available. These are dealt with in Chapters 12 and 13.

Finance brokers

While large development companies have the know-how to arrange their own finance, smaller development and property companies may find it advantageous to work through a finance broker who usually has connections with insurance companies.

The finance broker deals with specific propositions on a fee-paying basis. He obtains quotations for finance and advises on the relative merits of the different offers for the particular project in view. As a specialist, he may save the developer more than his brokerage fee.

IV RECENT DEVELOPMENTS IN THE PROPERTY MARKET

The boom years 1971–2

In the two decades following the Second World War government restrictions and the imperfections of the capital market meant that developers and property companies had to show ingenuity and flexibility in raising finance. As we have seen, merchant banks, UK subsidiaries of foreign banks and finance companies provided property finance when that was unavailable from the joint-stock banks.

In 1972 the Heath government decided to expand the economy and, with the new monetary policy of *Competition and Credit Control*, the money supply was increased. Much of this new money found its way into the property market via the banks, including the joint-stock banks, which could now compete openly with the merchant banks. Compared with institutional lending, which between 1970 and 1973 rose from £1,715 million to £3,269 million, bank lending increased from £71 million to £1,332 million. Moreover, the distribution of bank loans changed: in 1970 three-fifths went to the residential sector, but by 1973 this was less than one-quarter of the total, the increased lending having gone mostly to property companies.

There was no lack of demand. In an inflationary situation people sought to be owner-occupiers, and the institutions were willing to buy all completed developments. Not only was 3½ per cent an acceptable rate of return on prime property investments but, with a shortage of office space for occupation purposes, rents doubled within two years, thereby enhancing capital values still further. Between 1964 and 1974 the value of the Centre Point office block in London soared from £10 million to around £60 million even though it remained empty. Land Securities Investment Trust, the largest property company in the world, had similar windfall gains, the value of its portfolio rising from £658 million in March 1971 to £1,306 million in September 1973.

The collapse of the property market 1973–4

Property freeholds were now in part a speculative counter. The first check on optimism occurred in November 1972, when as part of its strategy to combat inflation the government froze commercial rents. Then in the summer of 1973 there was a loss of foreign confidence in the pound sterling, and the government's growth policy came to an end.

The steep rise in interest rates which resulted was catastrophic for developers. Buildings under construction fell in value, the situation being aggravated by rising construction costs and completion delays. Worse still, depositors with the fringe banks withdrew their money since they could obtain higher returns elsewhere, e.g. in local authority short-term loans. Thus these banks could no longer roll over loans to developers.

The storm might have been ridden out had the rent freeze not been renewed. The institutions now reappraised property as an investment, for continually rising rents, upon which their policies had been founded, appeared doubtful. The crisis in confidence, as institutions stopped buying property, engulfed both developers and banks, particularly the fringe banks. While property prices were rising, the liquidity risk of borrowing short and lending long for property development and acquisition seemed negligible. Now, when the banks wanted their money back, borrowers could not sell the property against which they had borrowed. In many respects the banks' policies had been far too liberal as regards 'deficit financing' by property companies, lending, for instance, at 14 per cent on controlled residential property showing a current yield of less than 5 per cent. As property prices tumbled, even the original lending base of four-fifths' valuation was not covered.

Many developers and property companies failed, e.g. the Lyon Group, the Stern Group and Bovis. But, in order to protect depositors, the government was more concerned with the banks. Although some, such as the Triumph Investment Trust, were forced into the hands of the Official Receiver, many (e.g. United Dominions Trust and the First National Finance Corporation) were rescued by a support operation, known as the 'Lifeboat', mounted jointly by the 'Big Four' banks and backed by the Bank of England.

Anti-property emotions produced two further blows. First, to deal with the windfall profits made by developers, in December 1973 a development charge on first lettings was imposed. This was a tax on capital gains before they were realised, but it was so ill-defined as to suggest that the Conservative government did not really know what it was doing. Second, in March 1974 a new Labour government came to power. Residential rents were frozen, and there was no easing of the restrictions on business rents. As a result, an orderly property market ceased to exist.

The wider repercussions

What the government had failed to realise when introducing its hotch-potch of measures was the extent to which property had become a vital part of the UK financial structure. The collapse in property prices involved a large part of the City. Not only could insurance companies pay less in bonuses on life and annuity policies but also pension funds could not keep pace with inflation and the value of assets of many banks fell. Much construction work also ended. Thus the liquidity crisis in property affected Stock Exchange optimism and share prices tumbled. Worse still, this loss of confidence occurred when world events were revealing the underlying weaknesses of the British economy.

The assumption behind the creation of the Bank of England's 'Lifeboat' was that the crisis was simply a short-term one of confidence: given breathing-space, properties could be sold off in an orderly manner, and confidence restored. But throughout 1974 high interest rates necessitated increased borrowing by the secondary and fringe banks, and this forced the sale of property. Thus the government, following pressure by the Bank of England and the institutions, announced in December 1974 that control on business rents would end. This partially lifted uncertainty surrounding property values, and confidence in first-class property as an investment was gradually restored.

Lessons to be learned from the crisis

The property crisis of 1973–4 has been described in some detail because important lessons can be learned from it.

First, banks must stick to recognised banking principles even when lending against property, in particular not borrowing short and lending long or being influenced by high, often speculative, prices.

Second, the property boom was largely the result of the easy-money policy of the Conservative government in its bid for growth. Real growth can only be based on a healthy balance of payments, and this requires sound financial measures to control inflation.

Third, governments must free themselves of the obsession that all property men are wicked. This simply leads to warped policy, e.g. rent control, rent freezes and taxation which bites into normal profits, with reduced development in the long run. This antipathy to property is reflected in the fact that, while many industrial firms, e.g. Norton–Triumph motor-cycles, British Leyland, Chrysler and Ferranti, received assistance when in financial difficulties, the government stood aloof from the troubles of the Lyon Group even though it was building factories in Assisted Areas!

Fourth, policy proposals, especially as regards taxation, should not be announced until they are definite. The hurried introduction of the half-baked development charge did much to throw the whole property world into disarray.

The present position

As the institutions began once more to buy prime properties, an orderly property market was re-established towards the middle of 1975. But the secondary market has remained dull, largely because many development and property companies are still selling to repay the banks. In addition, the banks, as already pointed out, are following a much more conservative lending policy, reinforced by stricter government control of the money supply.

Even prime office properties are unlikely to reach their peak prices of 1972–3 in the foreseeable future. Not only have rents fallen in most city centres but also gilt-edged security yields are now higher.

While it is still possible to obtain finance for approved developments, the difficulty lies in finding projects to give a profitable return on a borrowing rate of around 15 per cent. Moreover, expected future profitability has resulted from (i) doubts as to whether rents will continue to rise at their previous rates, (ii) the new development land tax, and (iii) the uncertainties resulting from the Community Land Act 1975. It seems likely, therefore, that for the time being most development will be by way of refurbishment, which, provided it does not increase original space by more than 10 per cent, is not subject to development land tax.

FURTHER READING

R. Ashton, 'The End of the Freeze', *Estates Gazette*, 22 February 1975.

J. Bridel, 'The Commercial Mortgage Market', *Estates Gazette*, 8 October 1977.

Centre for Advanced Land Use Studies (CALUS), *Urban Renewal* (London: CALUS, 1972) ch. 6.

J. Harvey, *Modern Economics*, 3rd edn (London: Macmillan, 1977) chs 6, 20–2.

W. Lean and B. Goodall, *Aspects of Land Economics* (London: Estates Gazette, 1966) ch. 6.

N. E. Shaw, 'A Banker's View of Property', *Estates Gazette*, 24 August 1974.

9
Comprehensive Redevelopment

I THE NATURE OF COMPREHENSIVE REDEVELOPMENT

Why certain redevelopment has to be 'comprehensive'

Comprehensive redevelopment takes two main forms: (i) slum clearance, occurring mainly in the 'twilight' zones of older towns; and (ii) city-centre redevelopment, providing modern shops and offices.

In both cases redevelopment has to be comprehensive rather than piecemeal. First, the scale is such that, by formulating a unified plan, complementarities can be arranged. With slum clearance housing can be linked with local shops, schools and open spaces, while consideration can be given to accessibility to the main shopping and civic centre and to places of work. Similarly, with city centres complementarities are possible between shops and between offices. Second, the most advantageous scheme usually involves the reorganisation of the infrastructure in order to improve accessibility through better or new roads, transport facilities, off-street parking and pedestrian precincts, and to provide public services such as sewers, open spaces, civic offices, libraries and technical colleges.

Post-war growth in comprehensive development

For a variety of reasons, the post-war period has seen an upsurge in the scale of slum clearance and city-centre redevelopment:

(1) War bombing, which devastated large areas of many towns, provided the opportunity for complete redevelopment.

(2) Housing conditions, particularly in the twilight zones, were unacceptable to the new philosophy of the Welfare State.

(3) Redevelopment of many town centres had become economically viable, the value of the cleared sites exceeding the value of the buildings in their current uses. The reasons for this change in relative values were:
(a) full employment and economic growth had increased spending power, benefiting shops (particularly multiples selling goods having a high income-elasticity of demand) and 'service' industries as opposed to the older basic industries;

(b)   the growth in government services and the desire of prosperous manufacturing firms for prestige offices increased the demand for first-class office accommodation in large buildings;

(c)   a retailing revolution towards supermarkets and multiple stores;

(d)   improved accessibility for the new car-shopper, e.g. through better road systems and parking facilities, added to the profitability of new shopping centres;

(d)   investment demand for prime properties by the institutions pushed up capital values.

(4) Local authorities began to take a wider view of their planning functions, moving from a restrictive approach towards the more positive objective of maximising net social benefit. Many authorities therefore initiated urban renewal to achieve the greater social benefits of a comprehensive scheme as opposed to individual piecemeal development.

There were thus powerful economic forces making for redevelopment. Moreover, when the brakes on private developers were removed with the ending of building licences in 1954, the new development companies functioned in a highly professional way. Local authorities also supported or initiated urban renewal. Not only did schemes have financial advantages, such as increased rateable value, but socially they accorded with the new philosophy of the Welfare State and so, except in periods of economic stringency, were often helped financially by central government.

II   COMPREHENSIVE REDEVELOPMENT BY PRIVATE ENTERPRISE

The developer accepts the entrepreneurial role of uncertainty-bearing. As we saw in Chapter 6, he has to recognise development potential, formulate the scheme which will realise the greatest net benefits, obtain planning permission, assemble the site, raise the necessary finance and get the development constructed.

These functions have to be fulfilled whether the development is undertaken by private enterprise or by a local authority. Both have their own particular strengths and weaknesses.

Advantages of development by private enterprise

Development by private enterprise, whether by a development company, property company, construction firm or even an insurance company, has the following advantages:

(1) Sole responsibility for the development rests with the developing

company. This results in quick decision-making, effective administration and rapid completion.

(2) Since it accepts all the risks and is dependent upon the profitability of the scheme, the company is competitive in its approach.

(3) The developer secures the equity interest, subject to any conditions laid down by the institution providing finance.

(4) Considerable expertise has probably been acquired in previous developments. In contrast, a local authority developing a city centre may only be undertaking a one-off project.

(5) A developer with a record of successful projects can arrange finance. Even the infrastructure, such as local authority offices, may be covered, but here the going rent appropriate to a first-class covenant will be required.

(6) Where a single private developer is responsible for the complete project, many social costs and benefits will be allowed for in the scheme evolved; for example, accessibility and complementarity are promoted since these add to profitability. In short, externalities are 'internalised'.

Moreover, the local authority can impose its own ideas, both in prior consultations and through its planning requirements. For example, in the three-acre development south of Southwark Bridge, Laing Development Co. agreed to include residential accommodation which would contribute to the fulfilment of Southwark's housing responsibilities.

Disadvantages of development by private enterprise

Not only does the individual developer undertaking a comprehensive scheme run into practical difficulties but his objectives may also conflict with the interests of the local authority. We will deal with each problem in turn.

Comprehensive redevelopment encounters obstacles in acquiring many separate interests. First, interests have different owners and, particularly with leases, expire at different times. Indeed, fragmentation of ownership has been increased through the breaking up of estates under the Leasehold Enfranchisement Act 1967 and even by the sale of council houses. Second, the developer is not buying interests in a perfectly competitive market. A development may be held up by one owner refusing to sell or using his monopoly power to exact an exorbitant price. Eventually the local authority may have to be asked to invoke its powers of compulsory purchase, when further delays result if a local public enquiry has to be held. Moreover, in return the authority may require some equity interest, for instance limiting the lease on land acquired to ninety-nine years.

Furthermore, the private developer cannot change the existing lay-out of roads in order to produce a better development. Thus either the development conforms to an ossified road structure or the help of the local authority has to be sought to modify it.

More important for the optimum allocation of land resources are the situations where the objectives of the developer and the interests of the local authority do not coincide.

First, because he seeks to maximise his money profit, the private developer prefers to undertake only the profitable parts, concentrating on building offices, shops and possibly residences. This leaves the local authority the task of providing the unprofitable infrastructure of sewers, roads, transport facilities, public conveniences, schools, etc. Nor can this difficulty be dismissed by regarding the local authority's spending on the infrastructure as the capital necessary to secure the extra flow of revenue resulting from increased rateable values. For the fact is that, because the developer concentrates on the profitable parts of the development, he can bid more for the land he requires than if the non-profit-earning parts had to be included. As a result, when the local authority buys land for the infrastructure, it is forced to pay the market price set by the private developer. Redevelopment by the local authority avoids this difficulty. If, however, it does not wish to take this responsibility, a solution is still possible provided there is sufficient difference between the value of the cleared site and the present value of the buildings on it. Planning consent can be conditional upon the developer providing infrastructure land or even on meeting some of the infrastructure cost.

Second, unlike the private developer, the local authority is concerned with the social costs of *not* developing. In deciding whether to rebuild residential accommodation in twilight zones, for instance, the private developer bases his estimates on the rents which can be charged. Given the restrictions imposed by the Rent Acts, such rebuilding is highly unlikely. In other words, on a private benefit and cost basis of assessment, the value of the resources in their current use still exceeds the value of the cleared site. In contrast, the local authority has to take account of the external costs of *not* clearing slums – the social problems resulting, the acceleration of decay, the spread of decay to adjacent areas, etc. Thus the local authority would develop earlier than the private developer.

Third, only the local authority can initiate comprehensive redevelopment where the originating motive is to provide a new road system.

III REDEVELOPMENT BY THE LOCAL AUTHORITY

In view of its interest in comprehensive development, should not the local authority assume the entrepreneurial role and itself be responsible for urban renewal? Such a solution, however, faces strong criticism.

(1) Development by the local authority means that administrative functions are placed in the hands of the body which, through its planning powers, is acting in a quasi-judicial capacity. Thus there is the danger that

the authority, in order to ensure the commercial success of its own investment, will refuse planning consent for development elsewhere.

(2) The authority may be motivated more by civic pride or political dogma than economic considerations in taking responsibility for development. In a large scheme there are bound to be intangibles which are difficult to measure in money terms, and so some subjective interpretation is inevitable. It must be remembered that councils are political bodies, and political philosophy will affect their assessment as to who should undertake commercial schemes.

(3) It is questioned whether council organisation – through departmental chief officers, committees and council meetings – is the right one for commercial decision-making and maintaining the impetus of large development schemes. In contrast, the private developer can make quick decisions as he monitors the scheme throughout the construction period.

(4) The local authority may find difficulty in obtaining the scarce development specialists. Since it is only concerned with a one-off scheme, it cannot offer long-term contracts at the high salaries such specialists command, and is therefore outbid by private developers.

(5) In accepting the role of uncertainty-bearing, the local authority takes responsibility for possible losses. Whether the authority should accept this risk when a private developer is willing to do so is questionable.

(6) Because of central government restrictions, the local authority may not be able to borrow sufficient finance for the scheme. Its cheapest form of borrowing is through bills and short-term loans in the money market, but the Treasury restricts the use of these for capital expenditure. Long-term loans may be obtained from the Public Works Loans Board (again subject to government limitation), by the public issue of stock, or by borrowing from abroad. The latter, however, can be expensive since, unlike the foreign loans of the nationalised industries, they are not guaranteed by the government, while there is always the danger that a sterling devaluation will increase the interest and amortisation burden. Smaller sums of capital may be available through local loans, a budget surplus on its revenue account, and even from the proceeds of its own lotteries.

IV PARTNERSHIP ARRANGEMENTS BETWEEN LOCAL AUTHORITIES AND PRIVATE DEVELOPERS

Co-operation between local authorities and private developers

In the past many highly successful comprehensive redevelopments have been carried out by private enterprise, e.g. Regent Street, Grosvenor Square, Belgravia. However, today both the private developer and the local authority have realised that, because of the difficulties encountered, neither can function satisfactorily independently of the other. Thus co-operation has evolved.

In its earliest form the local authority simply prepared an outline plan within which existing owners developed and provided any public works or buildings. While such a loose arrangement allows the local authority to minimise outlay, risk and responsibility, it has disadvantages. Not only does diverse ownership of interests create practical difficulties, but the authority also has no means of recouping the capital cost of the unprofitable parts of the scheme.

Co-operation nowadays, therefore, usually takes some form of partnership scheme whereby the local authority and other interested parties, particularly the developer, share the common proceeds. In this way the authority, while not accepting full responsibility for redevelopment, participates in the financial rewards of a scheme to which it has contributed.

Forms of partnership

The exact terms of the partnership will vary according to each party's commitment and relative bargaining power. For instance, on the one hand the developer may need the compulsory-purchase powers of the authority; on the other the local authority seeks the developer's expertise and sources of finance. As a result, the partnership may take a variety of forms:

(1) *Agreements wth landowners and developers under section 52 of the Town and Country Planning Act 1971*. These agreements supplement normal planning control. They regulate the phasing of development and may cover such matters as contributions towards the authority's costs in making development possible or the transfer of sites to the authority for community facilities.

(2) *Trusts for sale, and syndicates*, in which landowners join with the local authority in assembling and disposing of land for development in accordance with a comprehensive plan.

(3) *A joint company between landowners and the local authority*. The joint company is a device by which interested landowners can join with a local authority to acquire and dispose of their land when serviced, thus giving both landowners and the local authority a share in the equity arising. Alternatively, *special equity-sharing arrangements* can be made for making payments to landowners wholly or partly linked to the profits made in disposing of their land.

(4)   *Comprehensive land assembly by the local authority from its own resources.* Here the local authority acquires the land and provides the infrastructure. The site, or parts of it, are then leased to individual developers. Such rights can be sold by tender, though political issues are involved when land has been acquired by compulsory purchase. Covenants can be included to provide for standards of development and rent reviews.

This method has advantages to the local authority: (i) less capital outlay than if it were responsible for developing; (ii) less responsibility for development decisions, since these are decentralised among the individual developers; (iii) retention of over-all control of the development plan: (iv) the cost of the infrastructure can be covered by the proceeds of the sale of leases; (v) an equity interest can be retained by periodic reviews of the ground rent (perhaps as a proportion of the full market rent) and through the reversion of the land at the end of the lease. Nevertheless, the authority has to remember that if the project and the infrastructure are to be financed largely by private capital, it can only be undertaken if an adequate proportion of the scheme is allotted to profitable commercial uses, e.g. offices. Thus the Knightsbridge renewal scheme fell through because office development was restricted.

(5)   *A joint company between the local authority and developers.* The joint company represents a means of integrating the powers of the local authority and the expertise of the developer in a specific development scheme. The authority assembles the land (if necessary through compulsory-purchase powers) and provides the infrastructure; the developer recognises the 'highest and best' use, arranges finance and gets the buildings constructed. Even so, there are difficulties to be surmounted.

First, there must be a fair and generally understood procedure for selecting the developer to be involved in the joint company. Second, the actual sharing of the equity can depend mainly on the relative negotiating strengths of the parties concerned. The equity is most usually divided in proportion to land ownership or the original capital contributed, or according to the initial ratio of ground rent to rack rent. Third, where institutions have provided finance, they may also require a share of the equity. Although the loan is backed by a local authority, and is thus closely akin to fixed-interest gilt-edged stock, the institutions' development finance has to come from funds allocated for property development, where the prime objective is to provide a hedge against inflation.

Steps in the formation of a partnership scheme

Let us assume that the initiative comes from the local authority. The authority provides a plan showing the area for development and the means of access, and indicates what it requires in the scheme. Developers are then invited to participate in the proposed development. The authority checks on the ability of those who accept, and chooses about half a dozen to prepare an outline submission together with the financial basis upon which they will proceed. Although this involves each developer in a considerable amount of work and expense, it is less onerous than preparing a detailed submission.

Usually developers attend before the local authority and enlarge upon their ideas. One developer is then selected, and detailed discussions are held on the type of development as well as the financial terms.

Co-operation along these lines has certain advantages. First, the two parties get a better understanding of each other's requirements, so that they can evolve a scheme which is mutually satisfactory. Second, the local authority can weigh up the pros and cons of requiring the developer to provide certain civic amenities at his own expense, particularly as regards its effect on the return on capital invested in acquiring the site. Third, the selected developer can undertake detailed surveys of demand in order to assess the shopping and office space required and the recreational facilities which can be supported. Fourth, the local authority can assemble the site, if necessary declaring it an area of 'comprehensive development' and obtaining compulsory powers. Should a public enquiry be necessary, the developer's demand survey will provide support for the scheme.

As a result of these detailed negotiations, a *building agreement* and *form of lease* are drawn up. The building agreement is the basic document, defining the precise contents of the scheme. Accompanied by a set of plans, it sets out how the cost of those parts of the scheme for which the authority is responsible are to be determined and whether any buildings are to be erected by the authority.

The *form of lease* covers the terms upon which the local authority will lease the site to the developer upon completion of the development. It deals with (i) the ground rent, and (ii) the respective responsibilities of the local authority and the developer for the future maintenance of the project.

Ground-rent terms can vary. Thus, if a ground rent is charged during the construction period, the developer will treat it as a cost when tendering. This could make the scheme more expensive; because finance is at its highest risk during the construction period, the developer would have to pay a higher rate of interest than the local authority. The dominant aim in determining the terms of the ground rent, however, will be to allow the authority to participate in the profits of the scheme. Nowadays this goes much further than fixing a ground rent with periodic rent reviews to guard against inflation. Usually local authority leases combine: (i) a basic ground rent at a level which gives the developer a satisfactory yield on his total capital expenditure, e.g. 2 or 3 per cent above the basic borrowing rate; and (ii) rent-review provisions. The latter may be complicated. For instance, since all units may not be let immediately, reviews may not operate until a few years have elapsed. Moreover, there is the problem of whether the ground rent should vary in its proportion to rack rent over time. It is argued that since the developer took the initial risk and that this increases with time, he should derive the greater income from the project as time goes by. Thus the proportion of ground rent to rack rent should remain constant and not increase. Finally, if the institutions providing finance want a share of the equity, it complicates the rent-review clauses.

Provision also has to be made for the cleaning, security and maintenance of shopping centres. Making the local authority responsible reduces the developer's costs, but it may lead to inadequate services since such centres require higher standards of cleanliness and greater security against vandals than do ordinary streets. Should this lead to the developer eventually having to take over, the additional service charges to tenants may be resented.

The future

In the near future comprehensive redevelopment is likely to be affected by restrictive government economic policies, both monetary and fiscal. In order to control inflation and to re-establish confidence in sterling, the government has had to limit the money supply and raise interest rates. Thus bank lending has been restricted, while 12 per cent on government stock tends to be a more attractive yield to the institutions than returns on development finance. In any case the high cost of borrowing has meant that few development schemes are financially viable.

Nor is the private sector's reluctance to develop likely to be made good by the public sector. High interest rates are just as damaging to local authority schemes, because of the burden of servicing interest payments. Moreover, the Conservative government is committed to reducing the Public Sector Borrowing Requirement and direct taxation. In practice, cuts in public spending fall heavily on local authorities and, since their essential services cannot be easily reduced, it is new capital expenditure, e.g. on land assembly, school building, road improvements, etc., which will have to be pruned.

The conclusion is that, in the near future, there is little possibility of local authorities extending their role as developers. Consequently, with schemes for comprehensive renewal at present unattractive to private enterprise, city-centre redevelopments are likely to be shelved.

FURTHER READING

M. Ash, 'Development Agencies and the Community Land Bill', *Estates Gazette*, 19 June 1975.

A. W. Davidson and J. E. Leonard (eds), *Urban Renewal*, Property Studies in the United Kingdom and Overseas, No. 3 (London: Centre for Advanced Land Use Studies, 1972) ch. 6.

Department of the Environment, *Report of the Working Party on Local Authority/Private Enterprise Partnership Schemes* (London: HMSO, 1972).

J. Ratcliffe, *Urban Land Administration* (London: Estates Gazette, 1978).

10

Public-Sector Development: Cost–Benefit Analysis

I THE FUNCTIONS OF COST–BENEFIT ANALYSIS (CBA)

Welfare and 'Pareto optimality'

The object of an economic system is to allocate scarce resources in such a way that society's welfare is maximised (see Chapter 1). But welfare is subjective to the individual person and thus impossible to measure cardinally. Only in the narrow Pareto sense, therefore, can we say that the reshuffling of resources will result in a *definite* welfare improvement: at least one person is made better off without anyone being made worse off.

For practical purposes, however, this requirement is too restrictive. Securing benefits for some persons almost invariably involves costs to others. We can allow for this by saying that a *potential* Pareto improvement exists when those who gain from a change can fully compensate those who lose. The improvement is only 'potential' because welfare may be affected by the inherent income redistribution underlying the change when compensation is not actually paid (see p. 140).

Property development represents a reallocation of resources to increase welfare. In the private sector it takes place through the market system; in the public sector decisions have a political content, but a technique referred to as cost–benefit analysis (CBA) may be used to impart objectivity. Whichever method is used, it must be evaluated on the welfare test: does it allocate resources to produce a Pareto-optimal situation? That is, is it one where it is impossible to increase welfare by a further reshuffling of resources?

Weaknesses of the price system

With the price system, individuals indicate their preferences in the market. The demand curve reflects the benefit expected to be received from different quantities of goods and services. Similarly, the costs of supplying these quantities are shown by the supply curve. Resources are allocated on the basis of the equilibrium price which results.

But, as we indicated in Chapter 1, the free price system can achieve the maximum net benefit for society only under highly restrictive conditions, and then subject to the existing distribution of income. The fact that such conditions do not apply in real life and that welfare could possibly be increased by redistributing income provide grounds for government interference in the market mechanism. Such government interference is considered in more detail in Chapter 13.

The nature of government decision-making

Action by the government may take the form of regulation (e.g. building regulations to reduce fire hazards), taxes or subsidies (e.g. grants towards the maintenance of historic buildings) or by the government itself providing goods and services. It is with the latter that we are chiefly concerned in CBA. Government responsibility for roads, bridges, airports, parks, amenity land, new urban areas and housing means that decisions have to be made as regards the allocation of land and land resources. Is investment in a new motorway justified? Which site shall be chosen for a new airport? Should land be purchased for the National Trust? Should housing be provided by rebuilding or improving existing houses?

The difficulty is that, since many of these goods are provided free or below market price, indications of the desirability of investment through a price system are either non-existent or defective. Moreover, allowance has to be made for 'spillover' benefits and costs. For instance, the usual cost–revenue criterion may be inappropriate when there is unemployment, for then the real cost of resources may be nil when consideration is given to the 'multiplier effect' of employing them. The government, too, may have to pay more attention then the private sector to the wishes of unborn generations. Therefore, some other basis of decision-making has usually to be adopted.

Finally, government decisions may rest mainly on subjective political considerations. For example, in order to obtain a 'social mix' council housing may be provided in an expensive residential area. Such a procedure, however, has serious defects in dealing with public investment. First, the one-man, one-vote principle does not weigh votes according to the intensity of welfare gained or lost. As a result, the simple majority decision allows two voters marginally in favour of a scheme to outvote one who strongly opposes it in spite of the fact that the sum of their benefits is less than the costs inflicted on the single opponent. Second, political decisions are essentially subjective. Economic efficiency in resource allocation requires that objective criteria should be used as far as possible. Third, the extension of government involvement in the economy has increased the burden and complexity of decisions which have to be made at government level. Decentralisation of decision-making is desirable.

The role of CBA

CBA is a technique which seeks to bring greater objectivity into decision-making. It does this by identifying all the relevant benefits and costs of a particular scheme and quantifying them in money terms so that benefits and costs can each be aggregated and then compared.

In particular, CBA is likely to have its main use in the public sector where: (i) price signals are inadequate to guide investment decisions; (ii) 'spillover' benefits and costs are important because of the magnitude of the schemes; and (iii) the welfare of unborn generations has to be allowed for.

II   THE PRINCIPLES OF CBA

Quantifying in money terms

Since welfare is subjective to the individual, it cannot be measured cardinally in order to aggregate the welfare of individuals. The nearest we can come to surmounting this difficulty is to say that benefits are commensurate with willingness to pay (WTP) in terms of money. This can be justified as follows.

A consumer maximises benefits from his expenditure when

$$\frac{MU_A}{MU_B} = \frac{P_A}{P_B}$$

If, for instance, the marginal utility (MU) of the last unit of A is five times that of the last unit of B, he will buy an extra unit of A provided that the price of A is less than five times the price of B. Thus benefits derived are indicated by WTP, i.e. the sum of money which a person will pay for a good or service rather than go without it. The market demand curve aggregates individuals' WTPs.

Benefits as measured by WTP are shown in Figure 10.1. DD_1 is the demand curve. Assume a constant-cost supply curve, PS. The price will then be OP, and people will buy OM. Benefits derived equal $DOMR$, but total expenditure will be $POMR$, giving a consumers' surplus of DPR. Consumers' surplus must therefore be included with benefits, especially with large indivisible projects. But for goods which are bought in quantity in the market, calculating consumers' surplus involves ascertaining the demand curve for all goods. Because of the difficulties involved, it is usual to value the benefits in terms of total expenditure.

Benefits have to be compared with the costs of obtaining them: in other words, what people would be willing to pay to avoid the projects going

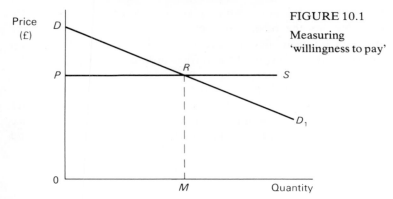

FIGURE 10.1

Measuring
'willingness to pay'

ahead. In the above example, the costs are equal to *POMR*, the cost of the factors which have to be diverted from the best alternative project. In practice, costs also are measured in terms of quantity times price (and with an upward-sloping supply curve there is a producer's surplus). If benefits exceed costs, the project should go ahead.

A simple public investment problem

Assume that a large area of sandy beach can be reached only by a narrow lane branching off the main road some five miles away. As a result, visitors, even though they are mostly local, find it necessary to travel to the beach by car. No parking is permitted on the approach lane, but the local farmer has converted a field adjacent to the beach into a car-park.

A parking fee is charged which the farmer feels maximises his profits, for he really wants to sell the car-park field for as high a price as possible, using the proceeds to expand his farming activities. The car-parking fee is £1, at which 10,000 cars park annually, leaving considerable spare capacity. The only cost, which is incurred irrespective of the number of cars parking, is £2,000 for two attendants employed for four summer months to collect parking fees and clean the toilets. The farmer is currently asking £80,000 for the car-park.

Because the lane to the car-park is so narrow, all waiting is prohibited by double-yellow lines each side. The council has to employ two wardens, costing £5,000 a year, to ensure that the no-waiting restriction is observed. Even so, frequent hold-ups mean that the return journey averages thirty-two minutes.

The council estimates that if it took over the car-park and made parking free, the cars using the park would increase by 10,000 a year. The increased visitors would require extra toilets costing £20,000, but these could be supervised and cleaned by the existing two men since nobody would be needed to collect parking fees. The extra traffic would also necessitate widening the approach lane at a cost of £170,000. After the road improvements the return journey to the beach would only take twenty minutes. It is estimated that the twelve minutes saved is worth 20p per car journey. Moreover, the two traffic wardens employed at £5,000 each would no longer be necessary.

The scheme has a further advantage for the council: enlarging the town's park some eight miles distant and costing £50,000 need no longer be proceeded with since people are likely to prefer the beach once car-parking is free. Finally, it is assumed that there is full employment and no inflation.

The CBA approach

In all cost–benefit analysis it is necessary to:

(1) *List all relevant items.* These will include spillover effects of the proposal, e.g. the cost of extra toilets and road-widening, the saving on the extension to the town's park. Care must be taken to avoid double-counting: thus the farmer could not include the loss of his land and the loss of parking fees, because the former is simply the capitalised value of the latter.

(2) *Value expected benefits and costs,* deciding whether any allowance is to be made for the more distant future.

(3) *Discount the future flow of benefits and costs* in order to obtain their capitalised present value. This involves choosing an appropriate rate of discount (see pp. 150–4).

(4) *Appraise the project* by setting off aggregate benefits against aggregate costs. This can be done according either to the Pareto criterion of seeing how different parties gain or lose or by a direct comparison of additional benefits and additional costs.

The Pareto balance-sheet

The parties to this public investment in a car-park are the farmer, the existing parkers, the additional parkers and the taxpayer. What are their respective gains and losses?

The *farmer* receives £80,000, but loses a net income of £8,000 a year.

Existing parkers save £10,000 a year on fees, and twelve minutes on the return journey valued at £2,000 a year.

New parkers have so far provided no firm indication of the value of car-parking benefits to them. It is therefore necessary to estimate their WTP. The situation is shown in Figure 10.2. We know that the maximum price any would pay would be just under 100p, and that the last would come only if there were no charge. Assuming that the demand curve is

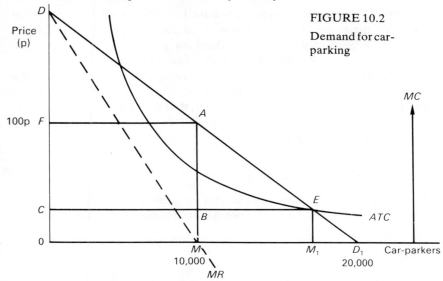

FIGURE 10.2
Demand for car-parking

linear, we thus have the total WTP of new parkers equal to the triangle AMD_1, in money terms £5,000 a year. If we assume that this represents their demand when the journey takes thirty-two minutes, the saving in time through the road improvements provides these additional 10,000 cars with an extra benefit of £2,000 a year.

Taxpayers have to bear the costs of the investment: £170,000 for widening the road and £20,000 for the additional toilets. But there are gains: £50,000 is saved through not having to enlarge the town's park, and the two traffic wardens at £5,000 a year will no longer be required; since there is full employment, they can easily find jobs elsewhere.

TABLE 10.1

	Gains (£)		*Costs (£)*
Farmer		Profit lost	80,000
Sale proceeds	80,000		
Existing parkers			
Fees saved	100,000		
Time saved	20,000		
New parkers			
Parking benefits	50,000		
Time saved	20,000		
Taxpayers		Land	80,000
Saving on town park extension	50,000	Toilets	20,000
Traffic wardens	50,000	Road widening	170,000
Total benefits	370,000	Total costs	350,000

Annual future revenues and costs have to be discounted to the present to obtain their current capital value. Assuming a discount rate of 10 per cent, these perpetual flows are valued on a ten years' purchase. We therefore have the Pareto balance-sheet shown in Table 10.1.

Since those who gain can compensate those who lose and still show a net increase in benefits of £20,000, the local authority should undertake the project. It should be noted, however, that the viability of the scheme arises only because spillover benefits, chiefly the saving on enlarging the town's park, have been included.

Additional benefits and costs approach

In practice, CBA usually concentrates on *additional* benefits and costs only, shown in Table 10.2. The net increase in benefits is still, of course, £20,000.

TABLE 10.2

	Benefits (£)		*Costs* (£)
Existing parkers	100,000	Road-widening	170,000
New parkers	50,000	Land	80,000
Costs saved:		Toilets	20,000
Parkers' time	40,000		
Traffic wardens	50,000		
Town park	50,000		
Total	290,000	Total	270,000

Possible constraints

A CBA itself involves costs and therefore should not be undertaken if these are likely to be greater than the margin of doubt as regards net benefits.

But even if CBA is carried out, the project, although acceptable, may run up against obstacles. Thus the council's car-park scheme above could only go ahead if funds were available. In practice, there may be *budget constraints*. Public-sector borrowing may be limited through balance-of-payments difficulties; or financing the scheme through taxation may not be possible because higher income-tax rates may have disincentive effects or additions to indirect taxes may add to cost-push inflation. A budget constraint means that projects have to be ranked, with available funds being apportioned among them so as to secure the maximum net benefit possible. This ranking problem was discussed in Chapter 6.

Some projects may be subject to *legal constraints*, involving easements, covenants or even the responsibilities of public bodies as laid down by statutes, e.g. for common land. A costly and time-consuming private bill procedure may be necessary in order to proceed with the scheme.

More important, the project may encounter *administrative or political difficulties*. Not only may more than one local authority or public body be involved but they may also be motivated by different interests or political views. Thus the National Trust would probably oppose an electricity scheme which took pylons over land for which it was responsible.

Finally, the project may be opposed on *distributional* grounds, being deemed to benefit the rich to the exclusion of the poor. For instance, if it were located in a prosperous region rather than one of high unemployment, it could conflict with government regional policy.

Difficulties with a CBA

Our simple example of the car-park obscures conceptual and practical difficulties which are inherent in any CBA. These include:

(a) allowing for the distributional effects of a project;
(b) adjusting market prices to allow for indirect taxes, price controls, and so on;
(c) estimating the 'willingness to pay' for intangibles which are not priced in the market;
(d) incorporating intangibles;
(e) choosing the appropriate discount rate; and
(f) providing for risk and uncertainty in estimates of future benefits and costs.

We now examine these in more detail.

III THE PROBLEM OF DISTRIBUTIONAL EFFECTS

It would be rare for a public project to qualify on the strict Pareto principle of some gainers but no losers. We can adapt the car-park scheme above as a possible example. Suppose the farmer knows the demand curve, DD_1 (see Figure 10.2). His costs as stated are all fixed, with the average total cost curve a rectangular hyperbola (ATC) and the marginal costs nil up to the point of capacity (MC). Profits are maximised at a parking charge of OF (100p) with the number of cars restricted to OM (10,000), where $MC = MR$. Now assume the council faces the same demand curve and the same cost conditions. It could purchase the site from the farmer and extend car-parking to OM_1, charging price OC where revenue just covers the same total costs. There has, however, been a net benefit increase given by the triangle *ABE*. Moreover, since the farmer has been fully compensated in money, no problem of income redistribution arises.

However, in our original example of the car-park, users, although willing to pay, were given the benefit free, the cost being borne by taxpayers. The former gain; the latter lose. There is thus some redistribution of income.

The difficulty is that the gainers may be rich people having, as is generally assumed, a lower marginal utility of income than poor people; on the other hand, the losers may be poor people with a high marginal utility of income. In the car-park project, for example, the gainers were car-owners who had sufficient leisure time to take a trip to the beach, whereas the losers, the taxpayers, may include many old people who could ill-afford an increase in their rates.

While we cannot completely overcome this difficulty of income redistribution, it is possible to deal with it up to a point. If the change in income redistribution is small relative to the CBA gain, it can be ignored. Alternatively, a weighting system can be used. Thus, to assess the welfare of the car-park scheme, we should apply a low weight to the richer car-parkers' benefit and a higher weight to the poorer taxpayers' losses in order to reflect their relative differences in marginal utility of income.

However, since there is no cardinal measure of utility, any weights chosen must have an element of subjectivity. In other words, if we are maximising a project in the light of whether it increases welfare, CBA can never be completely objective: politicians must eventually decide subjectively.

This problem of distributional effects crops up in various forms. Country-lovers may lose pleasure through electricity pylons intruding on the landscape. If they were fully compensated, there is no loss of income so the problem of measuring their marginal utility of income does not arise. The difficulty, a frequent one, is in identifying such losers; as a result, compensation is not actually paid. We therefore have to consider the distributional effects. Similarly, when estimating benefits to future generations, e.g. of a conservation policy, as compared with costs to the present population, some allowance ought to be made for the fact that future generations are likely to have a higher income.

IV   ADJUSTING MARKET PRICES

CBA expresses benefits and costs in money terms. To do this it has to give a price to identifiable units. This raises two problems:

(1)   Where a good is traded in the market, to what extent can we use the market price?

(2)   If there is no market for the good, for example because 'free riders' cannot be excluded, how can we ascribe a price to it?

In this section we are concerned with the first problem; the second is considered in section V. In order to avoid complicating the discussion, external benefits and costs will be ignored.

Possible deficiencies in market prices as reflecting opportunity costs

Where market prices reflect the true opportunity cost to society of using resources in a particular way (assuming no externalities), they can be used to estimate the cost of a project.

However, in the real world it has to be recognised that prices in the market may not accurately reflect opportunity cost. This may be the result of imperfect competition, indirect taxes and subsidies, or controls which interfere with the free operation of the market mechanism. In these circumstances it is necessary to consider whether some adjustment is both desirable and practical.

Imperfect competition

Under perfect competition price = marginal revenue = marginal cost = the cost of the good to society. Where there is imperfect competition, however, price is higher than marginal revenue, though the latter is still equated with marginal cost. Thus, price exceeds opportunity cost to society. Similarly, in factor markets the value of the marginal product at the quantity employed is higher than the factor reward.

Suppose in our example of the car-park that the tarmac for the road was supplied by a monopolist. In order to maximise his profits, he would charge price OP per ton (see Figure 10.3). On the other hand, marginal cost would be only OC per ton. We should thus value the tarmac at OC, the opportunity cost for this amount.

There are, however, two major difficulties. First, there is the practical one of estimating marginal cost. Second, there is the conceptual problem of the 'second best'. Given that the 'first-best' allocation of resources by marginal-cost pricing in all markets is unattainable, do we ensure a 'second-best' solution by adopting marginal-cost pricing solely in the public sector? We cannot be certain. If, in the existing situation, there is the same degree of distortion between price and marginal cost in all markets, adopting marginal-cost pricing in only one part of the economy could lead to an allocation of resources further from the Pareto optimum. In short, while there may be a single optimum position given all the necessary conditions for Pareto optimality, there may be many 'second-best' possibilities, and if the 'second best' is only obtainable in practice we may be making things worse by tinkering with the system in the hope of

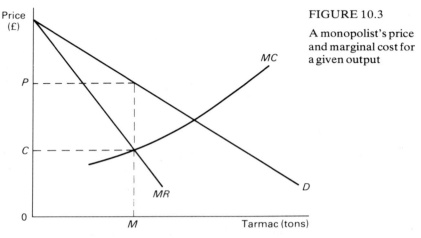

FIGURE 10.3

A monopolist's price
and marginal cost for
a given output

attaining what is really impossible. Having served this warning, however, there is a strong possibility that a move to bring prices more into line with true opportunity costs *would be* in the right direction.

It should also be noted that marginal cost is not acceptable when, in a situation of decreasing costs, total costs are not covered. It has been suggested for such a case, therefore, that the principle of a two-part tariff pricing system should be followed, a sum being added to marginal cost by way of a fixed standing charge.

Indirect taxes, subsidies and market controls

Opportunity cost is represented by factor cost. It is argued that market prices should be adjusted by subtracting indirect taxes, e.g. for petrol saved by the construction of a motorway, and adding subsidies, e.g. for the value of agricultural produce lost. The snag with this procedure, however, is that taxes deducted have to be recouped on other goods, thereby distorting their prices. There is thus a case for calculating benefits and costs at current market prices.

Similarly, physical controls may keep prices below market price, e.g. rent control. Such controlled prices cannot therefore be used for accounting purposes.

Moreover, prices may be distorted by controls elsewhere, e.g. through quotas. Suppose, for instance, that a land-reclamation project allowed a crop of potatoes to be grown. In valuing this crop it should be remembered that the price of potatoes is to some extent the result of the Potato Marketing Board's policy of restricting the potato acreage. Similarly, prices of imports may be artificially lowered by a protection policy aimed at maintaining a higher exchange rate than that which would prevail in a free market.

Should adjustments be made to market prices?

While market prices may not reflect true opportunity costs, the obstacles to making the necessary adjustments are formidable. The cost of obtaining the necessary information may be too high to be worth while. Consistency in the adjustment made would be difficult to attain throughout the public sector. Nor is there any guarantee that the 'second-best' allocation would be achieved.

Because of such problems, some economists have rejected correcting market prices. Others, however, consider that adopting a straight marginal-cost pricing rule gives consistency to accounting procedures and corresponds more closely to the costs which CBA is seeking to measure.

V PRICING NON-MARKET GOODS

Market prices may not be available. This occurs with:

(1) *Public goods*, where 'free riders' cannot be excluded (e.g. street-lighting, land, radio programmes) or where it is decided to make no charge (e.g. public parks, bridges). Here the cost is covered by taxation or a non-discriminatory poll tax, neither of which reflects true 'willingness to pay'.

(2) *Intangible externalities*, e.g. noise and congestion cost, human lives saved, the pleasure derived by passers-by from flowers and trees in private gardens or from a walk in Hyde Park.

Both the above enter into CBA calculations, and thus it is necessary to ascribe 'shadow' or surrogate prices to them so that benefits and costs can be quantified in money terms.

But formidable difficulties exist, the nature of which can be indicated by considering a few specific examples.

Recreation

In our example of the car-park we were able to estimate the benefits (WTP) of a trip to the beach from an existing market. However, for many recreational facilities, e.g. the Lake District, Hadrian's Wall, the National Gallery, there has been no previous market. How, then, do we derive a demand curve?

One method would be to devise a questionnaire in which people state how much they would be willing to pay for the facility. Nevertheless, difficulties may arise in obtaining a representative sample, while replies may lack accuracy because of respondents' subjectivity.

A second possibility is to adapt prices from a parallel facility where charges are made, e.g. for admission to the grounds of a stately mansion. But for many activities, e.g. fell-walking, such an alternative is not available.

The usual method, therefore, is to see how demand varies with travel costs, both in money and time. The greater the distance travelled to the facility, the greater the travel costs; thus demand should fall with distance. To allow for differences in density of population in the catchment area being studied, the number of trips per thousand of the population for different zones is derived. Suppose the following figures are obtained:

Zone	Trips per 1,000 population
1	300
2	100
3	60

To simplify, let us assume that: (i) travel costs from zone 1 average £1; (ii) an outward movement to zones 2 and 3 each adds £1; and (iii) there are one thousand people in each zone. We can now derive a demand curve as follows:

Price (£)	Trips made from zone			Total trips
	1	2	3	
1	300	100	60	460
2	100	60	—	160
3	60	—	—	60

From the demand curve we can estimate WTP.

This approach, although based on revealed market behaviour, presents difficulties:

(a) What should be the unit priced? Whole-day trips, half-day trips or hours spent enjoying the facility?

(b) If the car is the main mode of travel, then the number of trips should be related to every 1,000 *car-owners* of the population.

(c) Some allowance ought to be made for the average number of persons brought by each car.

(d) Where the journey is made by car, the assessment of cost presents problems. If the car is used mainly for business, then only the marginal cost (chiefly for petrol) will be the real cost of the journey. On the other hand, if the car is used exclusively for recreation, a proportion of overheads should also be included.

(e) At what price should travel time be valued (see below)?

(f)   How should costs be adjusted if the actual journey to the facility also gives pleasure?

(g)   How is the cost to be apportioned if more than one recreation centre is visited on the journey?

Valuing time saved

Transport improvements usually result in reducing the time spent in making a journey. What price do we put on this benefit?

Where it is working time saved, e.g. deliveries by lorry, and it results in extra work being done, the employer's valuation should be accepted: that is, it would include savings on overheads as well as on wages.

But time saved may simply mean that people get to work quicker, thereby increasing their leisure time. For people who choose how many hours they work, the marginal utility of leisure and work time would be equal, so that again time saved should be at the earning rate. However, there are two qualifications. First, some deduction should be made for any disbenefit of work, e.g. monotony. Second, for most people a straight choice between an extra hour's work and an extra hour's leisure is not available. In practice, therefore, leisure time has to be valued arbitrarily as a proportion of the earning rate, and in fact 25 to 50 per cent is usually taken as being the value of time saved.

An alternative approach is to take the value which people put on time indirectly when they incur higher costs in order to save it. This value may be indicated in different ways, as follows:

(a)   People may pay a higher price for their housing in order to be nearer their work. The snag here is that the higher price may reflect quality differences or nearness to non-work facilities.

(b)   The route chosen may reduce time but at a higher cost, e.g. the toll to cross an estuary by ferry. To be accurate, however, the assessment would have to be confined to regular users having perfect knowledge.

(c)   Car-drivers may trade speed against petrol consumption, etc. However, they may not know the exact cost involved, may enjoy driving at speed, or choose their speed for safety considerations.

(d)   One mode of travel may be faster than another but more expensive, e.g. a taxi as opposed to a bus. Comfort considerations, however, may enter into such a choice.

Some allowance should also be made for the fact that as productivity increases over time so will the wage rate; thus the value of leisure time will tend to increase over time.

Human life

Such projects as road improvements reduce deaths and accidents; others such as airports increase them for people in the vicinity. How can a money value be given to human life? More specifically, how do we value loss of life? Here again there are alternatives, each presenting its own difficulties.

First, the present value of future expected earnings can be calculated, with additions for suffering endured and the grief experienced by the family. However, this ignores the consumer's surplus a person enjoys in spending his income.

The second alternative measures the present value of *net* output of the dead person, i.e. the flow of future earnings less consumption. This method, however, presents moral difficulties, for it implicitly assumes that society's objective is maximising total GNP. Fortunately, society does not require a person to justify his existence on economic grounds. Unlike the worn-out horse Boxer in George Orwell's *Animal Farm* who was sent to the knacker, retired people are not disposed of because their death would represent a net gain to society! Society takes human feelings into account.

A third method assesses the value placed on human life by society through its political decisions. For instance, if a compulsory safety-belts costing £X saved Y lives, the value of human life is at least £X/Y. However, the fundamental objection to this approach is that it is a circular argument: the economist should really be justifying the cost of compulsory safety-belts in terms of the value of lives saved!

A fourth measure, the sum a person insures his life for, does not measure the value of life, but simply reflects a man's concern for his family's future in the event of his death. A bachelor, for instance, might have no life insurance, but he still values his life! Indeed, in practice, insurance may be taken out merely to obtain a house mortgage!

The real difficulty with all these methods is that they break with the criterion of a potential Pareto improvement: that there is still a gain after all losses have been compensated for. The second method highlights this snag, for the fact that society could gain from the death of a retired person arises simply because the latter receives no compensation for the loss of his life. Since such compensation is probably infinite, any project which saved one life would cover its costs!

However, it must be remembered that, in practice, we are not concerned with *one* person's certain death. What we have to compensate for is the extra *risk* of death to which all affected persons are exposed, e.g. as the result of the increased traffic of a new airport. Those concerned are: (i) the additional air passengers; (ii) their relatives; and (iii) people living around the airport. The value of the risk to the first can be disregarded, since it can be assumed that travellers have allowed for this in buying an air ticket. Indeed, as regards the third group, care must be taken to avoid double-counting since compensation may already have been carried out through the price system, e.g. in a lower price for houses in the vicinity of the airport which has induced residents to accept the risks involved. Otherwise, an insurance figure can be accepted as the necessary compensation required by the second and third groups except that, since people tend to underestimate, this figure may be somewhat inadequate.

VI PRACTICAL PROBLEMS IN DEALING WITH SPILLOVER EFFECTS AND INTANGIBLES

Spillover effects present practical problems. Which spillovers should be included? In aggregating costs and benefits, how much weight should be attached to the shadow prices of intangibles compared with true market prices?

The problem of which spillovers should be included is concerned, first, with the difficulty of distinguishing between real changes and distributional effects, and, second, on deciding the cut-off point.

Real changes and distributional effects

Spillover effects can be classified into real changes and distributional or transfer effects. *Real changes* are those that affect the performance of other inputs (e.g. an additional large office building in the City of London could increase traffic congestion and thus lower the efficiency of road transport) or the pleasure of others (e.g. a motorway, which creates a noise nuisance to nearby residents). Obviously such effects should be taken into account, and Chapter 13 considers different ways in which the government can do so.

Distributional or transfer effects refer to those effects of individual projects which result in shifts in *prices* to other parties. Thus an increased demand by tourists for hotels in London will lead to higher wages of catering workers, not only in hotels but also in restaurants and cafés. Other things being equal, profits of the latter will be reduced.

Are these effects part of the cost to society of increasing hotel services? Consider what has happened. The higher wages of catering workers will cause restaurants and cafés to reduce their demand for them. The restaurant itself will now earn a lower economic rent, while variable factors will drift to more profitable uses. But what all this means is simply that maximising consumers' economic welfare has pointed to a better 'basket' of products from a reshuffling of resources. Although painful for some, such readjustments must occur in a changing economy. In any assessment of the costs and gains of public development, there is no reason why the government should consider distributional effects except that, on grounds of equity, it may feel some compensation is called for.

Similarly, does an allowance have to be made for changes in the prices of substitute and complementary goods and services which result from some public development? For example, road and rail transport are to some extent substitute products. If the government, by instituting a new road-building programme, reduced the profitability of British Rail, should this be allowed for in assessing the economic viability of investment in new roads? A private monopolist with many lines of production would obviously take into account such interactions when introducing changes. Should not the government do the same? Quite apart from the obvious difficulty of trying to trace the endless chain of effects throughout the whole field of government action, the answer is not entirely clear. The action of the monopolist may not be the appropriate criterion for the maximisation of consumers' economic welfare since there may be other spillover effects which he does not take into account. Thus the government, for instance, may require the price of North Sea gas to be raised relative to that of coal in the interests of full employment, conservation of reserves and a long-term fuel policy dependent on coal reserves.

It is easy to be tidy and logical in theory but far harder to implement ideas in practice. In real life it may be extremely difficult to sort out real effects from distributional effects. For example, if a by-pass road isolates formerly thriving shopkeepers and involves them in loss of trade, does this represent a real cost or simply a transfer item? Seemingly the latter, for the physical productivity of shopkeepers has not been altered. Or has it? It could be argued that in this case planning has affected the locational pattern of shop services so that production potential has suffered because they are now in the wrong place. If we accept this reasoning, such losses must count as real effects which should be included in any reckoning.

In most cases these effects are not likely to be of great significance and are often offset by changes in the opposite direction (e.g. in the case of the new road, production potential elsewhere may increase through being more advantageously located).

To sum up, the gains and costs of a project should include the value of any real spillovers. But changes in values and prices which merely reflect relative changes in the conditions of demand and supply are beside the point. Thus, in choosing between alternative public projects, the government should not act like a giant monopoly, seeking to maximise over-all profits from its many activities, but should assess each case on its merits, taking into account real spillover effects. Pure redistribution effects are outside the question of economic efficiency, though the government can make a political decision to allow for them on the ground of equity.

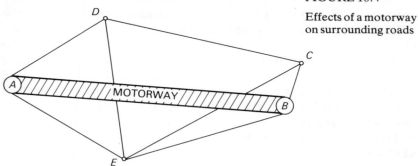

FIGURE 10.4

Effects of a motorway
on surrounding roads

The cut-off point for spillovers

In considering spillovers there is also the difficulty of deciding the cut-off point and whether any allowance should be made for unforeseen costs and benefits.

In Figure 10.4, for example, a motorway is built from *A* to *B*. Do we include only the benefits of travellers from *A* to *B*? It is likely, however, that it could reduce congestion for travellers from *B* to *C* and from *E* to *B*. Indeed, such routes could be extended, so where do we stop? The further we go, the more difficult it is to distinguish all beneficiaries. Moreover, certain spillovers have to be decided, as Mishan (1972) points out, by reference to what 'men of goodwill' regard as 'reasonable'. Thus while environmental spillovers from the motorway would certainly qualify, the envy which some people not owning a car might feel as they saw others using the motorway to get to the seaside would have to be excluded.

Nor can all spillovers be foreseen. The motorways around Los Angeles have saved the white-tailed kite from extinction. The reason is that the shrubs and grass of the broad shoulders and central dividers provide relative safety for the mice and lizards, the staple diet of the kite, for no man in his right mind ever sets foot in these areas. Alternatively, there could be unforeseen external costs. The Aswan Dam, for instance, reduced the flow of fish food from the Nile into the Mediterranean, giving rise to the real costs of fewer fish and, by affecting the livelihood of fishermen, having distributional effects. Moreover, since this was not confined to Egyptian fishermen, it raises the problem of whether, in a world where countries are becoming increasingly dependent on one another, spillover effects should be limited to the national economy.

The weighting of intangibles in aggregating benefits and costs

Market prices at factor cost, in so far as there is perfect competition, reflect true opportunity costs. In comparison, shadow prices are derived indirectly, and to that extent are somewhat suspect. Should we, when aggregating, therefore treat market and shadow prices equally? The difficulty becomes more real when shadow prices form a high proportion of total costs and benefits. Thus, in our example of the car-park, the £70,000 benefits obtained by new parkers was based on an estimated demand curve derived from the price paid by existing car-parkers. Had this shadow price been overestimated by 30 per cent, the scheme would not have been viable. Actual CBAs have shown the margin of error to be much smaller and crucial. Thus, while the Roskill Commission estimated that the Cublington site for the Third London Airport would be £158 to £197 million cheaper than Foulness, only a 1 per cent error in total benefit or total cost figures could have made Foulness the lower-cost site.

VII CHOOSING THE APPROPRIATE DISCOUNT RATE

The 'real' rate of interest

If we postpone current consumption, resources can be used for investment in capital equipment. This produces greater output in the future: that is, there is growth. The gain is increased future consumption. We can thus speak of a rate at which current consumption can be transformed into future consumption. Starting from consumption C_0, this is shown by the transformation curve TT_1 in Figure 10.5.

However, future consumption is valued less highly than present consumption. This is because: (i) people generally suffer from myopia; (ii) future income is less certain since there is always the risk of death; and (iii) future income is likely to be greater than present income, and thus the marginal utility of present income is higher. This preference which people generally have for present as opposed to future consumption is referred to as *time preference*, and is shown by the indifference curve SS_1.

A function of an economic system is to bring people's time preference into line with the actual opportunity cost of transforming current consumption into future consumption. Given a perfect market, perfect competition, perfect knowledge and no externalities, the free market system can produce a rate of interest which achieves this. We shall refer to this as the 'real' rate of interest.

In Figure 10.5 the transformation curve TT_1 shows that if XT is not consumed but invested, consumption in year 1 can increase by MK. That is, the net productivity of capital, k, equals

$$\frac{MK}{XT} = \frac{MX - KX}{XT} = \frac{MX - XT}{XT} = \text{slope of } TT_1 - 1 \text{ at } X$$

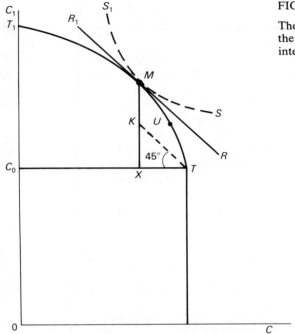

FIGURE 10.5

The determination of the 'real' rate of interest

Similarly, SS_1 can be regarded as a society indifference curve between C and C_1. At any point the marginal rate of substitution of C_1 for C is equal to the slope of SS_1. Since, however, people prefer C to C_1, this slope will equal $1 + s$, where s is the weighting to be attached to C compared with C_1. But s is really society's rate of time preference, and so $s =$ slope of $SS_1 - 1$.

Given our assumptions, the market will produce a unique or 'real' rate of interest, i, represented by the slope of RR_1, which equates the time preference of society (the individuals comprising the market) with the profitability of available investment opportunities. This means that $i = s = k$. In Figure 10.5 equilibrium occurs at M, where TT_1 just touches SS_1, the highest indifference curve attainable by society.

Any other point on TT_1 would put society on a lower indifference curve. Thus point U represents underinvestment compared with society's time preference, for the opportunity-cost rate of return is greater than the time-preference rate required. This disequilibrium between investment and saving would cause the rate of interest to fall until there was equilibrium with RR_1 at point M, where the net productivity of investment would be in line with society's time preference.

Complications

In practice, the conditions necessary for a unique, equilibrating rate of interest are not fulfilled.

First, many different rates exist, reflecting differences in risk (the small private company would have to pay a higher rate of interest than a large public company) or in imperfections in the capital market (the only source of funds to the small private company may be a bank, whereas the large company could float a loan on the capital market).

Second, money rates of interest may be affected by monetary influences as opposed to being determined solely by real forces – the return on investment and time preference. Monetary influences would include external pressure on the exchange rate or changes in the demand for money for liquidity purposes.

Third, actual money rates of interest may be higher than RR_1 because the reward for saving is reduced by taxation and inflation.

Selecting from the rates offered in the capital market

With different rates to choose from, which is the most appropriate for assessing public-sector projects?

One view is that discounting should be at the rate of interest at which the government can borrow to finance such schemes: that is, the yield on long-term gilt-edged securities. However, the government borrowing rate tends to be low because it is a 'riskless' rate. But public projects are not free from risk, e.g. *Concorde*, and the rate of discount should reflect this. Even if the project is financed from taxation, the opportunity cost is the rate which the taxpayer could have obtained had the money been left with him to invest.

Therefore, it is argued that because resources for investment are not unlimited the opportunity cost of a public project is the equal-risk project in the private sector which has to be forgone. Thus the appropriate rate of interest is what a large public company would have to pay for funds to finance such investment, e.g. the current debenture rate.

Only if lower risk is inherent in public projects should a lower interest rate be used. It can be argued that this lower risk does in fact exist. Because so many public projects are undertaken, risks are spread: greater losses on one project can be averaged out by gains on others. Thus the government (as it were) carries its own insurance. Moreover, not only are risks spread over projects but also the cost of any error in estimation is distributed among so many taxpayers that the actual risk borne by each is so small as to be acceptable. Thus discounting projects at a slightly lower rate than in the private sector is justified.

Projects financed out of taxation

It should also be noted that many projects are financed, not out of borrowing, but out of taxation. Here the true opportunity cost of capital would necessitate tracing the taxes back to their source and discovering the value of them to the original owners. Suppose, for example, that firms paying corporation tax could obtain a 25 per cent rate of return by ploughing back their profits. This would be the opportunity cost of capital raised by such taxation. Alternatively, if taxes force firms to borrow in order to carry out investment, then the opportunity cost of funds to the government is the cost of such marginal, private market borrowing. A study conducted in the USA using 1956–7 data produced an opportunity cost of funds raised through taxation equal to approximately double the bond rate prevailing at the time. No similar study has been conducted in Britain, but if similar conditions prevailed it would produce a 'target' rate of interest for evaluating publicly financed projects much higher than the long-term rate on gilt-edged securities.

The social time preference rate

Apart from allowances for differences in risk between public and private projects, the problem is complicated by time-preference considerations.

First, society's time preference is not the same as the sum total of individual time preferences. It can be held that individuals suffer from myopia, a deficient 'telescopic faculty', so that they fail to appreciate how much they would benefit from future as opposed to current consumption. Moreover, individually they would prefer to save more but will not do so unless they are sure that others will also save more. This proviso is covered where society acts for individuals.

Second, society as a whole is an undying institution, and the government, which is responsible for society's decisions, is therefore concerned with the welfare of future generations, making decisions (as it were) on behalf of those still unborn. Such decisions are of particular importance when a project has an 'irreversible' cost, such as the demolition of a historic building, the destruction of the natural beauty of the Lake District, the complete exhaustion of a mineral stock or the wiping out of a particular species of animal, bird or plant. As the Ecology Party put it in the 1979 General Election: 'We do not inherit the land from our fathers; we borrow it from our children.' Thus in comparison with individuals, who have a limited time horizon, society has a lower time preference.

Both the above arguments therefore give further justification for discounting public projects at a lower interest rate than that arrived at through the market.

FIGURE 10.6

The allocation of
investment resources
between public- and
private-sector
projects

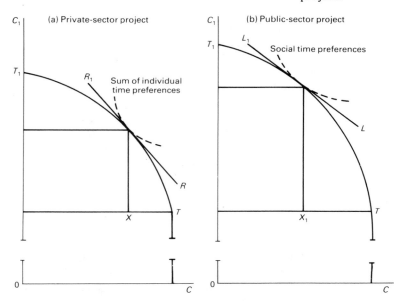

Providing for risk and uncertainty through the rate of interest

While all the methods suggested in Chapter 6 for allowing for risk and
uncertainty in appraising projects can be applied to public-sector
schemes, the above discussion suggests that choosing an appropriate rate
of interest will be the one usually followed. In practice, governments fix a
minimum rate of return which must be achieved for public-sector investment to be acceptable.

However, if public projects are discounted at a lower rate than in the
private sector, it will divert resources towards public investment, e.g.
producing energy from coal (a public project) rather than from oil
(mainly private-sector investment). This is shown in Figure 10.6, where
differences in risk and time preference between the private and public
sectors are shown in the transformation curves and indifference curves
respectively. The equilibrium real rate of interest is therefore lower in the
public sector (LL_1) than in the private sector (RR_1). As a result, investment in the public sector is greater (X_1T) compared with the private
sector (XT).

VIII   AN APPRECIATION OF THE ROLE OF CBA

Applicability of CBA in the public sector

With the tendency of public-sector expenditure to increase in relative importance, it is essential, since resources are limited, that such expenditure obtains 'value for money'. The difficulty is that financial criteria may be either non-existent or inadequate in the public sector to assess the viability of projects. CBA is designed to assist such decision-making. Public projects often involve the allocation of land resources; thus the technique of CBA can be applied to evaluating planning applications, comprehensive redevelopment proposals, motorway construction, the siting of an airport, and so on. In particular, spillover benefits and costs are fully allowed for.

Limitations of CBA

Nevertheless, as our analysis has indicated, CBA runs up against serious conceptual and practical difficulties. These tend to weaken its effectiveness as a tool for decision-making. The following considerations are of particular importance.

First, CBA cannot be used where political decisions dominate. For instance, how much is spent by Britain on defence will depend upon subjective views as to how far the Soviet Union's expansionary aims are a threat to Britain and to what extent such expenditure can be trimmed in order to extend the social services. Similarly, proposals for comprehensive education are advanced, at least partly, on the subjective grounds that they would promote a more integrated society, and expensive local authority housing may be provided in areas of high land values, e.g. Hampstead, in order to achieve a 'social mix'. While social factors can be identified, it is often impossible to measure them satisfactorily.

Second, CBA may be difficult to apply to certain decisions. Consider, for instance, a local authority which has £1 million to spend on a swimming pool. The decision rests between: (i) one swimming pool of Olympic standards which, while it could also be used by local people, would bring prestige to the town; (ii) three smaller swimming pools, suitable for inter-school galas; and (iii) six very small pools specifically designed for children learning to swim. The advantages of each are largely immeasurable by CBA techniques, the result being that councillors would have to decide subjectively (and perhaps on political lines) by voting at a council meeting.

Similarly, a firm CBA decision cannot be applied where a project involves irreversible decisions, e.g. the survival of a species of animal or plant. In such cases it is impossible to estimate a current economic cost since it would deny the opportunity to choose to future generations.

Third, CBA cannot deal objectively with the redistribution of income which results from a project.

Fourth, CBA encounters formidable difficulties both in measuring and aggregating intangibles. As a result, its validity is enhanced as the number of values obtained directly from the market increases, particularly if they are determined under conditions of near-perfect competition.

Fifth, there is always the problem of the cut-off point in deciding the benefits and costs to be included. The viability of a project could rest on this decision, and there is always the temptation for interested parties to extend the cut-off point in order to justify their particular preferences.

Finally, what passes as CBA is often in reality merely a 'cost-effectiveness' study comparing different methods of achieving a given end. CBA should not only compare the method of achieving an objective but should compare the likely returns from alternative uses of the resources. Thus, in the Roskill study, the decision to build a Third London Airport had been predetermined; the Commission merely examined the costs and benefits of alternative sites.

Conclusion on the role of CBA

CBA provides a rational technique for appraising projects where market information is either non-existent or deficient. But it must not make false claims for objectivity by dealing in precise sums. While it is an aid to decision-making, it is not a substitute for it. Its role is to present systematically all the information relevant to a decision, indicating the weight which can be placed on the accuracy of the calculations submitted. Drawing up such an agenda ensures that the claims of rival pressure groups are assessed and that all the relevant issues are fully debated before the ultimate political decision is taken.

Examples of the use of CBA in actual land-use decisions

While CBA as outlined above can be used in all public investment decisions, it has particular application to the allocation of land resources, where externalities are likely to loom large. Thus CBA studies have been undertaken for:

(a)   the construction of the M1 motorway;
(b)   the siting of the Third London Airport;
(c)   the resiting of Covent Garden Market; and
(d)   town planning in Cambridge (see Lichfield, 1966).

Rothenburg (1967) has also shown how CBA can be applied to decisions on urban renewal.

IX COST–BENEFIT STUDIES OF THE NEW COVENT GARDEN MARKET

The defects of CBA as a method of arriving at firm policy decisions is highlighted by two separate studies of resiting the old Covent Garden Market at Nine Elms.

The first was undertaken by A. J. Le Fevre and J. F. Pickering (1972), who used 1973 as the base year for their figures. They estimated that as a result of the growing direct links between the multiple retail chains and growers and the trend towards 'convenience' foods, the volume of trade passing through Covent Garden Market in 1973 would be only 75 per cent of that in 1959–60, and in 1981 it would be only 66 per cent. This assumption was then used as the basis for assessing future labour and equipment requirements.

TABLE 10.3

Costs	(£)
Land and building	30 m.
Capital equipment (assumption a)	100,000 p.a.
(assumption b)	260,000 p.a.
Benefits	
Sale of old site	10 m.
Saving in:	
Labour costs:	
assuming (a) a 10% reduction	
in the labour force	142,000 p.a.
assuming (b) a 25% reduction	
in the labour force	338,000 p.a.
Transport costs	207,000 p.a.
Waiting costs	705,000 p.a.
Wastage	126,000 p.a.

Their figures for the main costs and benefits were as shown in Table 10.3. Certain items are not given because the costs and benefits were assumed to balance within the heading. Nor did the study claim to be fully comprehensive – reduced congestion costs, environmental effects on residents and the loss of the individual character of the old site were considered to be of too small a magnitude to affect the general conclusion.

Discounting costs and benefits at 8 per cent (the current test rate for public-sector investment), and allowing for some reduction in annual equipment costs after 1981, gave a NPV under assumption (a) of − £7.6m. and under assumption (b) − £6.03m. Thus Le Fevre and Pickering concluded that on the basis of the assumptions made, 'the investment of £30m. in a new market at Nine Elms falls a long way short of proving a viable investment'.

How far has this conclusion been borne out in practice? The New Covent Garden Market transferred to Nine Elms in 1974 and the Covent Garden Market Authority commissioned Professor J. H. Kirk and Mr M. J. Sloyan to ascertain the position in 1976 after nearly two years of operation. As a preliminary to assessing their study, however, it should be emphasised that Kirk had previously disagreed with the conclusion of Le Fevre and Pickering, chiefly on the grounds that they had underestimated the value of the old Covent Garden site (which he put at £23m., to produce a net gain rather than a loss).

Valuation of the fifteen-acre Covent Garden site was complicated by the delay in deciding planning use and the listing of some 250 buildings. But largely on the basis of sale of 4.6 acres of land adjacent to the old market hall at the end of 1974, Kirk and Sloyan (1978) estimated the value of the released land at Covent Garden as £24.3m. Their other figures were based on costs actually incurred during the two years' operations and on empirical studies. For easy comparison with the Le Fevre and Pickering analysis, their figures are set out in Table 10.4 under similar headings.

TABLE 10.4

Costs	(£)
Land and building (net of the cost of that part	
of Market Towers let to non-market users)	36.2 m.
Capital equipment	600,000 p.a.
Benefits	
Value of the old site	24.3 m.
Saving in:	
Labour costs	804,000 p.a.
Transport and waiting costs	1,100,000 p.a.
Wastage and pilfering	1,420,000 p.a.

Using an eight-year purchase basis, Kirk and Sloyan estimated the annual value of the old site as £3m. The project therefore produced an annual return of £5.7m. on an outlay of £36.2m., equivalent to just under 16 per cent, an acceptable yield. Alternatively, if we discount the total annual *net* benefits of £2,724,000 at 10 per cent (a higher figure being chosen for 1976), the scheme shows a NPV of approximately £15m.

It will be observed that for all items Kirk and Sloyan's figures are higher than those of Le Fevre and Pickering. This is partly due to the rise in prices between 1973 and 1976. But Kirk and Sloyan were able to base their figures on observed costs, and these would reflect the fact that the volume of traffic actually increased by nearly 10 per cent during the Nine Elms site's first year of operation (compared with Le Fevre and Pickering's assumption of a gradual reduction in trade).

FURTHER READING

F. Barker and K. Button, *Case Studies in Cost–Benefit Analysis* (London: Heinemann, 1975).

J. H. Kirk and M. J. Sloyan, 'Cost–Benefit Study of the New Covent Garden Market', *Public Administration*, Spring 1978.

R. Layard (ed.), *Cost–Benefit Analysis* (Harmondsworth: Penguin, 1972) Introduction and ch. 1.

A. J. Le Fevre and J. F. Pickering, 'The Economics of Moving Covent Garden Market', *Journal of Agricultural Economics*, January 1972.

N. Lichfield, *Cost Benefit Analysis in Town Planning: Case Study of Cambridge* (Cambridgeshire and Isle of Ely County Councils, 1966).

E. J. Mishan, *Elements of Cost–Benefit Analysis* (London: Allen & Unwin, 1972).

D. W. Pearce, *Cost–Benefit Analysis* (London: Macmillan, 1971).

J. Rothenburg, *Economic Evaluation of Urban Renewal* (Washington, D.C.: Brookings Institution, 1967).

11

The Construction Industry

I THE NATURE OF THE CONSTRUCTION INDUSTRY

Definition

In order to achieve consistency in national income calculations, industries are defined according to the Standard Industrial Classification. 'Construction' covers the erection, repair and demolition of all types of buildings and civil engineering structures. Specialist subcontracting trades, such as asphalting, electrical wiring, flooring, plastering, roofing and plumbing are included, as well as the hiring of contractors' plant and scaffolding. Open-cast coalmining and the erection of overhead line supports and aerial masts are included largely for convenience reasons.

Certain points concerning this definition should be noted. First, while the civil and engineering establishments of public authorities are included, construction work, especially maintenance, carried out by other industries is not. Second, although building and civil engineering are treated as one, largely because their work overlaps, architects and surveyors working on their own account are excluded, being classified instead under 'professional services'. Third, and most important, the definition confines the construction industry to the *assembly* process. The manufacture of components and materials, such as bricks, cement, timber, doors and windows, comes under 'manufacturing', and quarrying gravel and sand under 'mining and quarrying'. Thus we have the incongruity that all on-site industrialised building is included, but components of off-site prefabricated buildings are not.

This means that the contribution of the construction industry to GNP is the value added to the inputs of materials and services from other industries. In 1979 this amounted to £10,237 million, approximately 6 per cent of GNP. Sometimes, however, the value of the finished products of construction firms is quoted. This gives a higher 'value of output', for it includes the cost of materials and components. Such is the basis of figures for Gross Fixed Capital Formation (expenditure on fixed assets), to which construction of buildings and dwellings contributed £16,114 million in 1979 (see Table 6.1 on page 69).

FIGURE 11.1

Construction
industry efficiency
and the rate of
redevelopment

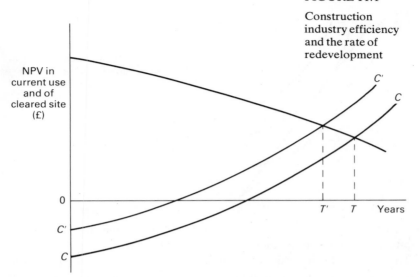

The relationship between the efficiency of the construction industry and
real property

Since activity in real property is concerned mainly with the construction,
adaptation and maintenance of buildings, an examination of the construction industry is essential to any study of real property. In particular,
we are interested in its efficiency, for this affects real property in a
number of ways.

First, an increase in construction efficiency will tend to accelerate
redevelopment. Thus in Figure 11.1 lower site-clearing and rebuilding
costs will, other things being equal, raise the value of the cleared site from
CC to *C'C'*, bringing forward redevelopment from year *T* to year *T'*.

Second, greater efficiency in construction will lead to a higher proportion of capital being combined with land. This is because capital, in the
form of buildings, is made cheaper relative to land. As a result, if both
factors are variable, capital is substituted for land. In other words,
development is more intensive. This is shown in Figure 11.2: increased
efficiency means that the price of capital falls from *OR* to *OR'*. As a
result, more capital, *OC'*, and less land, *OL'*, are employed, and more
units are built for a given outlay.

Where construction is on a fixed site a better or higher building will be
constructed (assuming no government planning or building limitations).
Greater construction efficiency raises the productivity of capital: in
Figure 6.4 (p. 89) the *MRP* curve moves from *MRP* to *MRP'*. Since the

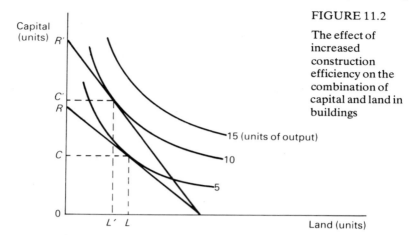

FIGURE 11.2

The effect of increased construction efficiency on the combination of capital and land in buildings

price of capital (the rate of interest) does not change, the amount of capital applied to the site increases from *OM* to *OM'*.

Third, a greater intensity of development will, given no change in the over-all demand for accommodation, tend to produce increased land values in the centre of the urban region compared with the periphery. In Figure 6.4 the rent that can be offered for a central site rises from *AiC* to *A'iC'*. In contrast, sites on the periphery (which are less capital-intensive) will benefit less from increased construction efficiency. This will be particularly true for certain types of building, such as offices, where higher structures are acceptable compared with other types of building, such as shops and flats. Moreover, since with a given demand for accommodation a larger proportion of it will be satisfied by the higher buildings on central sites, the demand for peripheral sites will fall. In other words, the *MRP* curve of peripheral sites moves towards the origin, so that they are either developed less intensively in their current use or put to a lower alternative use.

Criticisms of the construction industry

At first sight, many features of the construction industry seem to indicate inefficiency. Thus we can point to the cumbersome pricing procedures, the very high preponderance of small firms, the distribution of materials through builders' merchants, the large proportion of casual labour resulting in a high level of unemployment, the comparatively small increase in output per worker over time, the low level of mechanisation and a failure to adopt modern techniques of mass production.

Now, while some criticism may be justified, much is the result of a failure to appreciate the diverse activities of the construction industry, which ranges from large international companies performing all types of work to small, local, repair and maintenance firms. A study of the conditions of demand and supply relating to the industry reveals that its organisation is largely the response to economic factors. In other words, the critics are largely confusing technical efficiency with economic efficiency: they focus on the supply side, particularly as regards production methods, and fail to give adequate consideration to the special aspects of demand which face the industry.

II THE CONDITIONS OF DEMAND AND SUPPLY IN THE CONSTRUCTION INDUSTRY

As a prelude to examining the organisation and production methods of the construction industry, it is essential to draw attention to the main features of the demand for and the supply of the product.

Demand

The main features of demand can be summarised as follows:

(1) Because of differences of site, surroundings and users' requirements, most buildings are 'bespoke', tailor-made to the client's *individual specification*. To a large extent this determines the method of pricing (see later) and reduces opportunities for standardisation and thus of mass production.

(2) Since buildings are durable, nearly one-third of the value of the output of the construction industry is on repairs and maintenance (see Table 11.1).

TABLE 11.1

Value of output of the construction industry (according to spending), 1979 (£m.): Great Britain

	Private sector	Public sector	Total
New work			
Housing	2,763	1,754	4,517
Other	4,327	3,281	7,608
Repairs, etc.	—	—	6,836
Total	7,090	5,035	18,959

Source: *Housing and Construction Statistics.*

(3) Because the products are mainly capital goods, they are expensive relative to income and are thus usually purchased through borrowed

funds. Demand is, therefore, dependent upon the cost and availability of *credit*.

(4) Demand is particularly subject to seasonal and cyclical fluctuations. It tends to be bunched in the spring and summer months. More serious, however, is the effect of periodic recessions, for, as Table 6.1 (p. 69) showed, the construction industry accounts for one-half of Gross Domestic Fixed Capital Formation. Thus, as an industry producing investment goods construction is vulnerable to private-sector fluctuations in demand resulting from changes in expectations, a rise in the cost of borrowing or induced changes related to the level of income (the 'accelerator').

(5) Government policy is a further cause of unstable demand. Changes in taxes and subsidies can affect the rate of redevelopment. Thus the withdrawal of improvement grants for converting houses into flats for sale in 1974 was largely responsible for the 60 per cent contraction in the number of grants by the end of 1975. Of far greater significance, however, are the effects of using the construction industry as a major 'regulator' of the economy. Just under half the work of the industry is for the public sector (see Table 6.1). Thus when a cut in government spending is imposed the construction industry is the chief victim, for the major impact falls on capital projects such as new hospitals, roads, universities, local authority schools, housing, slum clearance and city-centre developments.

Table 11.2 and Figure 11.3 show how construction activity fluctuated over the period 1967 – 79. In 1976 spare capacity was running at 56 per cent; in 1978 it was still 25 per cent.

Supply

Several distinctive features of the construction industry are also evident on the supply side:

(1) Not only is it an *assembly industry* but also its operations, like those of agriculture, are *consecutive*. In contrast, most manufacturing industries can carry out all their operations concurrently.

(2) Instead of production taking place in a factory, it occurs on the *site* of the *finished* product. This gives rise to problems of protection from the weather, storing materials, moving labour and equipment and supervision of work.

(3) For most jobs *the minimum technical unit is small*. Thus a traditional house can be built by two bricklayers, two bricklayers' labourers, two general labourers and a carpenter, with other tasks, e.g. plastering, electrical work and plumbing, being subcontracted. Even large jobs can be completed by a relatively small labour force by putting out the work to specialist firms, i.e. by vertical disintegration.

(4) *Labour costs* form a high proportion, between one-third and

TABLE 11.2

Changes in construction activity 1968 – 79: selected activity indicators (1975=100)

	Construction output all work	New orders all new work	All construction employees	All housing starts	All housing completions	All improvement grants	Slum clearance demolished or closed	Cement deliveries	Brick deliveries
1968	117.9	142.4	116.6	122.1	132.2	79.9	143.0	107.0	133.4
1969	117.4	133.7	114.5	106.4	117.2	77.4	138.8	103.5	119.7
1970	115.2	131.1	106.6	98.8	111.9	112.4	135.8	102.0	117.4
1971	116.2	139.2	101.9	106.6	112.0	145.2	142.6	105.2	126.1
1972	116.9	146.3	101.8	108.7	102.0	229.9	134.1	107.2	129.8
1973	118.6	141.4	105.6	101.7	94.0	283.4	127.5	119.0	129.3
1974	106.3	101.1	103.2	78.1	86.1	187.6	83.1	104.2	92.7
1975	100.0	100.0	100.0	100.0	100.0	100.0	100.0	100.0	100.0
1976	98.5	105.5	97.5	100.8	100.7	105.5	97.6	92.6	98.4
1977	98.1	94.7	93.8	82.7	96.7	118.7	79.7	86.3	86.3
1978	104.8	98.8	93.3	82.0	89.2	114.1	65.9	88.4	93.4
1979	102.3	89.8	95.3	68.2	75.0	110.7	63.6	89.6	89.8

Source: Housing and Construction Statistics.

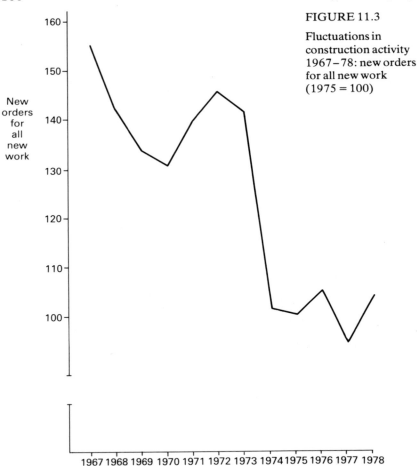

FIGURE 11.3

Fluctuations in construction activity 1967–78: new orders for all new work (1975 = 100)

one-half, of total costs. Skilled labour accounts for some two-thirds of total labour costs. Furthermore, although construction labour tends to be sheltered from international competition (apart from Irish labourers), the casual and cyclical nature of the work results in a high rate of unemployment. This is true even at the top of the boom, since there is often a time lag between the completion of one project and the start of another. As a result, unemployment in the construction industry forms a far higher percentage than unemployment of workers in general (see Table 11.3).

III PRICING THE PRODUCT

Efficient pricing of a project would ensure that the requirements of the client are met at the lowest possible price. To achieve this the building

TABLE 11.3
Unemployment rates (%) in selected industries, 1975 – 80 (August each year), Great Britain

	Agriculture, forestry and fishing	Mining and quarrying	Manufacturing	Construction	Gas, electricity and water	Transport and communications	Distributive trades	Financial, professional and miscellaneous services	Public administration and defence	All unemployed
1975	4.2	4.5	3.9	11.5	2.0	3.2	3.4	2.2	2.7	4.1
1976	5.4	4.7	4.7	13.2	2.6	3.9	4.7	2.9	3.7	5.3
1977	5.7	5.8	4.5	13.7	2.7	3.9	4.9	3.1	4.5	5.7
1978	5.6	6.6	4.5	11.9	2.4	3.7	4.7	3.0	4.6	5.6
1979	5.2	6.7	4.2	9.8	2.1	3.4	4.2	2.8	4.2	5.1
1980	6.6	7.3	6.6	14.8	2.2	4.5	5.9	3.8	5.0	7.0

Source: *Department of Employment Gazette.*

should be constructed by the most efficient firm at a price which just covers total costs. This implies competition between firms.

It is not easy to assess whether price is competitive. While the estimates of quantity surveyors and the experience of architects on similar projects may provide some guide, comparisons cannot be exact since most projects are different. To achieve individual pricing on a competitive basis, various methods are used.

(1)   *Tender*

The most common method is for firms to tender for the contract, the lowest tender, other things being equal, being successful. Certain points, however, should be noted:

(a) Competitive conditions in pricing the product require that many firms tender.

(b) In considering tenders account must be taken of the proven efficiency of firms. Normally the architect will advise. Ability to complete by a specified date is important. Moreover, under-pricing a project is not always to the advantage of the client. If the contractor runs into financial difficulties, delay results. Worse still, if another firm has to be engaged to complete, it may be in a strong position to exact a high price.

(c) Unlike manufacturers, construction firms working on a contract know the selling price of the product *before* production commences. The risk is incurred when tendering, and there is little possibility of adjusting the selling price (as in manufacturing) to cushion the effects of unforeseen difficulties.

(d) Since the construction process can cover a number of years, any fixed-price contract is, in time of inflation, fraught with danger. This risk is usually covered by the insertion of a 'rise and fall' clause to guard against cost increases. However, to some extent this reduces the contractor's incentive to shop around for the lowest-priced materials.

Tendering may be on an open- or a selected-list basis. With *open tender* the project is advertised and any firm which wishes to submit a tender can do so on the basis of the plans and bill of quantities supplied. This method ensures the greatest degree of competition. On the other hand, it does involve firms in unproductive work, for only about 20 per cent of tenders submitted are successful, a cost which is eventually reflected in the price of projects.

Selected-list tender partly overcomes this defect. A few contractors whose past work has proved their competitiveness and capability are invited to tender. An additional advantage is that time is saved in awarding the contract so that work can start sooner. Provided new firms, especially those with more progressive methods, can be added to the list, and collusion between the fewer firms involved can be eliminated, the selected-list tender method still ensures competition.

(2)   *Negotiated contract*

While tendering promotes competition, it relies largely on a separation of the design and construction processes. Yet a building may prove just as acceptable functionally and aesthetically, and be constructed at a lower price, when the design allows for the special techniques, skills and equipment of a particular contractor. Such co-ordination can be achieved through a negotiated contract. With this, a single contractor is chosen for a given project without competitive tendering, and he consults with the architect even at the design stage. Indeed, a negotiated contract may be the only form of pricing possible when the work involves processes which only the particular contractor can carry out.

However, because the removal of competition could lead to a higher final price for the project (which can be on a fixed-sum, cost-plus or bonus basis), the selected contractor is usually chosen on the evidence of his previous tenders and work.

A development of the system of negotiating further contracts with a firm which has proved satisfactory is *serial contracting*. Where other buildings of the same type are to be erected, there is a legal understanding that the firm will be given a series of contracts once the first has been completed successfully. This enables the firm to plan large-scale economies, and should therefore result in keener prices.

(3)   *The package deal*

Instead of appointing an architect, the client may go to a contractor offering an all-in comprehensive service from the design to the complete building at an inclusive figure. Thus the package deal is used mainly where a limited choice of design is acceptable, e.g. for factories and farm buildings, but it may be extended to offices and local authority housing.

The package deal enables the client to be certain of the initial capital cost of the building, and it usually results in greater speed of erection and lower costs. However, these may be partly offset if the client has to engage a specialist surveyor to advise him, or if he requires changes during construction, for then the contractor can largely dictate his own terms.

A variation of the package deal is the *design and construct* contract. The client's professional consultant prepares a brief of the buildings required, often with site lay-out plans. Each contractor then tenders on the basis of his own design and method of construction for that type of building.

(4)   *Fee construction*

In recent years certain contractors, e.g. Bovis, have introduced a 'fee-construction' arrangement. The contractor and client negotiate a fee for management services, the client covering the construction costs. This reduces the contractor's risks, but brings the client and contractor into close relationship. Keeping costs to a minimum, however, depends upon the contractor's professional integrity and his hope of further business.

(5)   *Speculative building*

A speculative builder resembles a manufacturer in that he produces buildings, chiefly houses, in anticipation of demand. He is particularly active when demand is rising, e.g. through increases in population or of real income. His estimate of the selling price of the building will largely determine his bid price for the land. Since the building process takes time, the success of his venture will mainly depend upon the price paid for the land in competition with other builders. Rising house prices, with other costs fixed, will increase economic rent on the land, and thus supernormal profit. It must be remembered, however, that the volatility of house prices (often resulting from an unstable financial background) makes speculative building risky. Hence many small builders undertake it as a supplement to their main contract work.

Conclusion

Apart from the physical imperfections of the market, awarding contracts by competitive tender does promote competition, though past experience has revealed some collusion between contractors. With the negotiated contract and the package deal, imperfect knowledge and relative bargaining ability may influence the price.

Furthermore, it is necessary to emphasise that competitive prices will only prevail if, on the supply side, firms are of optimum size. This requires continuity of work, enabling them to operate at full capacity. As we shall see, it is the lack of such continuity which is one of the major causes of inefficiency in the construction industry.

IV   THE STRUCTURE OF THE CONSTRUCTION INDUSTRY

The predominance of the small firm

Firms in the construction industry vary in size from the large civil engineering/building contractors, often undertaking such types of construction work as roads, bridges, office blocks, shopping centres and speculative housing estates, to the one-man labour only (lump) contractors such as bricklayers, plumbers, carpenters and jobbing maintenance firms.

The large construction firms can obtain the advantages of large-scale production. These include technical economies of specialised equipment and linked processes; commercial economies in buying materials; specialisation in management, such as their own surveyors and legal experts; the ability to raise finance on cheaper terms; and the spread of risks through diversification into many products, including international contracts. For the small or even medium-sized contractors, spreading risks is difficult since a single contract may account for a large proportion of their work.

In spite of these advantages, the small firm predominates, those with less than twenty-five workers (including the self-employed) covering 90 per cent of all firms (see Table 11.4). On the other hand, such small firms account in value for only 22 per cent of the work.

TABLE 11.4

The size and importance of private contractors in the construction industry, 1978

Total employment	No. of firms	(%)	Value of work (£m.)	(%)
Less than 25 employees	85,362	92.4	891.1	23.2
25 – 114 employees	5,032	6.2	721.6	21.6
115 – 599 employees	957	1.2	777.0	25.4
600+ employees	169	0.2	882.4	29.8
Total	91,520	100.0	3,272.1	100.0

Source: *Housing and Construction Statistics.*

This predominance of the small firm is a feature of all industries, including manufacturing. However, it is much more marked in the construction industry, a phenomenon common to Western European countries and the USA. The reasons are to be found on both the demand and supply sides.

Demand factors favouring the small firm

Demand is characterised by the preponderance of relatively small contracts resulting from the individuality of the product (for example, the single house or extension where the minimum technical unit is small) and the importance of minor repair work. Above all, there are the fluctuations in demand, referred to earlier, which induce firms to remain small and flexible rather than burden themselves with disproportionate high overheads resulting from under-utilised specialist equipment.

Supply factors favouring the small firm

Since production is on site rather than in a factory, the difficulties of supervision are greater. Even where construction is on one site, labour is more dispersed. With a large firm carrying out work on many sites, the difficulties of management control are magnified. As a result, management diseconomies of scale may soon outweigh technical, commercial and other economies.

Moreover, vertical disintegration in construction through the employment of specialist firms results from the consecutive nature of the operations and the lack of continuity of the work for specialised equipment. Thus we have comparatively small firms contracting for pile-driving foundations, roofing, electrical work, heating and ventilation systems, lift installation, and so on. Such subcontracting has advantages to the main contractor, for (apart from saving on overheads) it makes estimating easier and reduces his on-site supervision. On the other hand, it can increase the problem of co-ordinating the various construction operations.

Finally, as with many other types of production, many small businesses exist because the owner is prepared to accept a lower return in order to be his own boss. This is particularly true of the construction industry, where many jobs require little capital equipment or, if specialist tools and equipment are necessary, they can be obtained by hiring or subcontracting. Like most other businesses, however, builders find difficulty in obtaining capital to expand beyond a certain size, for their sources are, to all intents and purposes, limited to trade credit, personal savings, bank overdrafts and ploughed-back profit.

Many small builders try to operate on too small a cash flow, even though stage payments are received on an architect's certificate. Fluctuations in demand can prove financially crippling even for medium and large firms. Thus bankruptcies in the construction industry tend to be about twice as high as in other industries.

V   BUILDERS' MERCHANTS

The builders' merchant is the 'middleman' between the manufacturer of components and the builder. Few merchants now stock a full range of materials and components, and even the large chains hold only those having a high turnover. Instead we find specialisation: (i) stockists of heavy materials, such as bricks, breeze-blocks, cement, sand, aggregates, drain-pipes, etc.; (ii) smaller merchants handling components for the later construction stages, e.g. baths, wash-basins and kitchen fittings, or for repair work, e.g. tiles, slates, guttering; (iii) specialist shops dealing in ironmongery, glass, electrical equipment, glazed tiles, door fittings, etc.; (iv) local shops concerned mainly with finishing materials, e.g. wall coverings, paint, standard tiles and fittings, with their main customers being the 'do-it-yourself' enthusiast.

Merchants also vary in size. There are regional chains, e.g. United Builders Merchants (UBM), and large merchants who often supply small merchants and retailers. But the specialist wholesalers and shops mentioned above tend to be small.

For builders' merchants, the cost of ordering, transporting, holding stocks and serving customers is high, for not only are materials and components bulky and often fragile, but many also have only a small turnover. Indeed, it has been estimated that an 18 per cent mark-up margin is required just to cover these costs. In addition, there are cash discounts and normal profit to be taken into consideration, so that the final mark-up on manufacturers' prices varies between 30 and 50 per cent.

Yet, in spite of such charges, the merchant continues to exist simply because he performs essential functions which result from the peculiar characteristics of the industry: the large number of small firms, the high proportion of repair work, the consecutive nature of the construction process, and the difficulty of storing materials on site. In short, he represents another form of vertical disintegration in the construction process.

Functions of the builders' merchant

The functions of the builders' merchant can be summarised as follows.

(1) *Economising in distribution*

Where orders are small and numerous, it is more economic for manufacturers to distribute centrally through a wholesaler. Thus delivering in bulk to a merchant economises in transport and clerical work, while it is easier to assess the creditworthiness of a few established merchants than of individual builders. In his turn, the merchant breaks down the deliveries from manufacturers according to the requirements of the individual builder, usually economising in transport since one delivery to a builder may contain items from different manufacturers.

(2) *Holding stocks*

The merchant's function of holding stocks has advantages both to the individual builder and the materials' manufacturer. The builder is provided with an 'off-the-shelf' service, an important consideration where the demand for many jobs, e.g. repairs, cannot be anticipated, for it saves having capital tied up in storing components. Many merchants extend this service to larger projects. Because the consecutive nature of the building process gives rise to difficulties of storing materials and components on site, the merchant helps by phasing delivery.

Moreover, by holding stocks, the merchant enables the manufacturer to maintain the flow of components during periods of slack demand, thereby helping to stabilise prices. On the other hand, since the merchant does not fulfil the role of the dealer and speculate on future prices, fluctuations in the prices of building materials tend to be less than for agricultural products and minerals.

Finally, where materials, such as timber, have to be imported from abroad, the complications of foreign trade are shifted from the builder to the merchant.

(3)   *Transporting goods*

By arranging transport, the merchant relieves the small builder of the need to own a lorry for moving dirty and bulky materials, e.g. gravel, sand, bricks and heavy components. This allows the small builder to carry less overheads, operating merely with a van or even his own car.

(4)   *Granting credit*

Builders are usually given at least a month's credit in purchasing supplies, though a tighter control is exercised when interest rates are high.

(5)   *Giving technical advice and promoting new products*

By dealing with a large number of builders, the merchant knows which materials are successful. Where a builder is free of an architect's specification or, as in jobbing and maintenance work, can use his own discretion, suggestions from the merchant may be helpful. The merchant is often assisted in selling new products by technical information supplied by the manufacturer.

On the other hand, there is a tendency for merchants to hold 'conventional' goods, especially where new products are more fragile.

Recent developments

Recent trends in the construction industry have tended to increase direct dealing between construction firms and manufacturers. The increase in the size of construction firms, the growth in the number of large projects both in the private and public sectors, and (until very recently) the movement of local authorities towards direct-labour building, have meant that orders of sufficient size to interest manufacturers can be placed. Indeed, high-rise construction and system-building use components not normally stocked by builders' merchants. More manufacturers, too, are including installation in the price of their products, as with lifts, and heating and ventilation systems. Finally, many manufacturers have developed their own selling outlets, e.g. Marley, Magnet Joinery, often because of the reluctance of merchants to stock new products, and the resistance of builders to innovation.

Moreover, the tendency for the number of builders' merchants to fall has also resulted from rationalisation. Higher rates of interest have increased the costs of holding stocks, and merchant chains, such as UBM, tend to stock only standardised products having a short shelf-life, leaving it to smaller specialist merchants to hold other products.

VI LABOUR

Main characteristics

The construction industry employs some 1,267,000 people, nearly 5 per cent of the total working population. There is a high proportion of skilled craftsmen (55 per cent) and of male workers (92 per cent). The main features of the work-force, however, are the number of one-man, labour-only subcontractors, the high rate of unemployment and the low productivity per worker compared with other industries.

Labour-only subcontractors

Labour-only subcontracting predominates in house-building among carpenters, bricklayers and plasterers, who work either as individuals or in gangs. The main contractor provides the equipment and materials, paying the subcontractor for his labour only. The advantages claimed are higher productivity, less site supervision and flexibility. But among other motives for its growth has been the desire of employers and workers to reduce the burden of income tax, national insurance contributions, redundancy payments, training levies and, until it was abolished, selective employment tax.

This evasion of taxation, insurance, etc., through the 'lump' has presented serious administrative difficulties for the government. In addition, subcontractors work mainly on piece rates, so that they are unwilling to take on apprentices, the traditional means by which craftsmen are trained. Moreover, there is often uncertainty as to when the work will be performed and a failure to co-operate with other subcontractors. Finally, there is a tendency to neglect safety precautions, to waste materials and, with some gangs, to produce rushed, sub-standard work.

Unemployment

The rate of unemployment in the construction industry is usually between two or three times that of the economy generally, and this applies even in a construction boom. The industry is vulnerable to all types of unemployment except that arising from a contraction of international demand.

Normal (or casual) unemployment results from the high labour turnover as projects are completed. While the small building firm works with a few, but fairly regular, local employees, the civil engineering contractor operates on a national basis, accepting contracts wherever they are available. Only key workers are retained for the different jobs; other workers are engaged locally and are paid off on completion of the project. To some extent, employment could be made less casual by using machines to replace unskilled labour and prefabricated components to reduce site work. Nevertheless, the scope for such solutions is, as we shall see, limited, and so firms tend to restrict outside work during the winter months.

Frictional unemployment also occurs, some areas having surplus labour while others are suffering an acute shortage. The problem is not so serious with unskilled labour, Irish labourers, for example, moving to where they are required. But with skilled craftsmen there is both geographical and occupational immobility. Education and training of young workers is discouraged by the small pay differential between skilled and unskilled labour, the high rate of casual unemployment and the operation of the 'lump'. To overcome the difficulty, the larger contractors try to retain skilled workers on a permanent basis, inducing workers to go to different sites by travel bonuses and lodging allowances.

The industry is also affected by structural unemployment, resulting from long-term changes in demand for the goods made in a region or changes on the supply side through the introduction of new techniques. When an area is depressed there is less demand for construction work. To some extent unemployment may be alleviated by government regional policy, new industries being attracted to the region by improving the infrastructure and providing modern factories. The construction workforce is therefore given more time to contract by natural wastage.

It is cyclical unemployment, however, which hits the construction industry particularly hard since it is producing capital goods (see p. 164 and Table 11.2).

The prevalence of labour-only subcontracting and the high rate of unemployment have led to fragmentation of trade unions, with only about half the labour force being members. Most of these are employed by large civil engineering contractors and local authorities' direct-labour organisations and it is these which are most affected by any industrial action.

Labour relations and productivity

Productivity in the industry generally is discussed more fully in the next section. Here we consider labour relations: more precisely, obtaining the right quantity and quality of work from operatives.

The nature of the problem is illustrated by the 1976 *Report on Engineering and Construction Performance* published by the National Economic Development Office. A working party from all sides of the industry investigated work on large sites, and drew attention to poor site performance and bad industrial relations. For instance, on the Isle of Grain site, where the largest oil-fired power station in Europe was being built for the Central Electricity Generating Board from 1972 to 1976, workers who were paid for eight hours a day were giving only $2\frac{1}{2}$ hours actual time out of an achievable $6\frac{1}{2}$ hours. The result was that costs per worker-hour were increased from £3 to £10. In addition, there were prolonged stoppages through industrial disputes, the contractor, Babcock & Wilcox, eventually withdrawing from work outside its main contract of supplying the boilers.

Various devices have been tried to improve the situation. Better working conditions, such as weather protection, heating and lighting, can help, but these are not always practicable. Improvement in the quality of management, especially as regards site supervision, has a greater impact. Personal supervision, where the principal works with his operatives, has been shown to increase productivity by 15 per cent. This, however, is not possible with large civil engineering contracts, and here experiments have been made in keeping to few contractors (avoiding workers being disgruntled by the higher earnings of operatives employed by small subcontractors on piece-rates) and reducing the work-force of each site contractor to around 500. This allows closer supervision, ensuring that materials arrive on time, reduces non-productive time (for example, by better time-keeping), encourages a better team spirit through closer contact between management and labour, and increases effort.

The latter can be promoted by special devices. Where possible, piece-work can increase productivity, but allowances have to be made for site difficulties and differences in mechanisation, and there must be some underpinning by a basic rate to allow for bad weather. Target-bonus schemes can also be introduced where work can be attributed to specific gangs. Targets are set for particular operations and any saving on the target is shared in an agreed proportion with the workers concerned as an addition to the basic wage rates. The difficulty is that to some extent such schemes can reduce management control over output and, unless all gangs keep in step, the flow of work can be upset. Finally, length-of-service payments may be made in order to decasualise labour so as to improve labour relations.

VII PRODUCTIVITY

What are the facts regarding productivity in the construction industry?

Increased productivity means that a larger output is obtained for the same costs; or, alternatively, that the same output can be achieved at lower costs – that is, the supply curve shifts to the right. Since real property development is dependent on the construction industry, any increase in the industry's productivity is of vital importance.

Productivity is usually measured in terms of output per worker. The introduction of more and improved machines and the better training of workers normally increase productivity in all industries over time. Thus one yardstick is to compare changes in real output per worker over time with other industries. However, the figures, given in Table 11.5, are subject to qualifications. The figure for output per person employed is boosted for the construction industry compared with other industries by: (i) the higher rate of unemployment, certain industries carrying 'disguised' unemployment through a reluctance to put off workers; (ii) 17 per cent of its workers are self-employed compared with 7 per cent in industry generally; and (iii) male workers account for 95 per cent of construction labour compared with 64 per cent for the over-all working population. On the other hand, the figures are lowered by the high proportion (30 per cent) of repair and maintenance activity, which precludes the introduction of capital-intensive techniques used in new work.

Such qualifications are, however, unlikely to affect materially the main conclusion to be drawn from Table 11.5, that between 1969 and 1979 the increase in output per worker in the construction industry lagged behind that of the economy generally, and of certain industries in particular. Manufacturing industries provide the most appropriate comparison since the larger increases in productivity in certain other industries resulted partly from special circumstances. For example, over the period there was a reduction in the size of the textile industry with production being concentrated on the more efficient plant, while productivity in the gas, electricity and water category was boosted by natural gas. It should also be noted that the slower rate of increase in the construction industry is not confined to Britain: a similar phenomenon exists in other developed countries, e.g. the USA, France, Holland and Belgium.

One result of the slower growth in productivity in the construction industry is that the real cost of buildings will tend to increase relatively to costs in general. Thus, given no change in demand for its products relative to those of manufacturing industries, an increasing proportion of national resources has constantly to be devoted to construction. Such reallocation would be accentuated if demand for construction projects increased

TABLE 11.5
Changes in output per person employed 1969–79 (1975 = 100)

	1969	1970	1971	1972	1973	1974	1975	1976	1977	1978	1979
Whole economy	92.5	94.4	97.4	100.0	103.6	101.5	100.0	102.5	103.9	106.2	106.6
Manufacturing industries	88.0	88.6	90.6	95.8	104.1	102.6	100.0	105.4	107.1	108.2	109.7
Engineering	88.9	88.0	88.4	92.6	100.6	101.3	100.0	101.5	103.6	102.7	102.8
Textiles	80.6	83.6	89.7	93.3	100.9	97.0	100.0	105.2	106.6	108.5	109.7
Gas, electricity and water	70.7	76.4	82.7	93.3	101.8	101.0	100.0	103.1	108.8	111.4	116.4
Construction	111.3	116.2	119.9	117.3	111.4	102.3	100.0	99.1	101.2	105.1	103.5

Source: *Department of Employment Gazette.*

relatively to other goods, because (for example) of a high income-elasticity of demand for houses, shopping facilities, schools and motor-ways, or through an increased rate of household formation.

How can productivity be increased?

In manufacturing, increased productivity has resulted chiefly from mechanisation, innovation and the creation of a large demand permitting mass production. The relatively lower increase in productivity of the construction industry suggests, therefore, that there has been less progress along these lines. Two questions have to be answered: Why should the construction industry be slower in adopting such methods? Can we expect improvement in the future?

VIII   MECHANISATION

Table 11.6 shows that whereas the average worker in manufacturing uses fixed capital assets of £13,800 the average construction worker uses only £4,700, and this would be lower were the self-employed included. Moreover, the increase of 115.4 per cent over the period 1968–78 is largely explained by the low starting level. We have to ask: Why should construction be so labour-intensive?

Factors determining the substitution of capital for labour

Since mechanisation means providing workers with tools and power, it is really a substitution of capital for labour. The extent of such substitution depends upon: (i) how efficient firms are forced to be through competition; and (ii) the productivity and price of capital compared with the productivity and price of labour.

As we have seen, restricted local markets and imperfect knowledge may reduce competition for construction work. Nevertheless, some 50 per cent (by value) of such work is covered by fairly large contracts for which national firms compete by tender. Low mechanisation is therefore hardly the result of lack of competition.

It is necessary, therefore, to examine relative productivity and prices. Equilibrium will exist when capital and labour are combined to the point where their marginal rate of technical substitution equals their relative pieces (see Chapter 1). In Marshallian terms:

$$\frac{MPP_{\text{capital}(K)}}{MPP_{\text{labour}(L)}} = \frac{Price_{\text{capital}(K)}}{Price_{\text{labour}(L)}}$$

TABLE 11.6
Gross capital stock per employee (£000) at 1975 prices

	1968	1969	1970	1971	1972	1973	1974	1975	1976	1977	1978	Increase (%) 1968–78
Agriculture, forestry and fishing	14.1	15.7	17.1	18.9	19.8	19.8	22.3	21.7	24.8	25.6	26.4	87.2
Mining and quarrying	8.9	9.8	10.5	10.6	11.1	11.3	11.7	11.9	12.1	12.6	13.4	50.6
Manufacturing	9.2	9.4	9.8	10.5	11.2	11.4	11.7	12.6	13.3	13.4	13.8	50.0
Gas, electricity and water	81.5	88.2	94.4	100.3	108.4	113.7	114.4	113.6	115.0	116.9	119.1	46.1
Transport and communications	26.5	27.7	28.5	29.2	30.5	31.7	32.9	33.2	34.2	35.2	35.6	34.4
Distribution and other services	4.9	4.6	4.9	5.2	5.3	5.4	5.7	5.8	6.0	6.2	9.0	83.6
Construction	2.6	2.9	3.4	3.7	3.7	3.7	4.1	4.3	4.2	4.7	5.6	115.4

Sources: *National Income and Expenditure Blue Book*; *Annual Abstract of Statistics.*

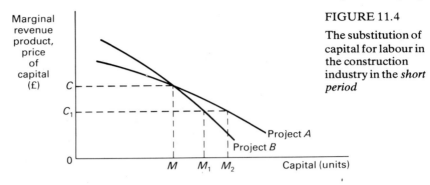

Marginal revenue product, price of capital (£)

Capital (units)

FIGURE 11.4

The substitution of capital for labour in the construction industry in the *short period*

As regards relative marginal physical productivity, i.e. the rate at which MPP_K falls as capital is substituted for labour, we must consider both the short period, where labour is assumed to be the fixed factor, and the long period, where both factors are available.

The short-period situation is depicted in Figure 11.4, where extra units of capital are added to a fixed supply of labour. Given perfect competition, the slope of the curve reflects substitutability. In project A, MPP_K drops off more slowly as capital is added because capital is a better substitute for labour than in project B. Thus a fall in the price of capital from OC to OC_1 leads to MM_2 extra capital being employed in project A but only MM_1 in project B.

The long-period situation can be analysed with the help of isoquants (see Figure 11.5). In Figure 11.5(a), because capital is a poor substitute for labour, a given fall in the price of capital from C_1L_1 to C_2L_2 leads to only MM_1 capital being substituted for labour. In Figure 11.5(b) capital is a better substitute for labour and the same relative price fall leads to NN_1 extra capital being employed.

In short, a fall in the price of capital relative to labour tends to produce a substitution of capital for labour. But the extent of this substitution will depend upon: (i) how good physically is capital a substitute for labour; and (ii) the extent of the relative price fall.

The possibility of physical substitution

When we examine the possible replacement of labour by machines in the construction industry we find reasons why it is limited. First, capital is not a good substitute for labour. Whereas a general labourer is flexible in performing the consecutive jobs on a building site, capital tends to be specific to one process. Nor is capital a good substitute for skilled workers, such as plumbers, carpenters, bricklayers and electricians, who form over one-half of the labour force. Second, the nature of the work of the industry as a whole limits the substitution of capital for labour.

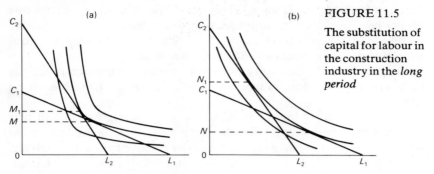

FIGURE 11.5

The substitution of capital for labour in the construction industry in the *long period*

One-third of all work consists of repairs and maintenance covering mostly labour-intensive jobs. Third, two-fifths of new construction is high-rise building where there is already considerable mechanisation with capital equipment, such as tower cranes, having replaced unskilled labour.

In practice, therefore, the substitution of capital for labour is only possible for unskilled labour engaged in low-rise construction, i.e. for about one-half of the labour force engaged in three-fifths of total *new* work. Such low-rise construction is mainly traditional house-building, where, as we shall see, the flexibility of the general labourer for performing many different jobs necessitated by the consecutive nature of building operations makes him cheaper than specialist machines having a low rate of use. Thus machinery is confined mostly to excavators for foundation-digging and site-levelling, all-purpose transport (such as dumpers and lorries) for moving soil and materials, and powered tools such as drills and saws.

The price of capital relative to labour

For any given fall in the price of capital, therefore, the substitution of capital for labour would tend to be confined to about one-fifth of the industry's operations. But, even within this one-fifth, the conditions of the industry's work are such that the price of capital relative to that of labour tends to remain high. The low utilisation rate of specialised machines results from poor site organisation, delays and extra wear and tear due to bad weather, and the consecutive nature of building processes. It has been estimated, for example, that site utilisation of mixers is 30 per cent, of dumpers 66 per cent, water-pumps 26 per cent and excavators 70 per cent, though this can vary between jobs – cement-mixers, for instance, being more fully employed on road construction. Hiring machines or employing specialist firms for certain processes is not the complete answer to keeping down capital costs. Hiring is still relatively expensive because of a low hiring rate, which, for example, for mixers is 76 per cent, for dumpers 80 per cent, for water-pumps 56 per cent and for excavators 90 per cent. And vertical disintegration of processes, e.g. by obtaining ready-mixed concrete from a specialist producer, can increase the problems of dovetailing processes and of site organisation.

Added to this, the frequent and wide fluctuations in the level of activity in the construction industry increase the risk of expensive machines lying idle.

The net result of low utilisation of machines, high wear and tear resulting from bad weather and the necessity of moving machines from site to site all tend to make capital expensive relative to unskilled labour. This, together with the low physical substitutability of capital for labour, accounts for the low degree of mechanisation in the industry.

The possibility of increasing mechanisation

Changes in relative prices or in physical productivity as between labour and capital could lead to increased mechanisation.

First, a relative rise in wages, resulting from trade-union pressure or competition from other industries, would tend to produce a substitution of capital for labour. Thus bricks are now being delivered in packages or on pallets for mechanical handling.

Second, increased mechanisation could result if large firms, with their better organisation, became more important. For instance, improved organisation can reduce the high cost of a tower crane. Similarly, more large-sized contracts, e.g. for New Towns or local authorities, give greater assurance that an expensive machine will be used to capacity.

Third, a movement towards larger components (e.g. through off-site prefabrication) or towards high-rise buildings (e.g. through the high cost of central sites, greater productivity in high-rise building or the relaxation of height limits) would necessitate cranes, etc., for lifting.

IX   INNOVATION

In broad terms innovation covers new labour-incentive schemes, improvements in organisation, and the use of standardised components. The first was considered in section VI; here we concentrate on organisation and standardised components.

Obstacles to innovation

The characteristics of the construction process present formidable obstacles to innovation. The construction industry consists of small, local firms often sheltered from competition, and this is especially the case in housing. Even for other types of construction, differences in design, location and the degree of subcontracting make comparisons difficult, so that builders may not know whether new methods are cost-effective. Furthermore, with little significant change in the relative cost of factors, wide variations in the level of construction activity and the difficulties inherent in the piecemeal introduction of new methods when production involves consecutive processes, there has been little spur towards innovation. In any case, the preponderance of small firms means that knowledge of new and improved methods does not spread quickly.

Organisation

Improving the organisation of the construction project can be examined with reference to the integration of the design/construction process and securing continuity of operations.

In Britain construction is marked by the diffusion of responsibility for the finished product, and this is particularly evident in the division between design and production. Although design and supervision is the responsibility of the architect, the main contractor is responsible for the actual construction, though some subcontractors may be appointed by the architect or even by the owner of the building. This division adds to the problems of organisation and site management.

Integration of the design/construction process requires the client, architect, quantity surveyor and main contractor to work closely together from the beginning. In this way the particular strengths of the builder can be harnessed and the most economic materials, consistent with the functional design of the building, chosen. Indeed, discussions with the client may reveal that a building based on dimensional co-ordination incorporating standardised components is acceptable. The main snag of such integration of the complete process is that work cannot be put out to competitive tender.

Because construction consists of consecutive processes, careful programming is necessary to ensure continuity of operations, the arrival of specialist firms and materials on time and the best use of machines. However, the programme must have some flexibility. For example, inside work can be kept in reserve against bad weather, initial overtime limited so that there is scope for making good delays, and work outside the main programme, e.g. garages and paths, held back in case delays occur through unforeseen difficulties or modifications to the original plans.

Programming the basic processes can be tackled in a number of ways. In its simplest form it may simply mean planning operations around the task which takes the longest time, e.g. laying the foundations and building the main walls. Or the construction process may be based on ensuring that the minimum technical unit is fully employed, e.g. about seven men in building a house, with other operations being subcontracted. A third method is to simplify the construction process by using new materials (e.g. ready-mixed concrete and light-weight hollow concrete units larger than the brick), employing specialist forms and incorporating prefabricated units in order to reduce the number of operations on site.

Where the building is large or of a non-repetitive type, *critical path analysis* can be used. Figure 11.6 shows in simplified form how this approach can be applied to the construction of a bedroom-garage extension to a house. The project is represented on an arrow diagram in which the arrows represent the different activities and the pattern of the diagram shows how these activities must be interrelated. This decides *how* the project must be carried out: all activities represented by incoming arrows must be completed before any of the activities represented by outgoing arrows can start. A second decision will then cover how long processes will take to complete; but it should also be noted that only the critical path activities are worth expediting if an earlier completion is required.

Standardised components

The use of standardised components, such as windows, doors and roof trusses, reduces costs by allowing factory production and eliminating much craft labour on site. Factory-produced components are cheaper because they can be mass produced with specialised tools, the organisation does not need to be dismantled (as on a site), workers can be provided with cover from bad weather and with heat and light, and expensive skilled labour can be replaced by machines. In addition, the reduction in variety eases the stocking problem, while interchangeable spares make repair jobs cheaper.

Standardisation of components can be carried further by *dimensional co-ordination*, a systematic method of relating the size of components to facilitate their use together. It is based on a module of chosen dimensions which, in multiples and sub-multiples, provides the required sizes of all components, e.g. bricks, breeze-blocks, windows, doors, panels and floor slabs, in a logical progression. The advantages of dimensional co-ordination (which took a big step forward with metrication) are a reduction in the number of components, the elimination of wasteful cutting, and higher productivity through factory production and quicker assembly on site.

X   MASS PRODUCTION

The nature of 'industrialised building'

In manufacturing, one way in which costs have been reduced has been through the creation of a mass demand, usually by persuasive advertising.

FIGURE 11.6

Simple critical-path
analysis diagram

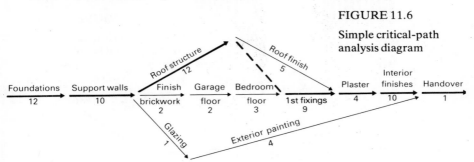

Notes:
(a) figures denote the time (in days) for each activity
(b) total project time = sum of critical activities = 58 days
(c) non-critical activities have 'float' time, e.g. roof finish (4 days), glazing and
   exterior painting (30 days), brickwork and floors (5 days)

This has allowed the introduction of methods of production yielding
maximum economies of scale. Nevertheless, while the first requirement
of mass production is a large demand, technical conditions of production
must allow the process to be split into many simple and separate operations so that specialist machines and workers can be employed continu-
ously.

The construction industry has been based on what can be described as
'traditional building': that is, materials and components are purchased in
the market and then assembled on site into buildings designed for
particular or prospective clients. Recent trends have been towards substituting, where possible, 'system building'. This may simply refer to the
incorporation in the building design of prefabricated components. More
particularly, it may be limited to industrialised building, where (as far as
possible) the whole building process from design to the finished product is
based on factory techniques.

In essence industrialised building takes the form of designing a building
in which the components, such as walls, ceilings, floor panels, cladding,
concrete beams, etc., are repetitive, thus allowing mass production under
factory conditions with its attendant advantages (see p. 186). Furthermore, as much finishing work as possible is incorporated into the components, site work can consist mainly of their assembly into position with no
further work to be done. By this means it has been estimated that the
building of a house can be reduced from 1,800 man-hours by traditional
methods to 900 to 1,300 man-hours by industrialised methods, depending upon the particular system.

There are two main types of industrialised building: (i) 'open', where
the architect uses 'off-the-peg' components to achieve a design acceptable to the client; and (ii) 'closed', where design and components are one
system, the manufacturer of the components also being responsible for

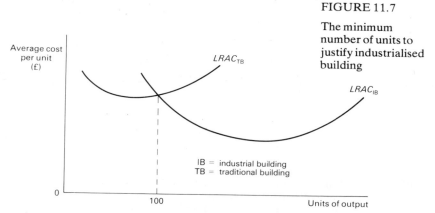

the erection of the finished building. As far as possible, components are produced in a factory, though with closed systems they may be made on site.

To be successful, industrialised building must be able to compete costwise with traditional building methods. However, costs must be interpreted broadly, allowing for speed of building, subsequent maintenance costs and such special government concessions as subsidies towards research and development or allowing local authorities to accept tenders slightly higher than those where traditional methods are to be used. The extent to which industrialised building can be cost-competitive depends upon conditions of demand and supply.

Demand

Industrialised building requires a demand which is both large and continuous. Thus in Figure 11.7, in order to secure the lower long-run average cost curve of industrialised building ($LRAC_{IB}$) resulting from design/construction integration, factory production of components and economies of scale, there must be a demand for at least 100 dwellings per period.

The difficulty is that, in the construction industry, total demand is simply an aggregate of small parcels: apart from New Towns and local authority housing, approximately 90 per cent of all contracts are for less than 100 dwellings. Increasing the size of contracts would only be possible if the variety of buildings were restricted to a narrower range. Yet private clients, especially house-buyers, demand a building which is satisfying functionally and aesthetically, since they feel that they are going to occupy it for a long time. Industrialised building, in contrast, is frowned upon as being uniform, a view mainly derived from the austere appearance presented by local authority flats built in this way largely because of the severe cost restrictions imposed.

Demand for industrialised building therefore has to come from those clients where some uniformity of product is acceptable and where the highest and best use of the site is not impaired by the erection of a factory-built construction. This has meant that in the private sector the method has been most successful for factories, hotels, farm buildings, small garages, house extensions and garden sheds. Nevertheless, in the public sector, where 'needs' rather than 'demand' is the dominant consideration (see p. 216), industrialised building has been significant in providing dwellings (particularly high-rise flats), schools (e.g the CLASP system – Consortium of Local Authorities Schools Programme), hospitals and universities. Even so, industrialised dwellings in 1971, their best year, accounted for only 33 per cent of the total of all new local authority and New Town dwellings completed.

Continuity of demand is a further requirement. Industrialised building involves capital investment, and this is likely to be uneconomic unless there is an adequate work-load over a number of years. Here the construction industry faces difficulties. First, particularly with regard to dwellings, the main product of industrialised building, tastes change (as, for example, the recent reaction against high-rise flats). Second, public-sector construction, the main source of industrialised-building orders, fluctuates. Not only do political swings influence public-sector housing programmes, but the latter are a major victim whenever cuts are made in government spending as a means of regulating the economy.

Supply

Even if demand is sufficient to justify mass production, the method will only be adopted if it results in a competitive saving in costs of production.

During the early post-war period the government encouraged experiments in the development of industrialised-building techniques since the method offered the possibility of a rapid increase in the number of dwellings. But too many systems resulted and traditional building retained a cost advantage until the number was reduced. However, by 1971 industrialised building had reversed the position. Nevertheless, this over-all cost advantage over traditional building had been lost by 1978. Furthermore, between 1973 and 1978 tenders for local authority industrialised dwellings fell from 13 per cent of total local authority dwellings to ½ per cent (Table 11.7).

Table 11.7 shows that at no time did industrialised building gain an overwhelming advantage. The reasons for this are as follows:

(a) If skilled craftsmen and wet finishes are to be eliminated in the assembly process, the components of factory-built systems must have greater dimensional precision than traditional materials. But the greater accuracy achieved by the use of steel, plastics, wood and concrete slabs

TABLE 11.7

Floor area and cost of construction: industrialised and traditional building (tenders approved for local authorities: England and Wales), 1970–8

	Industrialised				Traditional			
	Number of dwellings	Average area (sq. m.)	Average cost (£)	Average cost per sq. m. (£)	Number of dwellings	Average area (sq. m.)	Average cost (£)	Average cost per sq. m. (£)
Houses and bungalows								
1970	8,246	85.7	3,301	38.54	33,632	80.0	3,203	40.04
1971	6,951	84.4	3,620	42.84	33,663	79.1	3,673	43.50
1972	5,077	84.8	4,521	53.28	22,267	78.8	4,364	55.44
1973	10,529	85.7	6,112	71.37	28,249	78.9	5,852	74.16
1974	11,254	84.4	7,011	83.06	39,168	80.3	7,146	88.99
1975	10,696	83.7	7,901	94.39	47,324	81.8	7,880	96.33
1976	8,172	83.7	8,194	97.89	48,003	81.7	8,310	101.71
1977	1,197	78.3	8,822	112.67	26,656	80.8	9,326	115.46
1978	193	57.0	12,005	210.76	26,918	79.5	10,634	133.69
Flats in 1 to 4 storeys								
1970	4,568	59.6	3,405	51.13	23,320	54.3	2,953	54.36
1971	4,210	58.3	3,252	55.76	24,202	54.1	3,408	63.08
1972	3,485	57.2	4,169	72.87	19,866	54.0	4,181	77.50
1973	4,789	55.9	4,986	89.13	22,551	52.9	5,548	104.95
1974	4,109	55.9	6,271	112.18	30,404	52.6	6,483	123.25
1975	4,268	54.5	6,832	125.35	33,126	53.3	7,183	134.76
1976	2,866	55.0	7,482	136.03	35,522	53.0	7,555	142.54
1977	556	69.2	7,577	109.48	21,420	51.2	8,556	167.18
1978	52	54.4	11,319	208.21	20,592	51.4	9,693	188.59
Flats in 5 or more storeys								
1970	1,500	64.8	4,428	68.35	4,169	63.4	3,993	62.97
1971	752	65.2	4,443	68.14	3,426	59.2	4,756	80.19
1972	94	48.6	5,404	111.19	1,644	63.1	6,016	95.37
1973	180	61.6	6,527	105.92	1,832	58.4	8,643	147.90
1974	590	64.6	8,572	132.66	1,031	52.6	11,214	213.03
1975	88	48.6	9,393	193.27	1,215	57.4	10,723	186.93
1976	109	32.7	7,835	239.50	1,259	59.2	13,886	234.58
1977	—	—	—	—	620	63.8	14,478	226.83
1978	—	—	—	—	233	50.5	15,325	303.39

Source: *Housing and Construction Statistics.*

prepared under high pressure has to be weighed against their higher cost relative to bricks and concrete, especially as they are not as yet fully proven. Since materials account for about half the cost of a building and labour for one-third, a 25 per cent increase in the cost of materials would require a 37.5 per cent saving in labour costs just in order to break even as regards over-all costs.

(b) Factory-produced components increase transport costs through the extra journey of delivering them to the site and because the finished parts are usually bulkier and more fragile than the raw materials.

(c) A higher capital outlay is required, cranes for lifting being essential.

(d) Industrialised building tends to be inflexible. With traditional building, modifications are usually possible, both in actual construction and in subsequent use. In contrast, changes in industrialised building usually involve interference with the basic design. Thus, when experience necessitated new fire precautions for hospitals, they could only be incorporated in the industrially designed building at considerable expense.

(e) There is a tendency for industrialised building to eliminate the competition of tendering, a monopoly seller often being faced by a monopoly buyer.

(f) Traditional building can now make use of factory components through dimensional co-ordination.

Likely future trends

Industrialised building enjoyed a short-lived boom in the early 1960s, and by 1966 it accounted for 25 per cent of all dwellings (42 per cent of New Town and local authority housing). The Ronan Point disaster of 1968, however, produced a reaction against high-rise flats and led to an examination of their social disadvantages, such as the isolation of old people and their unsuitability for children.

In addition, recessions in the construction industry in 1968 (repeated during 1974–9) highlighted the risk of over-investment in fixed capital, thereby eroding any competitive advantage enjoyed by industrialised building.

Nor was industrialised building helped by rising standards of living and the swing towards owner-occupation, for building societies are more willing to lend for house purchase than for flats.

Finally, two advantages of industrialised building have been reduced in importance by recent developments. First, the easing of the housing situation and the swing towards renovation of older buildings have meant that there is now less emphasis on providing new dwellings quickly. Second, the high rate of unemployment in the construction industry has resulted in less stress being placed on increasing productivity.

On the other hand, future developments could renew interest in industrialised building. These include: higher land prices, which would encourage high-rise building; improved organisation and greater continuity of demand; a fall in the price of precision materials, such as plastics, relative to that of the traditional brick and concrete poured on site; a rise in relative wage rates or shortages of skilled craftsmen; a fall in the price of capital; and lower transport costs.

In the immediate future, however, such developments appear to be doubtful. Increases in productivity in the construction industry therefore are more likely to come from better labour relations, improved organisation and, above all, from the development of designs based on dimensional co-ordination incorporating, as far as possible, standardised, factory-made components.

XI   GENERAL CONCLUSIONS

The construction process is subject to a high degree of uncertainty from changes in government policy, the peculiar wishes of clients, dependence upon the performance of subcontractors and frequent bottlenecks in the supply of materials, components and skilled labour. In addition, there are always possible delays in obtaining planning permission, bye-law approval and arranging finance.

The organisation of the construction industry reflects these difficulties. Contracting firms tend to exist solely as organisations capable of building and they avoid committing themselves to one construction method or building type. Instead, flexibility is secured by adhering to simple and widely understood techniques, with a minimum of plant that can be fully employed through redeployment according to individual jobs. Advantages of specialisation are largely secured by subcontracting.

Improvements in productivity are therefore likely to come chiefly from the development of higher management ability within individual firms and from innovations in the industry generally. The latter will rest largely on the standardisation and factory production of components, designs based on dimensional co-ordination, and the reconciliation of competitive tendering with integrated design and production techniques.

Nevertheless, the extent and speed of such innovations will depend upon the degree to which standardised components prove acceptable and the extent to which fluctuations in the level of demand generally can be eliminated.

FURTHER READING

P. N. Balchin and J. L. Kieve, *Urban Land Economics* (London: Macmillan, 1977) ch. 10.

P. M. Hillebrandt, *Economic Theory and the Construction Industry* (London: Macmillan, 1974).

W. Lean and B. Goodall, *Aspects of Land Economics* (London: Estates Gazette, 1966) chs 20–4.

P. A. Stone, *Building Economy*, 2nd edn (Oxford: Pergamon Press, 1976).

12
Housing

I HOUSING POLICY

Why a housing policy?

Housing, like most goods and services, can be provided by private enterprise operating through the market. Indeed, the private sector still accounts for two-thirds of all housing, mostly through owner-occupation. What, therefore, are the economic grounds for interfering with the free operation of market forces in the provision of housing?

First, there is the maldistribution of income, some people having insufficient to secure adequate housing by bidding in the open market.

Second, there are external costs associated with bad housing. Some people may not allocate a sufficient proportion of their income to housing, preferring other goods, such as cars, drink, holidays abroad, and so on. As a result, slums are perpetuated, giving rise to ill-health, delinquency, vandalism, and so on.

Third, the government may consider that people generally underestimate the satisfaction they would obtain from extra housing. Thus housing, like education and social insurance, is treated as a 'merit' good, spending on housing being encouraged by subsidy or housing being provided directly through the public sector.

Fourth, public intervention is often necessary to accelerate new building, the renovation of dwellings and the elimination of slums. In particular, the government has had to take responsibility for dealing with the shortages resulting from the two world wars.

Unfortunately, much current housing policy has to be directed to rectifying mistakes made by past governments. Worse still, it is dominated by political considerations, which, as we shall see, have thwarted the formulation of a consistent policy and have ignored economic principles. In this connection it must be noted that there will always be a 'housing problem', for the same reason that there will always be an economic problem: resources are scarce relative to wants. What this chapter seeks to do is to see whether the application of economic analysis can help in ensuring that the resources we do have go as far as possible.

Difficulties of framing a housing policy

Governments find no difficulty in stating the ultimate aim of housing policy. Thus the Conservative government of 1970–4 considered that everyone should have 'a decent home with a reasonable choice of owning it or renting the sort of home they want' (*Widening the Choice: the Next Step in Housing*, Cmnd 5280, HMSO, 1973).

But while admirable in sentiment, such an aim conceals problems in the framing of actual policy. What, for instance, do we mean by a 'decent home'? The answer involves a subjective judgement, with policy being based on 'needs' rather than on 'demand' (see pp. 216–18). In any case the concept of what is inadequate or substandard changes over time as people's incomes increase and technical improvements, such as central heating, are made. Policy has therefore not only to define what is currently 'decent' but also has to decide to what extent it should antici-pate *future* minimum requirements. Thus spreading resources thickly on a limited number of houses by requiring councils to build to Parker–Morris standards must be balanced against the fact that it extends the time that many people have to continue living in really wretched conditions.

Again, choice in housing means that dwellings should be sufficient in number and variety to enable people to exercise their preferences of tenure as between buying and renting and, within the tenure, of location, space, number of rooms, design, and whether the house/flat is furnished or unfurnished. Such choice promotes people's freedom, eliminating interference in the way they use their homes and providing increased mobility. Here the price system can play an important role by reflecting such preferences (admittedly within the existing distribution of income) and stimulating production in response to them. Indeed, choice can only be really effective in a free market. Thus, with rent control, demand exceeds supply so that landlords can let *existing* dwellings irrespective of a tenant's real preferences. As a result, tenants may not get the improve-ments for which they would be willing to pay a higher rent. Similarly, council tenants complain at being refused permission to paint their front door in a colour of their own choosing or to keep pets.

Objectives of a housing policy

As a first approach, we can state the objectives and role of the govern-ment with regard to housing as follows.

(1)   *To obtain the optimal use of existing housing resources*
At any one time there is a given stock of housing to meet current needs. Often governments have been so preoccupied with new building pro-

grammes that present stock has been neglected by being allowed to remain unoccupied or to fall into disrepair. As we shall see, both types of neglect have resulted from the policy of rent control.

(2)   To ensure adequate housing for all households

Longer-term policy must aim at improving housing conditions. Consideration must be given to individual preferences as regards tenure, type and location of dwellings. Furthermore, policy must allow for a surplus of dwellings over needs to provide a 'pool' to allow people to change homes or for substandard houses to be replaced, and to cover ownership of second homes.

(3)   To guide the location of new housing

New housing should be located so as to take account of current shortages, employment opportunities, future changes in demand, the existing infrastructure and over-all strategic plans. In the past this has not always been followed, though the government is in the best position to co-ordinate plans. Thus in the London area concern has been voiced over a shortage of employment opportunities, partly the result of conflicting post-war policies of providing local authority housing in the inner areas (from which industry and offices have been forced to move).

(4)   To be responsible for the housing needs of special groups

Certain people, such as the frail and elderly, disabled and handicapped, must have their housing requirements co-ordinated with the welfare services. Some may need specially designed or adapted housing. Where residential care is required, it should be met as far as possible within the community rather than in a remote situation. The responsibility for such co-ordination must be with the central government and local authorities, supplemented by voluntary bodies.

(5)   To influence the policies of local authorities in allocating housing

If we accept that, as seems likely, rented housing will eventually be provided almost entirely by local authorities, the government must ensure that those people who under present methods of allocation fail to collect enough points and so find themselves at the end of the housing queue are not so penalised but have access to the rented council sector.

In pursuing its objectives the government must recognise that it must work within certain constraints, some real, others moral.

First, government spending on housing must take account both of the extent to which the Public Sector Borrowing Requirement (PSBR) can be increased and of competing claims on the public purse.

Second, a stable level of demand for housing is essential to an efficient house-building industry. The government must consider this in using monetary and fiscal policy in its general direction of the economy.

Third, policy should be fair as between tenants, landlords and owner-occupiers. This creates difficulties when, as at present, housing policy is used partly as a means of redistributing income, e.g. the 'fair-rent' scheme, where increases in registered rents fail to keep pace with the cost of repairs and inflation generally.

Definitions

Housing policy is concerned with the relationship between households and dwellings: a *household* is defined as 'two or more persons living together with common house-keeping, or a person living alone who is responsible for providing his or her own meals'; and a *dwelling* is 'a building, or part of a building, which provides structurally separate living accommodation'. (*Housing Policy: a Consultative Document*, HMSO, Cmnd 6851, 1977.)

II THE PROVISION OF HOUSING THROUGH THE PRICE SYSTEM

The dominance of the standing stock

As we saw in Chapter 4, an essential feature of housing is that, except over virtually very long periods, we are dealing with a stock: 20 million dwellings in Britain increase by only 200,000 a year. Even if the construction industry could raise its normal output by a third (which would be a considerable achievement), the rate of increase in the standing stock would only rise from 1 to 1.5 per cent per annum.

This 'stock' nature of housing has important implications as regards housing policy:

(a) In the short period (which may be many years) the only immediate solution to a housing problem is to restrict demand to the limits imposed by the fixed stock.

(b) In the short period, and in fully developed urban areas, the price of old houses determines the price of new houses. Thus the land price is a residual, and high land prices do not restrict the supply of housing (see pp. 37–40).

(c) If 'needs' are not covered by the number of dwellings available, resources must be diverted into house construction.

The process by which the housing stock is increased through the price mechanism will now be examined.

Equilibrium in the distribution of the standing stock

We will assume that housing is occupied either by tenants or owner-occupiers. This means that there are three parties: tenants, landlords (who can be regarded as investors) and owner-occupiers.

We deal first with the standing stock. This will be allocated according to preferences expressed through *demand* in the market for renting as opposed to owner-occupation. While the over-all demand for housing depends mainly on long-term factors (see p. 217), the choice between renting and owner-occupation will be influenced by the rent charged compared with the cost of mortgage repayments, the desire for independence from a landlord, pride of home ownership, possible capital gain, etc.

Let us assume: (i) initially the stock of dwellings is randomly distributed between renters and owner-occupiers irrespective of preferences; and (ii) there is perfect competition both in the housing and capital markets.

Because of pride of ownership, the desire to be independent of a landlord, or (in particular) because the rent charged may be little less than mortgage repayments on a house, some renters will wish to become owner-occupiers. On the other hand, some owner-occupiers may wish to sell and rent, preferring immediate capital. Since the stock was initially distributed randomly, households will now trade in the market to achieve their preferred positions. Suppose people show an increased preference for renting as opposed to owner-occupation. Prices of owner-occupied houses would fall, while rents paid by tenants would rise. Landlords would therefore buy owner-occupied houses and rent them out. As a result of increased rented accommodation, rents would start to fall until eventually equilibrium between renting and owner-occupation was established, rents being somewhat higher than in the initial situation.

Two further points can be made. First, since a landlord normally seeks to pay off his interest and capital within sixty years, the rent he expects would, other things being equal, be equivalent to mortgage repayments where the term of the mortgage was for sixty years. Second, since we have assumed perfect competition in the capital market, if he receives this rent, there will be a long-term equilibrium situation, for he will be obtaining the going rate of return on capital with no alternative investment offering a higher yield.

Suppose now there is an over-all increase in the demand for housing as opposed to other goods. Let us assume, too, that this increased demand occurs in the rented sector. Rents will rise and so will the yield to landlords. In the short term landlords can buy owner-occupied houses, renting them to tenants. But the yield on housing as an investment is now higher than the return on alternative investments. In the long term, therefore, landlords would provide the capital for building new rented housing. Eventually, with the additional supply, rents would fall back, and this would continue until equilibrium was restored, but still with rents higher than they were originally.

In practice, the model has to be adjusted for real-life conditions:

(a) Mortgages are usually shorter than sixty years, so that repayments are higher than rents.

(b) On the other hand, rents will be increased by items often ignored by the owner-occupier, such as (i) an allowance to cover normal profit, administrative costs and possible adverse changes in government policy, (ii) costs of repairs, which the owner-occupier often does himself, and (iii) a sinking fund to recoup his capital, whereas the owner-occupier's main concern is that the house will last his lifetime.

(c) A part of the rented market may be 'frozen' by the government, e.g. local authority housing.

(d) Because of building society 'rationing' (see later), finance may not be available for would-be owner-occupiers, especially those in the lower-income groups.

(e) Imperfections of the market mechanism and immobilities, e.g. fixed-term renting leases, mean that it takes time to achieve equilibrium.

(f) Legislative provisions, e.g. rent control, may on the one hand force people into owner-occupation, and on the other hand deter landlords from renting out accommodation.

(g) The pattern of taxation and allowances benefits the owner-occupier (see later) and penalises the landlord. Thus, since any provision for a sinking fund has to come from taxed income, the landlord is discouraged from making the improvements expected by the tenant, who may therefore move to the owner-occupied sector.

It should be noted, however, that the rate of interest will not affect the division of the housing stock between renting and owner-occupation. As we saw above, ignoring the repayment of capital, the rent to be paid equals the rate of interest: that is,

$$\text{Monthly rent} = \frac{\text{Yearly interest charges on the capital value}}{12}$$

If the rate of interest falls, the investment capital value of rented houses rises. Thus the interest charge remains the same, and rents are not changed. Since owner-occupiers will have to pay this higher capital value in the house market to obtain their houses, a fall in the rate of interest will similarly leave them in the same position.

In the long term a fall in the rate of interest is likely to benefit investment in housing, where yields extend further into the future as compared with most other forms of investment (see p. 77).

However, easier, as opposed to cheaper, credit is likely to induce a move from the rented to the owner-occupied sector since some frustrated renters can now move to their preferred position. Moreover, easier credit should stimulate new building in both the private and public sectors.

Of course, all the changes predicted above occur within the existing distribution of income. Thus 'the most preferred position' in the market for the poorest households will probably be older dwellings, inferior amenities, less desirable locations and more intensive occupation. It must be remembered that in the long term the poor will benefit from secular growth in income and in the housing stock for they will then be able to spend more on housing and so 'filter' upwards. On the other hand, it has to be recognised that 'slum clearance' may remove the preference option of cheap inferior housing from the very people it seeks to help.

The advantages of the free-market system in the provision of housing

Until the Second World War housing was provided almost entirely through the price mechanism, with 80 per cent of all dwellings rented, 10 per cent tied and 10 per cent owner-occupied. Local authority housing was virtually non-existent.

Such a free market in housing has advantages:

(a) Some accommodation is always immediately available, the quality enjoyed being determined by the rent people are able and willing to pay.

(b) Within their income limitation people can exercise choice in housing according to their preferences. Thus if one landlord will not allow them to keep a dog, they may try to find another who will, perhaps at a higher rent.

(c) Where the stock of accommodation is small compared with households, rents rise and people are forced to economise on space, e.g. by sharing houses. In the short term, using available accommodation more intensively is the only possible solution.

(d) High rents stimulate the conversion of large houses into separate flats and new construction. People at the lower-income levels benefit by being able to filter upwards.

(e)   No complex and expensive government machinery is necessary to build dwellings, allocate them or supervise day-to-day maintenance.

State intervention in the housing market

An active state housing policy really began with the First World War. Rents rose because house-building virtually came to an end, extra households were formed and general inflation occurred. Consequently, by the Increase of Rent and Mortgage Interest (War Restrictions) Act 1915, it was made illegal for landlords of unfurnished houses, or parts of houses let as separate dwellings, where either the rent charged in August 1914, or the net rateable value did not exceed £35 in London or £26 elsewhere, to charge rents higher than those charged in August 1914, except in so far as improvements had been made or the rates increased. The Act also prohibited calling-in of mortgages or raising mortgage interest rates on rent-controlled property. Security of tenure was given to occupiers in order to make the Act effective.

Although originally introduced as a purely temporary expedient, rent control eventually became the key-stone of government post-war housing policy, and we must therefore examine it in some detail.

III   THE ECONOMICS OF RENT CONTROL

The question which has to be answered is whether rent control is an improvement upon the free-market mechanism in allocating existing housing accommodation, supplying new dwellings and redistributing income. Economists tend to be critical, for the following reasons.

(1)   *It does nothing to solve the short-term housing problem*
In the short term there is a fixed stock of dwellings, *OM* in Figure 12.1. Let us assume that initially this fixed stock is 'rationed out' by a market rent, *OR*, which equates demand and supply.

Now assume that, through additional household formation, demand increases from *D* to D_1 but rent is controlled at *OR*. Two results follow. First, landlords cannot secure the extra economic rent, R_1RTY, arising through the increased demand for a fixed supply. Second, persons on low incomes (and others) *who are already occupying a rented dwelling* can, through security of tenure, continue to occupy it at the current rent. These are the sole advantages of rent control, though in recent years it has been argued that rent control reinforces a policy of wage restraint.

The difficulty is that, since nothing has been done to cause the existing

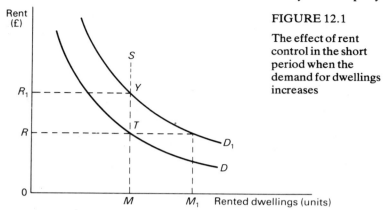

FIGURE 12.1

The effect of rent
control in the short
period when the
demand for dwellings
increases

stock to be used more intensively, demand continues to exceed supply.
Some households, represented by MM_1, simply have to double up in
existing dwellings.

(2)   *It allocates housing arbitrarily and often inequitably*

With a free-market mechanism the existing stock of accommodation is
allocated by the equilibrium market rent, for this is the 'price' where
demand just equals supply. This rent would be determined by people
bidding in the market, reflecting their preferences and income constraint.
However, inequality of incomes would generally mean that the poorer
households would suffer the worst housing conditions. Nevertheless,
instead of interfering with the price mechanism, and so denying consumer
preference, incomes should be redistributed in order to increase the
purchasing power of the poor. Taxation can appropriate the increased
economic rent received by landlords.

Whenever the price system is eschewed, some other means of allocating supply has to be used. Thus the government can divide the limited
stock of a good into 'fair' shares which are rationed out, or people may be
able to exercise some individual preferences within a limited-points
system. But because of the relatively small flow of new dwellings on to the
market, neither method is suitable for allocating housing. We can illustrate as follows.

When petrol was in short supply in 1979 rationing would have been
possible since new flows were constantly coming on to the market. As the
size of these flows changed, the ration could be varied. With housing,
however, people are occupying the fixed stock; they cannot be turned out
in order to implement the principle of 'fair shares'. Thus rationing can be
applied only to new building or the trickle of private, rented accommodation which becomes vacant and is re-let. With new building allocation is
achieved partly by building society policy (see p. 213) and, in local

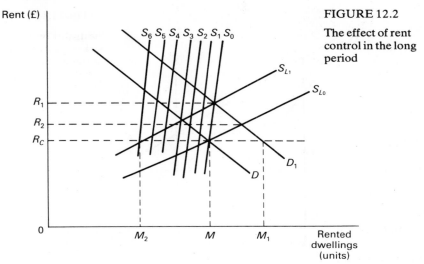

FIGURE 12.2

The effect of rent
control in the long
period

authority housing, by a points system; with vacant privately rented
dwellings personal contact with the owner or his agent dominates.

Initially, therefore, allocation of the housing stock is simply on the basis
of possession. As a result, rent control is related only randomly to the
income and needs of the individual, whether landlord or tenant.
Moreover, it increases the difficulties for many newly-weds and poor
people not already occupying a dwelling, for they cannot afford the
higher-priced free-market substitutes. Even where private landlords
re-let dwellings, they carry out their own 'rationing', preferring elderly
spinsters to large families and students, and, since the Rent Act 1974,
temporary foreign visitors to more permanent British families.

(3)   *It decreases the supply of privately rented dwellings*
In the long period the supply of dwellings would extend in response to a
higher free-market price; rent control obstructs this functioning of the
price system.

Indeed, supply tends to decrease, the long-period supply curve moving
to the left from S_{L_0} to S_{L_1} in Figure 12.2. First, as rented dwellings become
vacant, they are sold in the higher-priced owner-occupier market. Second, as repair costs rise relative to rents, houses deteriorate or remain
substandard. Third, where the accommodation is part of the landlord's
house, he may re-occupy it for his own use (see p. 205). Thus rent control
conflicts with the broad aims of housing policy.

The above arguments can be demonstrated diagrammatically. In Figure 12.2, when demand increases to D_1, the rent will rise to OR_1, but in
the long period will settle at OR_2. With a rent control at OR_C, demand

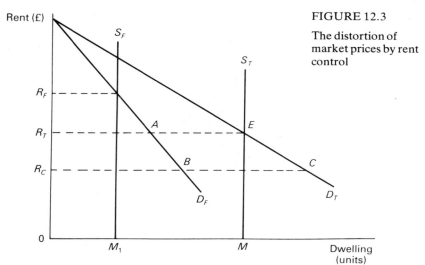

FIGURE 12.3

The distortion of
market prices by rent
control

exceeds supply by MM_1. Successive short-period reductions in supply, however, eventually give a long-period supply curve of S_{L_1}, with excess demand of M_2M_1.

(4)   *It distorts market prices, particularly within the housing market*

Households who cannot find dwellings to rent are forced to turn to substitutes in the uncontrolled owner-occupied sector of the market. The model, Figure 12.3, illustrates the results.

Assume a fixed stock of dwellings, OM. Everybody wanting a dwelling are in a queue, with people randomly distributed as regards preferences and income. (Alternatively, it can be assumed that all people have identical income and preferences.) The curve D_T represents their total demand curve. Further assume that a proportion of the demand, say one-half, is allowed to optimise consumption of housing at the controlled rent OR_c. Since one-half of the housing demand at any given price will be taken up by people at the head of the queue, the other half will represent people who have to bid for dwellings in the free sector. Thus the D_F curve, representing their demand, will bisect the horizontal between D_T and the vertical axis at all prices.

If there were no division of the market, total demand would equal the fixed supply at an equilibrium rent OR_T. If rent, however, is controlled at OR_C, demand in that half of the market which can buy at OR_C extends from AE to BC. Since this quantity of dwellings is supplied from the total stock, it leaves only OM_1 (supply S_F) for the free market, since M_1M equals BC. The result is that free-market renters have to pay a rent of OR_F. That is, those who are not fortunate enough to obtain rent-

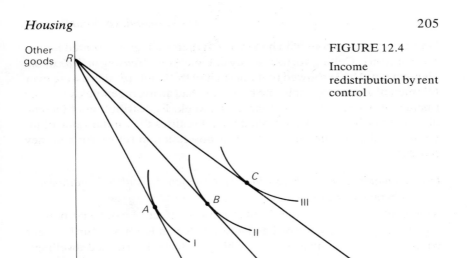

FIGURE 12.4

Income
redistribution by rent
control

controlled dwellings are forced to pay a higher rent than if the whole
market were completely free.

Three points should be noted. First, in practice, the extension of
demand from *AE* to *BC* may come about by under-utilisation of accommodation, e.g. through owner-occupiers not letting a part of their house
or old people retaining the same accommodation in spite of their children
having left home. Second, this means that any allocation according to
'needs' becomes inefficient over time, and this is perpetuated by the
rent-rebate system. Third, households who suffer most are those who do
not happen to be at the head of the queue and who cannot afford OR_F in
order to become owner-occupiers.

(5)   *It redistributes income arbitrarily*

We can transfer some of the information contained in Figure 12.3 to an
indifference-curve diagram, Figure 12.4. Let us assume that all households have identical tastes and income. If there were no rent control, the
price would be represented by the line RR_T, and all households would
optimise at *B* on indifference curve II; with a controlled rent RR_C,
controlled households optimise at *C* on the higher indifference curve III.
On the other hand, free-market households pay a rent of RR_F and
optimise at *A* on the lower indifference curve I. Yet there is no guarantee
with rent control that households who gain by being on indifference curve
III are more deserving than those who lose by being on I.

Moreover, similar arbitrariness is shown in the redistribution of income
between tenants and landlords. If prices generally rise over time, rent
control subsidises tenants at the expense of landlords. In 1915 many

landlords were persons who had invested their savings in a rented house. Even in 1961, Cullingworth's survey of Lancaster (*Housing in Transition*, Heinemann, 1963) showed that one-half of the landlords there were over 60 years of age, owned only one house and had an average weekly income (including net rents) of less than £10 a week. Redistribution of income also occurs when a rent-controlled tenant realises the capital value of his interest and gives the landlord vacant possession in return for a money payment.

(6)   *It creates vested interests which make it more difficult to formulate a coherent long-term policy*

Rent control has many undesirable 'spin-off' effects. First, by perpetuating shortages, rent control has fostered demands for yet further rent control, e.g. the Rent Act 1974, which controlled furnished dwellings. Second, to match the subsidy which controlled tenants enjoy at the expense of landlords, the government introduced further subsidies for owner-occupiers and council tenants (see later). Third, the resulting shortages led to a policy which is need-orientated rather than demand-orientated (see p. 216). Fourth, the artificially low rents produced by rent control and housing subsidies has generated an attitude to what is a 'reasonable' or 'normal' rent. Thus we have the 1965 Rent Act's concept of a 'fair rent' – to be determined by rent tribunals – but market shortages are ignored! It means that fair rents are fixed by controlled low rents – a form of economic incest: in other words, the concept of a 'fair rent' simply disguises rent control.

The difficulty is that, once subsidies and attitudes have been established, beneficiaries resist policy changes. Thus both the Rent Act 1957 (which aimed at some de-control of rents) and the Housing Finance Act 1972 (which switched local authority subsidies from housing generally to only those tenants needing them) met with such resistance that both policies were dropped.

(7)   *It distorts the allocation of resources*

One advantage of the price system is that, given perfect competition and the existing distribution of income, it allocates resources so that marginal private benefits equal marginal private costs. Unless there are spillovers, this is an optimum allocation, and one that is distorted by rent control.

Moreover, the evidence suggests that government policy directed to lower rents over the past sixty years has influenced people's views as to how much should be spent on housing. Thus when rents rise, people complain and look for government help; on the other hand, when car prices rise, people accept the rise and pay the higher price. Since expenditure on housing is too little, insufficient resources are attracted into the rented sector. For instance, over the period 1951–78 consumers' expenditure on housing averaged less than 12 per cent of total expenditure, whereas that on alcoholic drink and tobacco averaged 13 per cent and that on transport and vehicles over 10 per cent.

In the public sector, too, low rents have restricted the provision of housing. Increased subsidies, which are necessary if rents are not raised when costs are rising, add to the Public Sector Borrowing Requirement. Thus local authority housing suffers when cuts have to be made in the PSBR (as in 1976 and 1980).

(8)   *It hampers labour mobility*

Not only does rent control influence the distribution of land resources but it also affects the labour market. Whereas rent control tends to freeze the allocation of dwellings at a particular time, the optimum geographical distribution of labour is constantly changing. The difficulty arises because the subsidy implicit in rent-controlled housing is attached to the dwelling, not to the person, with only some rented dwellings enjoying the subsidy. Thus, unless the subsidy can be capitalised by giving the landlord possession in exchange for a money sum, it is usually lost on moving.

Worse still, rent control means that there is no alternative rented accommodation. Thus the only option is to buy in the owner-occupied sector at prices inflated by rent control!

(9)   *It involves administrative costs*

For example, rent officers need to be appointed to determine 'fair rents'.

Conclusions

Rent control simply mitigates 'the effects of shortage by giving comfort to sitting tenants at the expense of prospective tenants' (*Fair Deal for Housing*, HMSO, Cmnd 4728, 1971). Furthermore, it inhibits long-term solutions to the housing shortage. Not only is the supply of privately rented accommodation decreased but, by engendering the attitude that rents should be low, resources are also discouraged from flowing into extra housing.

Finally, by creating vested interests, rent control becomes difficult to remove. Progressive de-control, which started in 1923, was brought to a halt in 1939 when full control was once more re-imposed. Thereafter, rent control has remained as a permanent plank of housing policy. After the opposition to the de-control allowed for by the Rent Act 1957, no political party has had the courage to put forward such a policy. Indeed, it was not even mentioned in the Labour government's *Housing Policy: a Consultative Document* (Cmnd 6851, 1977). Instead, the system of 'regulated' rents has prolonged 'controlled' rents under another label.

The loss of privately rented accommodation through rent control, however, has resulted in the government having to distort the housing market in other directions. This has been done through subsidies to owner-occupiers and local authorities. It is to an examination of these sectors that we now turn.

IV THE OWNER-OCCUPIER SECTOR

The expansion of owner-occupation

Table 12.1 shows the rapid relative growth of the owner-occupied sector over the last sixty years. The reasons for this are as follows:

(1) *The shortage of houses to rent*, which has forced many would-be renters to buy.

(2) *A growth in incomes of skilled and white-collar workers*, which has enabled mortgages to be repaid over a twenty-five-year period.

(3) *The desire to keep up with the Joneses* as the trend towards owner-occupation developed.

(4) *Government financial policy*, which has increased the competitiveness of owner-occupation relative to renting. Thus, while the owner-occupier tends to ignore repair costs and amortisation of capital, a landlord has to allow for these in the rent charged, with amortisation having to be covered out of taxed income. In contrast, owner-occupiers enjoy tax concessions. Interest charged on mortgages up to £25,000 (in 1980) is exempt from tax, whereas rent has to be paid by tenants out of taxed income. Again, since the main residence of an owner-occupier is exempt from capital gains tax, it means that he enjoys a 100 per cent equity interest for a relatively small deposit, comparing favourably with the tenant whose rent increases with inflation.

TABLE 12.1
Distribution of the housing stock by tenure,
1914–78, Great Britain (percentages)

	1914	1947	1963	1969	1972	1975	1978
Owner-occupied	10	26	45	49	51	53	54
Local authority and New Towns	—	13	28	30	31	31	32
Private, landlord and miscellaneous	90	61	27	21	18	16	14

Note: in 1978, 54 per cent of dwellings in Scotland were rented from local authorities.
Sources: *Housing and Construction Statistics; Social Trends.*

(5) *The development of special sources of finance*, chiefly the building societies. Such finance is the subject of the remainder of this section.

Sources of finance for the owner-occupier

For most people, a house is an expensive capital good which can be purchased only by borrowing for a comparatively long period against the security of the house. Table 12.2 shows the main sources, and we shall study them in reverse order of importance.

TABLE 12.2
Mortgages (net advances, £m.): main institutional
sources, UK, 1972–8

	Building societies	Local authorities, New Towns, etc.	Banks	Insurance companies	All
1972	2,215	220	345	2	2,782
1973	1,999	401	310	121	2,831
1974	1,490	672	90	120	2,372
1975	2,768	755	60	67	3,650
1976	3,618	170	70	13	3,871
1977	4,100	33	120	22	4,275
1978	5,095	−91	270	47	5,321

Source: *Housing and Construction Statistics.*

(1)   *Insurance companies*
Insurance companies regard lending for house purchase partly as an investment but mainly as a means of extending their assurance business, since, in order to redeem the capital advanced, a borrower has to take out an endowment policy. While the rate of interest charged is usually about 1 per cent above that of building societies, the high marginal taxpayer can offset this by tax savings. First, the interest is paid on the full loan over the whole period, thus attracting a higher tax relief than a building society mortgage, where interest charges fall over time (see Figure 12.7 below). Second, endowment-policy premiums qualify for tax relief as a life insurance. Consequently, insurance companies lend mostly to better-off owner-occupiers buying more expensive houses, though the limit of tax relief on loans up to £25,000 has tended to reduce their advantage in this area.

(2)   *Banks*
Banks grant both short-term bridging finance and loans for up to twenty years. Usually the rate of interest charged is higher than that of building societies, while the amount advanced is limited to 50 per cent of the purchase price unless other adequate collateral can be offered. As a result, banks lend mainly to the better-off owner-occupier, and this aspect of house-purchase lending increased considerably in 1979.

(3)   *Local authorities*

Local authorities have increased in importance over the last decade, but recent limitations on the PSBR has restricted their lending. Unlike building societies, they will lend on low-priced older property, long leaseholds and flat conversions, even granting 100 per cent mortgages (though this may be offset by low valuations). They can thus be regarded as 'lenders of last resort'. Interest is about ¼ per cent above the Public Works Loans Board rate at which they borrow. Although somewhat above the building society rate, it is often fixed for the full term.

(4)   *Building societies*

Building societies were the first intermediary to specialise in providing finance for the owner-occupier with little capital. They originated as an attempt by the working man to help himself, a group of would-be owner-occupiers forming a society in Birmingham in 1775 to build houses which were allocated as they were completed. Once the last member had obtained his house (perhaps some ten years later) the society was disbanded. Eventually, however, lenders were found who did not want a house, and societies then became 'permanent'.

This background has largely determined the features of the present-day building society: (i) it regards itself as a 'social' institution; (ii) it is dependent upon borrowing short and lending long; (iii) it favours the owner-occupier at the lower-income end in lending. How these features have largely determined building society policy will now be examined.

The building society as a social institution. From their beginning building societies have never been profit-maximising institutions. This leaves them with a choice of objectives, such as sales maximisation or maximum rate of growth. Sales maximisation rather than profit maximisation would mean that mortgages granted would be OM_1 rather than OM in Figure 12.5. However, from their recent annual reports, there is evidence that building societies are concentrating on growth of business (as measured by deposits) and to this end they have established High Street offices convenient to depositors and which are open on Saturdays. Indeed, the extent of this development has so alarmed the planning authorities that they are withholding consent to change of use, alleging that such offices create 'dead' frontages in shopping areas.

Financial policy. Building societies are intermediaries for marrying finance to the building of houses. To do this they have to borrow funds, consisting of small, short-term loans, from private savers. Expansion has thus been dependent upon proven *financial stability* and *the ability to compete for such savings.*

Financial stability rests on overcoming the risk inherent in borrowing short and lending long. Normally withdrawals are covered by new

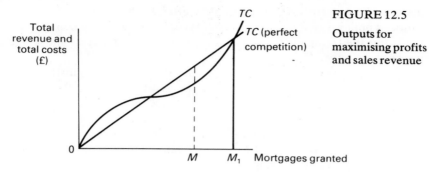

FIGURE 12.5

Outputs for maximising profits and sales revenue

deposits. Provided depositors retain confidence in being repaid on demand, there is unlikely to be a mass withdrawal. However, a building society must play for safety by maintaining adequate liquidity. This liquidity is provided by the intake of new deposits, repayments of existing mortgages (now equal to half the total inflow of funds), accumulated general reserves (corresponding to the undistributed profits of companies and now accounting for 3.5 per cent of deposits), and maintaining a high liquidity ratio in the form of cash and investments.

It is often argued that building societies need no longer add to general reserves. Not only do such reserves add to the cost of borrowing (30p of the interest currently paid by borrowers on every £100 going directly to general reserves), but in providing a safety-net they could blunt efficiency. In any case the government would hardly stand idly by should a building society face temporary liquidity problems. For their part, however, the societies claim that one purpose of the reserves is to cover the shortfall resulting from the time lag between raising rates paid to depositors and charging higher rates to borrowers, the latter often being delayed because of high administrative costs.

But it is the high liquidity ratio held by building societies which attracts the most criticism. Whereas 7.5 per cent is the legal minimum ratio, building societies rarely operate below 15 per cent, and in recent years it has been above 20 per cent. A lower liquidity ratio, it is maintained, would permit increased lending. Indeed, the high liquidity ratio is only possible because building societies do not have to compete with one another in granting mortgages. Building societies justify their high liquidity ratio as follows. First, liquid funds help them to maintain the flow of lending when deposits fall off. Second, such funds keep the society independent of government help. Third, much of the liquidity is notional since it is tied up in mortgages committed but not completed. Fourth, and most important, the societies must inspire confidence. Thus the high liquidity ratio is part of their optimum portfolio, an item to cover the time it takes to effect sales of houses where foreclosure is necessary and to provide against a possible fall in the capital value of investments (government and local authority securities). Certainly the building societies' cautious policy was vindicated in the crisis years of 1972–3 when they did not suffer the traumatic liquidity problems of many merchant and fringe banks.

Building societies *compete for deposits* with other savings institutions, particularly the National Savings Bank, Trustee Savings Banks and joint-stock banks. Their success has been based on: (i) an attractive rate of interest, particularly for the standard income-taxpayer since the interest payments are tax-free; (ii) different methods of saving to meet the needs of different depositors, e.g. insurance-linked savings; (ii) High Street branches convenient for depositors; and (iv) generous withdrawal terms of £100 on demand and complete withdrawal within three days (although one month is stipulated). This gives the lender what is virtually an interest-yielding current account lacking only cheque-drawing facilities, and means that joint-stock banks are competitive for funds only when the general level of interest rates is abnormally high, since the building societies are reluctant to raise their rates (see below).

Lending policy. In 1978 47 per cent of mortgages granted by building societies were to first-time buyers, 61 per cent of whom had an annual income of less than £5,000 (62 per cent were under 30 years of age). Thus building societies can be said to fulfil their stated aim of helping the small, first-time buyer as much as possible.

To do this they limit the size of loans, keep monthly payments as low as possible by extending the mortgage over twenty-five years, and hold down the rate of interest. The economic implications of these policies will now be considered.

Apart from the ceiling of £25,000 imposed by the government, building societies limit the *size of loan* according to the borrower's income. This limit is about twice the borrower's annual income, and, while an addition is usually made for a wife's income, little account is taken of the borrower's lifetime prospects. More important, this restriction on people's spending preferences forces buyers to live in a suburban property when, in order to avoid the cost of time and travelling, they might prefer to pay the higher price for a house or flat located centrally. Indeed, when taxation is taken into account, the distortion is aggravated: higher mortgage payments resulting from living nearer the centre are partly offset by reduced income tax, whereas higher fares have to be found out of *taxed* income. Thus the housing market is distorted, demand being diverted towards suburban or cheaper houses and away from town or more expensive properties.

So that monthly payments do not exceed 25 per cent of income, the *mortgage term* is normally from twenty-five to thirty years. In fact,

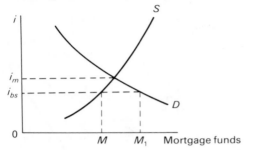

FIGURE 12.6

Building society
interest policy

through the inflation of money incomes, mortgages are usually repaid before the stipulated time.

The interest charged has to cover the interest paid to the depositor, tax paid to the Board of Inland Revenue, and a contribution to general reserves and management expenses. Even so, the rate is still below the going market rate for similar loans. This low rate is possible because building societies borrow relatively cheaply, seek to keep the cost of repayments down and are non-profit organisations.

The economic effect is illustrated in Figure 12.6. The demand for and supply of mortgage funds would be in equilibrium at a market rate of i_m. But building societies charge a lower rate, i_{bs}, with demand exceeding supply by MM_1.

Societies therefore have to 'ration' loans. They do this by imposing conditions which reinforce other policies, especially safety of capital. First, they discriminate between borrowers, giving preference to persons who have deposited with their society. Second, they discriminate in the type of property, those properties preferred enjoying a loan/value ratio of 80 per cent, with the less favoured having a lower ratio or even being refused a mortgage. In practice, freehold houses are preferred to leaseholds, the traditional three-bedroom house to one of advanced design, new houses to old, brick to wooden, houses to flats, and purpose-built flats to conversions. However, in recent years such preferences have not been rigidly adhered to, since, with rising prices, first-time buyers have had to settle for the cheaper types of dwelling. Third, repayments have to be in a manner determined by the society, usually equal monthly sums covering both capital and interest spread over twenty-five years (see Figure 12.7 overleaf).

Economic consequences of building societies' borrowing and lending policies. The above policies have important economic consequences:

(1) By their reluctance to raise the rate of interest paid to their depositors when banks and other competitors for funds are paying high rates, funds available for house purchase may be reduced. Moreover, this may be reinforced by the rationing conditions which societies pursue, for

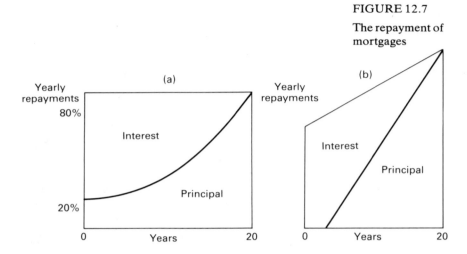

FIGURE 12.7

The repayment of
mortgages

these shield the societies from competition, permitting cautious and inflexible policies and even masking inefficiency.

(2) Borrowers cannot fully exercise their preferences. For instance, they may prefer a method of amortising the mortgage which takes into account the likelihood of a rising income in the future. The risks to the building societies would be small since house values are likely to continue to increase and so provide adequate collateral. In Figure 12.7, (a) is the method of repayment usually required by societies. But because of his pattern of income over time, a person may prefer (b) where, especially with inflation, the higher later repayments correspond to the lower marginal utility of a rising income. Pattern (b) should be acceptable to building societies provided that the rate of repayment ensured that the outstanding loan was adequately covered by the value of the property, which would be probable in view of the societies' loan/value ratio and the inflation of house prices over time.

Similarly, borrowers might be willing to pay a higher rate of interest if this allowed greater choice in the loan/value ratio or loan/income ratio or a relaxation of other conditions. The absence of such a choice must count as an imperfection in the housing finance market.

(3) The composition of the housing stock is affected. Since the purchase of most houses is through building society mortgages, speculative builders concentrate on the type of house likely to attract a mortgage, particularly the two- or three-bedroom house of traditional design.

(4) The building societies' condition for the grant of a mortgage that there shall be no sub-letting without approval not only reduces house accommodation available for renting but interferes with the borrower's freedom of choice.

To sum up, the development of building societies over the last fifty years has had two major effects: on the demand side it has permitted the growth of owner-occupation; on the supply side it has encouraged speculative builders to produce in anticipation of demand. Through their policies the building societies have definitely shaped the housing market.

Building societies and the national economy

Apart from the micro effects of their policies building societies influence, and are affected by, the main macro variables. As a result, they have an impact on the general performance of the economy.

First, because their depositors now account for almost half of net saving from personal disposable income, the facilities offered by building societies probably increase net saving.

Second, since the flow of loans has a direct effect on the level of house-building activity, building society policy influences investment. In particular, some control over the flow of mortgages could even out house-building starts, bringing greater stability to the construction industry. On the other side of the coin, building societies are not isolated from the effects of government policy, particularly monetary policy. As we have seen, when interest rates are high, they lose deposits to the banks. Moreover, high interest rates could deter investment and, with the resulting fall in national income, reduce the demand for owner-occupied houses – and, in doing so, dent the building societies' 'growth' objective.

Third, the investment of the building societies' general reserve and liquid funds has strategic importance. About one-third is allocated to local authority bonds, thus directly helping local councils to finance their activities, particularly housing.

Fourth, building societies can play a part in fighting inflation. The cost of mortgage repayments, an item in the Index of Retail Prices, is determined by the price of houses and the rate of interest charged. In the short term the price of houses depends upon demand, which in its turn largely rests upon the availability of credit. Consequently, building societies have to be careful about the amount they lend, as this directly affects the price of houses (and of land). Apart from raising mortgage repayments, a *rise* in the price of houses would tend to undermine confidence in the government's resolution to check inflation. Similarly, any reluctance of building societies to reduce the mortgage rate when interest rates generally are falling (as in 1977) would adversely affect the Index of Retail Prices, a major signpost for wage claims. At present the amount of credit to be allocated to house purchase is fixed monthly by a Joint Advisory Committee consisting of the societies, the Chief Registrar of Friendly Societies and representatives of the Department of the Environment, the Treasury and the Bank of England.

Lastly, because building society deposits now exceed those of the London clearing banks, they may, like them, have to be subjected to direct monetary controls in order to achieve money-supply targets.

V   LOCAL AUTHORITY HOUSING

The development of local authority housing

By the end of the nineteenth century concern over the effects of bad housing on health had led to the first tentative steps to dwellings being provided by local authorities. But the policy did not gather momentum until after the First World War.

In 1918 it was estimated that the deficiency of dwellings in England and Wales was some 900,000. Moreover, the continuation of rent control undermined the incentive to supply privately rented accommodation. Therefore, by the Town and Country Planning Act 1919, local authorities were required to prepare plans for providing housing to meet local needs. Rents charged were to be comparable with those of *rent-controlled* working-class dwellings. The policy thus reaffirmed the rejection of the market mechanism, and meant that local authority housing had to be (i) provided and allocated on the basis of 'need', not demand, and (ii) subsidised. The economic aspects of both these consequences will now be examined.

'Need' and 'demand'

Need measures the extent to which existing accommodation falls short of that required to provide each household with accommodation of a minimum specified standard irrespective of ability to pay. Making such an estimate, however, is not so easy as might appear at first sight. For one thing, projections of households are based on variables such as marriage rates and the size of family which are dependent upon changes in income and social attitudes. For another, 'need' is more than the difference between aggregate households and aggregate dwellings since both have to be subdivided and related according to size and location. Census returns and statistics from the Registrar-General provide the basic data. Above all, what is the 'minimum specified standard' presents practical and conceptual difficulties. How do we measure accommodation standards, by the family unit or by area per person? Really we should concentrate on the needs of the different types of family. For instance, a family of six requires less space than three households of two, while two adults and two children differ in their needs from one adult and three grown children. However, since such refined information is not available (especially for the future), standards are usually calculated on the basis of so many square feet or rooms *per person*. Similarly, what standard should be specified? Although this is basically a subjective decision, it cannot be divorced from the over-all level of income. Moreover, in formulating building plans a decision has to be made on whether to aim at a standard to overcome current overcrowding or a future standard which allows for income growth. When there is a deficiency of housing, the former tends to be paramount. In the long term, however, when only replacement of dwellings is called for, it is important to anticipate future standards, since dwellings have a long life.

To obtain the number of *households* the existing population is projected for the target year according to age and sex by applying birth and death rates and allowing for external migration. How many households which a given population will form, however, depends upon the marriage rate, the proportion of young people who live separately from their parents, and the number of old people who go to live with their children or are admitted to institutions. In addition, an attempt must be made to divide households according to size by applying statistics relating to the size of the completed family. Finally, since dwellings cannot be moved physically, an estimate should be made of the regional location of these different households in the target year. Naturally, the more distant the target year, the more inaccurate are forecasts likely to be, since data are influenced by changes in the level and distribution of income, immigration policy, internal migration, and so on.

Similarly, the stock of *dwellings* has to be estimated for the target year, taking into account new building, demolition, renewals and conversions. All are affected by changes in the level of national activity. In addition, information regarding the quality of dwellings – possession of the standard amenities and age – and their location is also important. Finally, not all the stock will be occupied by a separate household. Some 4 per cent is likely to be vacant to allow for mobility, while 1 per cent will be held for second homes, a figure which is likely to rise as real incomes increase. Policy is to provide housing units of sufficient quantity and quality and having regard to location for the households estimated.

Demand for housing is even more difficult to estimate, for this refers to an economic concept, *effective demand* – what people are willing and able to pay for housing. We are therefore concerned with: (i) preferences at a *price*; and (ii) the conditions of demand, depending upon income and income distribution, household formation, the cost and availability of credit, the price of substitutes, government policy as regards, for instance, rent control, subsidies, changes in tastes as regards flats or houses, expectations of future price changes, and so on. Demand represents the expression of people's preferences for different types of housing, within their income constraints, through the price system. There may be a loss of

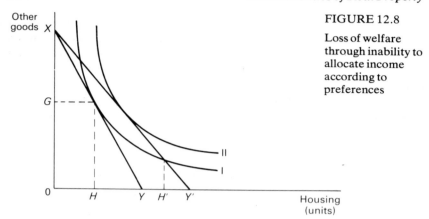

FIGURE 12.8

Loss of welfare
through inability to
allocate income
according to
preferences

welfare where these preferences do not coincide with what is allocated
according to 'needs'.

In Figure 12.8, for instance, at a market rent of XY a household would
purchase OH housing and OG other goods. The local authority charges a
subsidised rent of XY' but requires that the household occupies OH'
housing on a 'needs' basis. As a result, the household remains on the same
indifference curve I, but the taxpayer suffers loss of welfare through
having to cover the subsidy (provided it is not covered by knowing that
the poorer family is adequately housed).

However, the task of estimating demand for housing as a guide to
future policy is far from easy. One method is to apply past statistical
relationships between demand and house prices and rents, interest rates,
and so on. The difficulty here is that future demand may be different since
the conditions of demand change over time. Another method is through
direct enquiry, but this has limitations. Not only do people restrict their
estimates of demand to two or three years ahead, thereby providing little
guide for future policy, but such estimates tend to be related to the
artificially low rents they are used to.

The nature of housing subsidies

Subsidies enable certain households to enjoy housing services below the
cost of providing them through the free market. Such a broad definition
covers:

(a)   the transfer of income from landlords to tenants by rent control;
(b)   tax concessions enjoyed by owner-occupiers;
(c)   direct subsidies, consisting of:
>   (i)   central government grants to local authorities' housing
>   accounts

(ii)   rate fund contributions by local authorities
(iii) rent rebates and rent allowances to tenants on low incomes
(iv)   renovation grants.

Such subsidies have three broad objectives. First, they can be used to redistribute income more equitably, a decision which rests ultimately on a subjective judgement. Second, they can allocate more resources to housing than would be provided by the full price mechanism. This may be required because of the external costs of inadequate housing or because the government treats housing as a 'merit' good to which people should devote more of their income. Third, subsidies reduce the cost of housing, especially for local authority tenants, and may thus be a counter-inflation measure in taking the steam out of demands for higher wages.

These objectives may not always be compatible. Thus reducing landlords' income by rent control prevents resources going into the private rented sector, while subsidies to keep down the cost of living add to the PSBR. But there are certain economic propositions which are relevant to housing subsidies in general. We first state and examine these, and then consider to what extent they have been recognised in the implementation of policy, paying particular attention to subsidies given to public-sector tenants.

Economic propositions relevant to a subsidy

Proposition 1. Other things being equal, the subsidy should be given in such a way that consumers can obtain the highest possible satisfaction. Where the objective is to enable a consumer with limited income to enjoy a minimum standard of housing, a subsidy can either give him more income or reduce the price of housing. The former would appear to be the most efficient method since it enables the consumer to attain a higher indifference curve for a given subsidy expenditure.

This is illustrated in Figure 12.9. With his initial income the consumer attains indifference curve I, buying at point E other goods OG and housing OH. It is now deemed that OH housing is inadequate for his needs, and a subsidy is given to housing, reducing its price from PR to PV. As a result, the consumer substitutes other goods for housing, buying OG_1 and OH_1 respectively at F. But since the subsidy also represents an increase in income, a higher indifference curve, II, is attained.

Now suppose that, instead of the subsidy to housing (which equals FL in terms of 'other goods'), the consumer is given additional income (e.g. by way of Family Income Supplement or a negative income tax) so that he can still purchase OG_1 other goods and OH_1 housing. Since relative prices remain unchanged, this will be shown by moving the original price line further from the origin, TS, to pass through F. Since $TP = FL$ the income

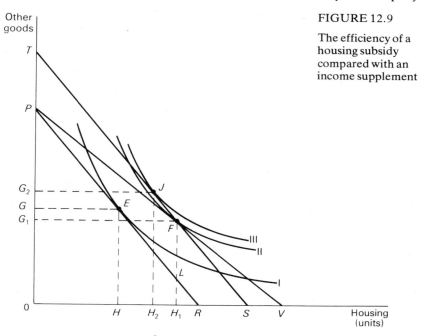

FIGURE 12.9

The efficiency of a
housing subsidy
compared with an
income supplement

subsidy costs the same, being just sufficient to allow the consumer to obtain the same amount of housing in each case.

The big difference, however, is that whereas a housing subsidy distorts relative prices at the same time as income is increased, an income supplement leaves the consumer free to attain his preferred position, *J*, without any accompanying price distortion. He therefore buys OG_2 other goods and OH_2 housing, achieving a higher indifference curve, III. In other words, there has been a Pareto improvement, for our consumer's welfare has increased and nobody is worse off since the same amount of subsidy is being paid.

But there is an important proviso: equilibrium at *J* is based solely on the consumer's private costs and private benefits. In practice, OH_2 housing may still be inadequate in that it gives rise to social costs, such as ill-health, delinquency and vandalism, which the consumer ignores or underestimates when some of his additional income is spent on other goods, such as drink and gambling. Social costs may therefore lead society to choose a *selective* housing subsidy rather than a *neutral* income supplement.

Other qualifications of the analysis are that *taxpayers* may prefer the subsidy to be linked to a 'merit' good (see above, p. 219), while if the supply of housing is inelastic the extra spending will drive up the price, reducing the amount that can be bought.

Proposition 2. If the main reason for housing subsidies is inadequate income, then they should be flexible with respect to changes in income. Two practical considerations follow from this proposition. First, the subsidy should be attached to the person and not, as with rent control, to the dwelling. Second, a negative income tax to achieve this would probably prove more flexible than rent rebates. Whereas the former would be automatically reassessed each year, the latter imposes an additional task on the local authority against the background of resentful tenants regarding it as a form of 'means test' not applied to the private rented sector where, through rent control, the subsidy is attached to the dwelling.

Proposition 3. The selectivity of any subsidy should be kept under review. The purpose of selectivity is to influence the allocation of resources. Thus housing subsidies are selective as between: (i) housing and other goods; (ii) local authority and privately rented housing, the latter enjoying no subsidy; and (iii) slum clearance and housing generally, the former attracting higher subsidies. This means that subsidies have to be adjusted with changes in housing needs and new directions in policy based on experience. For example, a switch from rebuilding to restoring inner-city dwellings can be promoted by reducing general housing subsidies in favour of improvement grants.

Proposition 4. Central government subsidies should not be so open ended that local authorities embark on extravagant housing projects. To this end, it is an advantage if: (i) the subsidy is on a unit basis (a given sum per dwelling) rather than a percentage (e.g. of cost or of the deficit on the housing account); and (ii) the local authority is responsible for a part of the total subsidy out of the rates so that there is a direct link between spending decisions and covering the cost.

Proposition 5. Public expenditure on housing should be related to the financial resources available, particularly as regards the government's other commitments, e.g. defence, health and education, and the size of the Public Sector Borrowing Requirement.

Housing subsidies 1918–78

Over the last sixty years so many Acts of Parliament dealing with housing subsidies have been passed that it is necessary to concentrate on the most significant, with particular reference to recent legislation. From this limited survey, however, there emerges the conclusion that the dominance of political considerations over the propositions stated above has made it virtually impossible to follow a long-term housing strategy.

The shortage of houses after the First World War led the government to introduce a housing subsidy in order to encourage housebuilding by both local authorities and the private builder. The situation is illustrated

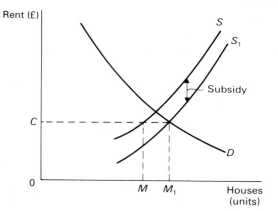

FIGURE 12.10

The effect of a
housing subsidy on
supply in the long
period

in Figure 12.10. At a controlled rent *OC* and supply *S*, *OM* houses are
available. In the long period a subsidy allows more houses to be supplied
at any given price, moving the supply curve to S_1. Now demand equals
supply, and OM_1 houses are available at the controlled rent.

The local authorities were given the real obligation of making good the
housing needs of their populations. Minimum standards were fixed, and
the subsidy covered the difference between annual costs (loan interest
and repayments and repairs) and rents plus the yield of a penny rate. But
the scheme included no inducement for local authorities to control
building costs (Proposition 4 above was ignored), and within two years it
was withdrawn.

The extent of the decline in housebuilding which resulted led to
subsidies being reintroduced in 1923. Provided a dwelling attained a
specified standard, both local authorities and private builders received,
without restrictions on selling prices or rents, either a lump sum per house
of £75 or £6 for twenty years. In addition, to promote slum clearance, the
Treasury bore half the losses incurred in such rehousing. Housing subsidies had now become selective, thus conforming with Proposition 3.
House construction revived. However, in 1924 the Labour government
made the private building subsidy conditional on houses being available
for letting at controlled rents, and within a few years private subsidised
building came to an end.

The general subsidy of so much per house was, after gradual reductions, withdrawn in 1933. But subsidies to clear slums and to reduce
overcrowding allowed the rate of local authority building to continue
almost unchanged.

An important concession of the Housing Act 1936 allowed all expenditure and receipts from local authority houses to be consolidated into a
single housing account. This meant that: (i) all rents could be averaged,
with earlier-built houses subsidising the later ones; and (ii) the subsidies

on later houses could be lower. It did, however, place local authorities which had built early in a strong position compared with late-starters and, more important, it ignored the effects of inflation, which increases the financial burden when earlier and cheaper houses have to be replaced.

After the Second World War the Housing Act 1946 granted local authorities a subsidy of so much per house but imposed a specified rate contribution. In 1949 *improvement grants* were introduced. However, as local authority building increased and the subsidy per house was raised to meet higher building costs, so the government's total subsidy bill became uncomfortably high. Hence in 1956 the general needs subsidy was abolished for *future* houses, except for one-bedroom dwellings, but selective subsidies remained for slum clearance and overcrowding. Although the obligation on local authorities to make rate fund contributions was also removed, such contributions nevertheless continued, and indeed increased.

But the government was moving towards greater emphasis on linking subsidies with the financial resources of both local authorities and households. Authorities which had many low-cost pre-1939 houses were favourably placed compared with those having predominantly post-war houses. From 1961 subsidies on new houses were fixed at two levels: £8 per new dwelling for sixty years, or £24 if the authority satisfied a test of financial need. For the first time the principle of a fixed subsidy for sixty years irrespective of changing needs over time had been breached.

Initially, the differing ability of council tenants to pay a full-cost rent was recognised by the government urging councils to adopt differential rent schemes. The two-rate subsidy was partly designed to put pressure on some Labour-controlled councils to raise rents. Local authorities were expected to charge a 'reasonable rent', twice the gross rateable value for 1956 (itself based on the 1939 letting value). If such higher rents would cover net expenditure (including loan servicing), only the lower £8 subsidy was payable. The test, which was not unreasonable as prices in general had risen by 177 per cent since 1939, was to be applied yearly, and local authorities were still free to decide their own rent policies.

Nevertheless, the new system had certain weaknesses. Subsidies were not related to the cost of land or building, which could vary from one area to another. More important, uncertainty about changes in interest rates, a substantial part of the cost of new housing, made planning by local authorities difficult. Above all, the system was at variance with the views of the Labour party. The Housing Act 1967 therefore introduced: (i) a basic subsidy for sixty years equal to the *difference* between annual loan charges for sixty years at a 'representative' rate of interest and charges calculated at 4 per cent of the 'approved cost' of dwellings of Parker–Morris standards; (ii) additional subsidies for high-rise dwellings, very expensive sites, special 'industrial' needs arising from the transfer of industry, additional building costs incurred to maintain the character of the area, and so on. In practice, the new subsidy virtually pegged the rate of interest at 4 per cent for all housing authorities and, in addition, covered their building and site costs. As such it was an open-ended commitment to local authorities, isolating their housing policies from the constraint of having to pay the market rate for funds. Proposition 4 was flouted, and housing subsidies rose accordingly.

The Conservative government's Housing Finance Act 1972 sought to restructure housing subsidies on sounder economic principles. A situation existed where the rents charged by different local authorities varied according to their individual policies, while vast differences still existed in their needs, mainly through subsidies carried over from past building programmes. As a result, the rent paid by council tenants depended upon the policy and needs of their particular authority, while that of tenants in the private sector rested on whether their dwelling was subject to rent control. The 1972 Act sought to put local authority and private tenants on the same footing by implementing Proposition 2. Thus:

(a)   remaining private controlled tenancies were to be brought within the scope of the Labour government's 1965 'fair-rent' criterion, with tenants who could not afford the 'fair rent' being given a rent allowance by the local authority (but covered by Treasury subsidy);

(b)   the same 'fair-rent' criterion was to be applied to council tenants, rent rebates being given where necessary; and

(c)   to cover the loss of rent, local authorities were given a *rent-rebate* subsidy equivalent to 90 per cent of any deficit in the housing revenue account, the percentage being reduced over time. The rest had to come from the rate fund subsidy of the local authority.

It should be noted that the proposed government subsidy helped those authorities faced with higher building costs since these would increase the deficit on the housing revenue account. But the Act antagonised vested interests. In order to limit the cost of the subsidy the freedom of councils to determine their rent charges was curtailed. On the other hand, tax subsidies to owner-occupiers were untouched. Above all, the resulting rise in local authority rents coincided with the government's policy of urging wage restraint. Thus an overdue measure became a political issue, and its reversal was one of the Labour party's election pledges of February 1974.

After an initial rent freeze, the revised policy of the Labour government was embodied in the Housing Rents and Subsidies Act 1975. This ended the year-long rent freeze, abandoned the last of the three stages of automatic de-control of rented dwellings in the private sector, and replaced the 'fair-rent' formula (a Labour government innovation of

1965) with 'reasonable rents' (a Conservative concept of 1961), which local authorities would be expected to charge. The Act also introduced a new pattern of general housing subsidy, consisting of a basic element, with possible additions depending largely upon the different levels of costs of different authorities. The stated object was 'to encourage vigorous and expanding housing programmes' by local authorities. Their cost, however, soon led to modifications. 'Reasonable rents' charged were often unacceptably low, the Greater London Council, for instance, having to raise its rents above the 1972 Housing Finance Act requirement in order to qualify for the high-cost element! Worse still, the percentage grants allowed on certain categories of expenditure enabled some authorities to exploit the system. Thus in 1976 the London Borough of Camden ranked third behind Birmingham and Manchester in housing expenditure for housing authorities, though in population size it came only sixty-seventh, while between 1965 and 1976 its housing subsidies rose from £633,000 to £20 million.

Such increases were a direct result of a policy which flouted Proposition 4. The over-all result can be seen in Table 12.3. Apart from annual revenue subsidies, local authority housing entails capital expenditure financed by borrowing from the central government. While Table 12.3 shows the increase in government housing expenditure at current prices,

TABLE 12.3

Government revenue subsidies and expenditure on
housing, 1968–79 at current prices (£m.)

	Housing revenue subsidies				
	Central government to				Total government expenditure on housing
	Local authorities	Public corporations	Local authorities	Total	
1968	134	13	84	231	1,157
1969	155	15	96	266	1,208
1970	192	18	103	313	1,319
1971	224	23	82	329	1,310
1972	245	52	40	337	1,509
1973	285	45	58	388	2,328
1974	535	56	149	740	4,209
1975	763	76	212	1,051	4,460
1976	941	164	196	1,301	5,117
1977	1,017	210	179	1,406	5,142
1978	1,145	257	242	1,644	5,073
1979	1,364	275	332	1,971	6,099

Source: *National Income and Expenditure* Blue Books.

such spending has also increased in real terms, as the following index
(1977−8 = 100) shows:

           1973−4   88
           1976−7   111
           1977−8   100
           1978−9   103

This increase was a major contributor to the rise in the Public Sector
Borrowing Requirement (see Chapter 13). Since it seems that the PSBR
has to be reduced irrespective of which party is in power, cuts in
government housing subsidies appear to be inevitable.

VI   HOUSE-RENOVATION GRANTS

In contrast with subsidies to owner-occupiers and local authorities considered so far (and which are directed mainly to new housing), renovation
grants aim at improving older buildings on economic, social and aesthetic
grounds. Originally introduced in 1949 to make good the ravages of war,
they have been extended and are now covered by the Housing Act 1974.
There are four kinds:

   (1) *Improvement grants* can be provided at the discretion of local
councils to improve older houses having a useful life of at least thirty
years, or to provide additional dwellings by the conversion of houses into
flats. Rateable-value limits confine the grants to the lower end of the
market.
   (2) *Intermediate grants* can be claimed from councils as a right to
provide any missing standard amenity – bath, wash-hand basin, sink, a
hot and cold water supply for these, and a water closet.
   (3) *Special grants* at the discretion of the local council for basic
improvements to houses in multiple occupation.
   (4) *Repair grants* at the discretion of the local council for repairs to
dwellings in Housing Action Areas (HAAs) and General Improvement
Areas (GIAs). Normally these grants cover 50 per cent of the cost to a
given ceiling, but up to 75 per cent in HAAs and 60 per cent in GIAs.

   In general such grants have, to a large extent, been made necessary by
rent control. Given an opportunity-cost return, investment to cover
repairs and provide better amenities would be forthcoming. Nor has tax
policy helped, since no allowance is given for a sinking fund to write off
the capital value of residential property.
   As the emphasis of policy has changed from slum clearance and

rebuilding to refurbishing existing houses, improvement grants should play a more significant role. Yet here again the achievement of objectives has been frustrated by the intrusion of doctrinaire politics. Until 1974 such grants were attached to the type of dwelling: if it were substandard, it qualified for an improvement grant. Thus grants could be claimed by owner-occupiers, private landlords and developers, with no means test. In practice, private landlords took little advantage of improvement grants. The increase in rent of 12½ per cent allowed on the landlord's portion made the improvement uneconomic, for it could not be written down as an investment allowance for tax purposes. Thus grants were claimed mostly by local authorities and owner-occupiers, the latter often to refurbish country cottages as second homes.

But the rise in dwelling prices in 1971–2 made improvement with the help of grants profitable for specialist developers, who converted substandard houses into flats and resold to owner-occupiers. In doing so they fulfilled the purpose of the grant – improving or adding to the housing stock. Although only the owner-occupier sector was satisfied directly, accommodation was set free indirectly in the local authority sector. In the short term such developers were making super-normal profits helped by these improvement grants. But since super-normal profits are often in practice difficult to distinguish precisely from normal profits, it might have been prudent to allow them to fulfil their role in a competitive market of inducing greater output. Increased demand for unimproved houses would raise the price of their basic factor of production – substandard houses – while the increased supply of conversions would reduce the price of the finished product, so that eventually super-normal profits would disappear.

However, the thought of even a small developer being able to make a profit by providing housing was too much for the new Labour government. Thus the Housing Act 1974 imposed discriminatory conditions. An owner-occupier could obtain a grant only for his main residence, and had to remain there for five years, or refund part of the grant. There was justification in this exclusion of country cottages, since (as second homes) they did not rehouse an extra family, while there is no reason why houses should be subsidised for recreational use. Also, private developers had to certify that the dwelling would be available for letting for at least five years, and the local authority could impose the condition that letting should be at the registered rent.

These latter conditions, which still hold, are both illogical and unwise. They are illogical because the owner-occupier can make the super-normal profit if he is prepared to undertake the role of developer. Yet, as with housebuilding, few would-be owner-occupiers have the expertise of the developer (especially when it comes to converting large houses into separate dwellings) or access to capital (since building societies are unwilling to lend for this purpose). In short, many owner-occupiers prefer to avoid the risks of developing and pay extra for a 'package deal'. The letting conditions are unwise in that the limited grants and low registered rents inhibit improvement since a higher return on capital can be obtained elsewhere. The result can be seen in Table 12.4. While a large part of the fall after 1973 can be attributed to the slump in the housing market, it is noticeable that no subsequent reversal of the trend has occurred with private landlords. The United Kingdom is still left with over two million dwellings without a bath or inside toilet. Thus the Housing Act 1974 provides a good example of the effect of applying a blinkered anti-profit philosophy to real property and of the necessity to take action elsewhere to offset the effects of preventing (in this case, by rent control) the market from fulfilling its essential functions.

TABLE 12.4

House-renovation grants by tenure approved 1961–78, UK
(000 dwellings)

	1961	1966	1971	1972	1973	1974	1975	1976	1977	1978
Local authorities and housing associations	43	34	95	141	192	126	67	89	113	122
Owner-occupiers	65	56	92	157	188	128	73	64	75	81
Private landlords	26	27	48	72	76	48	22	18	18	14
Total	134	117	235	370	456	302	162	171	206	217

Source: *Social Trends.*

VII   HOUSING POLICY

The present housing situation

Table 12.5 shows that there is now a crude surplus of 950,000 dwellings over households. While this situation has been brought about largely by new building, it has been helped by the unexpected fall in the rate of household formation since 1971.

What these figures disguise, however, are problems concerning location, the condition and age of the housing stock, the optimal use of housing resources and the extent to which future needs are being anticipated. We will briefly consider each in turn.

The over-all crude surplus of 4.5 per cent of the housing stock (in 1979) does not accurately reflect conditions in different localities. Because industry and people are more mobile than houses, the surplus in certain

TABLE 12.5

Housing stock and households 1967–79

Year	New construction	Slum clearance	Other gains and losses (net)	Net increase in housing stock	Total housing stock at end of year	Total number of households	Net increase in number of households	Crude surplus of housing over households	
	(000)	(000)	(000)	(000)	(000)	(000)	(000)	(000)	(% of dwellings)
1967	415	−95	−30	290	18,370	18,090	210	280	1.5
1968	425	−95	−30	300	18,670	18,290	200	380	2.0
1969	380	−90	−30	260	18,930	18,490	200	440	2.3
1970	360	−90	−20	250	19,180	18,690	200	490	2.6
1971	365	−105	+20*	280*	19,460	18,900	210	560	2.9
1972	330	−90	−20	220	19,680	19,080	180	600	3.0
1973	305	−85	−10	210	19,890	19,270	190	620	3.1
1974	280	−60	−10	210	20,100	19,460	190	640	3.2
1975	320	−65	−5	250	20,350	19,650	190	700	3.4
1976	325	−60	−5	260	20,610	19,840	190	770	3.7
1977	315	−50	−5	260	20,870	20,020	180	850	4.1
1978	290	−45	−5	240	21,110	20,190	170	920	4.4
1979 (est.)	240	−40	—	200	21,310	20,360	170	950	4.5

*Includes increase of 32,000 due to changes in the definition of dwellings used in the 1971 Census.

Source: Nationwide Building Society (compiled from Social Trends, Housing and Construction Statistics, Census Reports, Housing Policy Technical Volume (Part II)).

growth regions, e.g. South-east England and the Greater London area, is so slight that they must be regarded as areas of housing stress. The difficulty arises because surplus houses in one area cannot be moved to localities where they are most needed. Moreover, even within regions some surplus is necessary to allow people to change houses and to provide for the rebuilding of slums and old houses. In addition, some allowance must be made for second homes, a trend which is likely to increase as people enjoy higher real incomes.

Dwellings also have to be judged as regards their quality. The current situation (1980) is that one-third still lack one or more of the basic amenities, while about one-half are over thirty-five years old.

The main criticism of the current housing situation, however, is that policy has obstructed, on both the supply and demand sides, the optimal use of existing housing resources. Rent control and the difficulty of regaining possession of a dwelling even from unsatisfactory tenants has led to residential accommodation remaining unoccupied (e.g. above shops) where it has not been possible to sell for owner-occupation. Moreover, owner-occupiers themselves have been discouraged from letting surplus accommodation by income tax and, above all, the liability to capital gains tax on that part of their house which has been let when they come to sell. Unfortunately, no accurate figures are available to quantify such private-sector under-occupation. But in the local authority sector it was estimated in 1979 that some 100,000 dwellings were standing idle, partly on account of slack housing department management and partly as a result of government financial stringency which denied councils the grants necessary to bring houses already purchased up to standard. In addition, rent control has extended the demand for rented accommodation in both the private and public sectors. Thus periodic surveys by the Greater London Council have revealed that some 14 per cent of their dwellings are 'under-occupied' on the definition that tenants (mostly parents whose children have left home) have two or more rooms above their requirements.

On the demand side preferences have been distorted by government policies of rent control, tax concessions to owner-occupiers and subsidies to local authority housing. Table 12.1 above showed the decline of the private rented sector (now extended to furnished accommodation), and this has forced households to become owner-occupiers (rather than renters) or to join the housing lists for local authority dwellings. Furthermore, while in the owner-occupier sector the market has been free to indicate the type of dwelling preferred, local authorities have had to rely on their own estimates of consumers' preferences since no equilibrium price has operated. In a number of respects these estimates have proved defective, notably as regards wholesale clearance and rebuilding rather than renovation of existing properties, the splitting-up of established communities and rehousing in unwanted tower blocks.

Nor have the needs of special groups been fully met. While housing for the aged and handicapped has been fairly successfully provided as an extension of the welfare services, government policy has largely ignored the demand for accommodation of single persons. Moreover, because of rent control, the market has also failed to respond, except for those better-off young professional people who can afford to buy small flats. The problem is most serious in growth areas, such as London, to which young people are attracted.

Because of their increasing incomes, young persons are likely to be a major cause of household formation in the future. Yet planning by the government has been largely confined to the development of New Towns or the expansion of selected existing towns. In contrast to its success in South-east England, there have been miscalculations in the North-east and Scotland, where industries based on the New Towns have failed to expand and have even declined, e.g. Skelmersdale and Bathgate. Even in Inner London difficulties have resulted from providing dwellings there but starving workers of job opportunities by encouraging (even forcing) offices and industry to move out – a policy which has had to be reversed.

Suggestions for future policy

The above survey of the current housing situation in Britain suggests that government intervention in the housing market over the past sixty years can hardly be justified by the results. The basic reason for the lack of success is that it has failed to follow a long-term strategy based on sound economic principles. Instead, political considerations have dominated. Labour governments have distrusted the market economy and held an in-built bias against the private ownership of property. Conservative governments have feared that by reverting to the price system in rented accommodation they will on aggregate lose votes. Thus, even in 1980, what is regarded as a right-wing Conservative government has no plans for phasing out rent control in its policy proposals. Professional institutions have been equally timid: the latest housing survey by the RICS – *Housing: The Chartered Surveyors' Report* (1976) – barely referred to the case for phasing out rent control.

Yet the market mechanism has proved effective in, for example, the provision of television sets and motor-cars. In both there exists a choice between: (i) the particular model purchased, reflecting people's preferences within their limited income; (ii) buying outright, purchasing on hire purchase, or renting; (iii) different retailers and/or renting companies, all of which can vary in the prices charged, initial shop service, guarantees and after-sales service.

It is submitted that the same preferences as regards the type, quantity and quality of housing could be exercised by households by greater reliance on the market mechanism. Supply would respond to price. This would involve a long-term strategy of removing rent control and over-hauling subsidy policy as regards both owner-occupiers and local authority tenants. The effects of rent control have already been analysed. It has delayed the solution of the housing problem by giving rise to a situation where demand exceeds supply, the supply of rented accommodation has gradually decreased, labour has found difficulty in moving to new regions, the true cost of housing has been disguised, people being influenced into devoting too low a proportion of their spending on satisfying their housing needs so that resources have not been attracted into housing, and consumers have been unable to exercise their preferences for improvements by offering higher rents on an economic basis. Similarly, subsidies to owner-occupiers and council tenants have distorted market prices since tenants of private housing whose rents are not limited by regulation are in an inferior position. It is noticeable that in West Germany and the USA, where rent control has been virtually abolished, there is no acute housing 'shortage'.

Even subsidies towards renovation have not been fully effective through the intrusion of political bias and administrative predeliction towards rebuilding. But renovation could often have been cheaper and quicker. Suppose, for example, that it costs £25,000 a dwelling to rebuild but only £10,000 to renovate, and that the restored dwelling has a life of twenty years. At a 14 per cent rate of interest, the £15,000 saved has a capital value of £206,145, which, depending upon the rate of inflation, should provide sufficient to rebuild to the conditions then required. Furthermore, bulldozing down the twilight zone destroys established communities. Not only that, but because housing is used more intensively in the twilight zone, it deprives poor people of the type of accommodation they can afford near their employment in the city centre. More emphasis should therefore be placed on rehabilitation rather than rebuilding.

Difficulties of implementing the above policies

The main difficulties in moving towards policies as suggested above are political. Those who gain – rent-regulated tenants, owner-occupiers and council tenants – outnumber the losers – landlords and tenants paying market rents. A policy based on ending rent control is therefore a potential vote-loser.

Thus the change will have to come gradually. Initially steps can be taken to end control in: (i) areas where there is no housing stress; (ii) the upper rateable value limits; and (iii) furnished lettings. These liberating methods would indicate the extent to which regulated rents were below market rents, and suggest how quickly it would be feasible to extend de-control.

But to be successful the policy would need a bipartisan approach, the lack of which has bedevilled housing policy since the First World War. The omens are not favourable. Already (1980) the Labour Opposition has announced its intention of dismantling the Conservative government's Housing Act 1980. This seeks to encourage institutions to provide better-class housing by allowing them to charge market rents free from security of tenure and to allow landlords to regain possession of dwellings let at regulated rents on short leases ('shortholds'). Thus even such modest reforms are likely to die stillborn, for, after the experience of the past sixty years, a positive commitment to accept them by the Labour party if returned to power would be a prerequisite for people to invest in rented residential property.

The gradual ending of rent control would have to be accompanied by a phasing out of current forms of housing subsidy, the logical step being to adopt the principle of attaching subsidies to people according to their over-all needs rather than to the type of house occupied.

The benefits of the successful implementation of such policies would be immense. Preferences could be effectively expressed through the market, supply could respond to market signals, administrative controls (e.g. rent officers and rent committees) could be dismantled and decision-making decentralised. And, not least, it would leave local authorities free to concentrate on their essential housing functions in a mixed economy – slum clearance, building for special needs, e.g. sheltered housing for the aged, providing temporary accommodation for homeless persons, examining planning consents and exercising compulsory-purchase powers for social projects.

FURTHER READING

J. B. Cullingworth, *Essays on Housing Policy* (London: Allen & Unwin, 1979).

A. J. Merrett and A. Sykes, *Housing Finance and Development* (London: Longman, 1965) ch. 1.

F. G. Pennance and W. A. West, *Housing Market Analysis and Policy* (London: Institute of Economic Affairs, 1969) ch. 2.

R. Robinson, *Housing Economics and Public Policy* (London: Macmillan, 1979).

D. C. Stafford, *The Economics of Housing Policy* (London: Croom Helm, 1978).

13

The Government and Real Property

I INTRODUCTION

Welfare and the price system

In Chapter 1 we saw that, *given certain conditions*, the price system is efficient in allocating property resources in that: (i) those goods and services are produced which are most preferred by society; and (ii) it is impossible to reshuffle resources in order to produce more goods and services.

But, since the necessary conditions do not always hold, complete efficiency is not achieved. In any case the *allocation of resources* is concerned with only one aspect of the economic system – that relating to the field of microeconomics. Consideration must also be given to the over-all economic framework in which the allocative process works – the level of employment, the stability of the price level, the rate of economic growth and the international trading position – topics which are the concern of macroeconomics. As we shall see, policy aimed at the over-all *stability of the economy* has its impact on real property.

Finally, the welfare of a society also depends upon the *distribution of income*. As we saw in Chapter 1, this presents difficulties in formulating policy since it is impossible to measure cardinally the satisfaction which a person derives from extra income. Even so, measures are taken to promote a more equitable distribution of wealth, and these, too, affect the real property market.

Britain's 'mixed economy'

The weaknesses of the price system as a means of organising the production of goods and services has led to some countries adopting a 'command economy' where the basic economic decisions are made by an overriding state. But this, too, has disadvantages, notably the difficulty of estimating individual preferences, and the loss of individual freedom, usually political as well as economic, which results.

Thus Britain has adopted a 'mixed economy' which leaves most economic decisions to the price mechanism but has the government taking measures to remedy the defects. It is these remedies and their impact on real property which is the subject-matter of this chapter.

Broadly speaking, the government has three objectives: (i) stability of the economy; (ii) efficient allocation of resources; and (iii) equity in the distribution of income. The first is mainly pursued by its general macro measures, and we begin by showing the impact of these on the real property market. Equity in the distribution of income, however, is basically a political decision, and so our discussion of this aim is largely confined to simply noting some of the implicit redistributive effects of certain policies followed with regard to real property, e.g. in planning, conservation, the selection of (and methods of) charging for public, collective and merit goods (e.g. housing), direct subsidies (e.g. rent allowances) and, above all, in taxation (e.g. rates).

Our main attention, however, is directed to the government's attempts to allocate real property resources. This it does through taxation and subsidies, physical controls (e.g. planning, building regulations) and public ownership (e.g. housing, land nationalisation). Here the problem is approached by examining in more detail the reasons for market failure in the allocation of real property resources. We then proceed to a more thorough analysis of certain of these policies which are specifically related to land: taxation of real property, planning controls and land nationalisation.

The role of the economist

Because many objectives are incompatible, government measures often have negative side-effects. For instance, an anti-inflationary policy may lead to the unemployment of some resources. On the other hand, some measures may be complementary in that they help more than one objective. Thus a road-improvement scheme to relieve traffic congestion may give work to the unemployed. Usually, however, one objective has to be 'traded off' against another. Mr Harold Macmillan has likened the role of the government to that of a juggler whose task is to keep many balls in the air at the same time. Some balls are going up because they have recently been given special attention, while others which have been relatively neglected are on their way down.

In the last resort actual policies chosen are a matter of judgement and therefore rest on political views. The task of the economist is to identify possible economic reasons for government intervention and to analyse the likely consequences of different measures, leaving it to the politician to decide where the balance of advantage lies. Space does not permit a detailed analysis of the likely effects on real property of all policies. In the main we simply indicate the effects of different measures in the context of the reasons for them. Nevertheless, certain policies which are directed to real property in particular are treated more exhaustively.

II   STABILITY OF THE ECONOMY

Stabilisation policy seeks to achieve (i) full employment, (ii) a stable price level, (iii) an adequate rate of growth, and (iv) a healthy balance-of-payments position. The measures taken to achieve these ends normally take the form of short-term adjustments to the economy generally, but (as such) affect real property both directly and indirectly. They can be classified under three headings: monetary, fiscal, and physical controls.

(1)   *Monetary policy*
Monetary policy operates by varying the cost and availability of credit. There are, however, two distinct views as to the emphasis which should be placed upon it in managing the economy.

The Keynesian approach is that full employment is dependent upon there being adequate aggregate demand for the goods and services which can be produced when all available resources are fully employed. To secure this, the main weapon must be fiscal policy (see later). Monetary policy can supplement this but only indirectly: an increase in the money supply, by increasing liquidity, lowers the rate of interest, which in its turn stimulates investment spending, one of the components of aggregate demand.

In contrast, monetarists place much more emphasis on the direct effect of increases in the money supply, especially when there is inflation. They hold that, at least in the short term, a part of any increase in the money supply may be spent on goods and services and not concentrated entirely on financial assets. Thus, after a time lag, prices rise. It follows that instead of monetary policy being relegated to a subservient role it assumes crucial importance in the fight against inflation. The money supply must not be determined solely by short-term considerations: any increase should be limited on a yearly basis and directly proportionate to the increase in real output. Within this over-all ceiling rates of interest would be allowed to find their own level in the various sections of the money and capital markets.

Although the monetarist view is still disputed, it is now implemented by most Western governments. But restricting the money supply results in a rise in interest rates, often to uncomfortably high levels (see later).

A rise in short-term rates, by putting up the cost of advances, is felt immediately by developers and construction firms. In addition, it is often accompanied by selective credit controls, restricting the ability of the banks to lend for real property activity (see later). Building societies are also affected. Being reluctant to raise their mortgage rates, they are sluggish in offering more to depositors, with the result that funds are diverted to competing borrowers, chiefly the banks and local authorities. Thus housing activity falls as mortgages are more strictly rationed (see Chapter 12).

When the rise is extended to the long end of the market, the effects are more fundamental, affecting both new construction and the investment market. Since expected yields on real property extend far into the future, discounting at a higher rate leads to a greater proportionate reduction in their present values than for investment projects where the cost has to be recouped within about five years. This would tend to hold back private-sector development, especially by property companies, thus affecting the construction industry directly. In the investment market the higher yield on government bonds makes them more attractive compared with assets such as mortgages and real property. Particularly for loans against property, therefore, the lending institutions such as insurance companies and pension funds will require a higher return. But since they have a steady inflow of funds they may take a long-term view with respect to inflation and so continue to invest in freeholds, either by financing new development or by purchasing existing buildings. Eventually, however, higher relative returns to be obtained elsewhere will push up yields on all real property interests. Such lowering of capital values will discourage new construction by developers.

Nor is the public sector, which is responsible for one-half of all Gross Fixed Capital Formation, immune from higher interest rates. Local authorities can only afford to raise funds on the same scale by increasing the rate poundage to cover the higher cost. Reluctance to do this because of its political unpopularity means that, instead, they curtail their housing and other construction programmes. The nationalised industries, too, postpone their construction projects as the cost of servicing them rises. Above all, the central government may be forced to contract its spending (see below).

(2)   *Fiscal policy*

Fiscal policy rests on the Keynesian view that cyclical unemployment is the result of an inadequate level of aggregate demand. Thus increased government spending and lower taxation to allow more private spending would expand aggregate demand. In short, a budget deficit could be used to reduce the level of unemployment.

Keynes recognised that this meant an increase in the National Debt, in present-day terms the Public Sector Borrowing Requirement (PSBR). But for Keynes, writing in the depression of the 1930s, this presented few real problems and in any case was of minor significance in comparison with the benefits of reduced unemployment.

But the 1970s has seen a somewhat different situation. Not only has unemployment risen uncomfortably high, but it has been accompanied by inflation, a condition often referred to as 'stagflation'. Since inflation makes British exports uncompetitive and leads to imports replacing home-produced goods, it can be one of the causes of unemployment. Thus successive governments have given priority in their economic policy to fighting inflation. This brings budgetary policy into direct conflict with monetary policy, as follows.

By 1976 the government's social policies had produced a PSBR of over £9,000 million a year. Reducing this by higher taxation was hardly possible since high rates of direct taxes were already having disincentive effects, while higher indirect taxes could prove inflationary by leading to demands for higher wages. In this situation the PSBR can only be covered by creating money or by borrowing.

Initially an excess of government spending over taxation is achieved by the government paying its employees and contractors from its deposits at the Bank of England. Eventually this extra cash increases the eligible reserve assets of the joint-stock banks, allowing them to expand their total deposits, including advances.

But resorting to the 'printing press' in this way cannot be a permanent solution. The government has to cover its PSBR by borrowing. Even so, if it does this through the cheapest method, the sale of Treasury Bills, it runs into difficulties. The major holders of Treasury Bills are the joint-stock banks, and they buy them as the increased offering by the authorities forces up the yield. Such purchases, however, add directly to the banks eligible reserve assets, allowing them, as above, to increase their deposits. In other words, short-term borrowing involves an inflationary increase in the money supply.

As a result, the government has to rely on long-term borrowing, selling medium- and long-term bonds in the market to the non-bank sector, the institutions and private purchasers. Since such sources of funds rely mainly on current saving, this method is not inflationary. The difficulty, however, is that extra bonds can only be disposed of at a lower price, i.e. by a rise in the long-term rate of interest. This has the over-all effect of discouraging investment, thereby increasing unemployment and retarding the rate of growth. Nor is this all. Interest payments on this borrowing add to the PSBR. Furthermore, inasmuch as higher interest rates attract funds from abroad, the money supply is increased.

In practice, therefore, fiscal policy cannot proceed independently of monetary policy. Usually the government compromises by: (i) increasing borrowing at higher interest rates; (ii) setting a ceiling on the increase in the money supply; and (iii) reducing public-sector spending in order to relieve the pressure from a high PSBR. All three policies affect the real property market.

As we have seen, high interest rates discourage new construction in both the private and public sectors and have repercussions in the investment market, where real property yields eventually rise in sympathy. Similarly, the reduction in the money supply makes borrowing more difficult, and is thus felt by developers and construction firms. But, particularly in the short term, it is the direct curtailment of government spending which has the greatest effect on construction activity. Current spending is mainly contractual, e.g. National Debt interest, or obligatory, e.g. EEC contributions and social security payments. In so far as financial stringency reduces the government's current demand for real property, it may only be reflected in a slowing down in the acquisition of office space by the government's Property Services Agency. Thus cuts fall mainly on the central government's capital expenditure, with projects such as new motorways and university extensions being put into cold storage. Similarly, spending restrictions are imposed on local authorities, either by reductions in government grants or by refusing loan sanctions. Again the major impact falls on capital spending – city-centre rebuilding, improvements in infrastructure, new housing, etc.

While fiscal policy to stabilise the economy concentrates on the relationship between over-all government spending and revenue, it must also consider the impact of the individual taxes levied. A redistribution of the tax burden may influence the over-all level of consumption spending. But it is the allocation of resources which is mainly affected by selective taxes (see below).

(3) *Physical controls*

Particularly when the rate of inflation has been increasing uncomfortably, the over-all strategy of the government has had to be reinforced by physical controls. Some of these, such as restrictions on the amount by which prices, wages and dividends can be increased, are general in their application. In this connection it is interesting to note that rents of commercial and industrial property have been treated favourably, for (apart from a brief period in 1973) they were not subject to control. Thus prime properties with annual rent increases of 15 per cent compound afforded a better inflation-hedge than blue-chip equities whose dividends, until 1979, were limited to a 10 per cent rise.

On the other hand, in the selection of particular controls, real property has fared badly. Rent control has been retained for dwellings, partly to reinforce the government's anti-inflation policy. Moreover, between 1940 and 1953, and again in 1966, licences for building work were required.

But it is in the operation of monetary policy that real property has been singled out for special attention. Controlling spending by a rise in interest rates suffers from two main defects. First, it is non-discriminatory in operation. For example, while higher interest charges may lead to the curtailment of local authority housing programmes, office development may be so profitable that it is hardly affected. Second, higher interest rates are unpopular politically, largely because they eventually affect mortgages. Thus, until 1971, the government held down interest rates, restricting spending by requesting the banks to be selective when granting credit, and refusing it for the development and purchase of real property. And, while the intention of the policy of *Competition and Credit Control* (introduced in 1971) was to allow market forces to allocate a predetermined supply of credit to its various uses, the increase in the money supply fuelled the property boom of 1972 and conflicted with the government's policy of prompting growth through the expansion of manufacturing and exporting industries. Hence the government reverted to requesting the banks to discriminate against real property transactions when granting loans.

More recently the government limited the rate of interest which banks could pay on deposits of less than £10,000 so that they did not compete funds away from the building societies, which (by maintaining lower rates) help new owner-occupiers in particular.

III   THE ALLOCATION OF RESOURCES

The efficiency of the price mechanism

In Chapter 1 we saw that, in allocating resources, the price system could be inefficient for a number of reasons. First, competition may be reduced by physical defects in the market mechanism or through decisions being based on imperfect knowledge. Second, competition may not be perfect. Third, factors of production are often unable to move smoothly in response to price changes. Fourth, in addition to the private benefits and costs upon which individual consumers and producers base their decisions, there may be external benefits and costs. Fifth, it may be necessary or desirable for certain goods and services (usually termed 'community', 'collective', 'public', and 'merit' goods) to be provided by the government. Finally, an 'efficient' allocation of resources through the price mechanism only applies to the existing distribution of income: that is, a redistribution of income may increase welfare.

Government intervention in the real property market

All the above possibilities occur in the real property market, providing grounds for government intervention.

(1) *Physical market defects and incomplete knowledge*

As was pointed out in Chapter 2, the government can reduce physical defects in the real property market by simplifying conveyancing procedures, e.g. through the National Land Register, and by reducing stamp duty and other dealing costs.

Imperfect knowledge can result from difficulties of obtaining information, the limited time horizon of individuals, or uncertainty as to future conditions. As regards the first, the government can advertise (e.g. the advantages of Development Areas and expanding towns) and call for information and publish the results, e.g. *Housing and Construction Statistics*. Furthermore, by insisting on a high standard of competence being observed by the relevant professional bodies, the layman can proceed with a greater degree of confidence in the advice which is given.

With regard to the future, the government may override market information because it considers it has 'superior' knowledge to people deciding on their own. Thus, in expressing the wishes of unborn generations, the government may discount future benefits at a lower interest rate or impose physical controls, e.g. conserving areas of natural beauty through the National Trust, designating conservation areas, listing buildings of special architectural or historic interest and preventing the export of important works of art (see also pp. 101–5).

But probably the main way in which the government can improve knowledge is by providing a background of certainty against which private decisions can be made. It can do this, for instance, by zoning areas for different types of development and stating general principles governing its planning consents (see pp. 260–3). Such certainty tends to increase land values in aggregate.

(2) *Imperfect competition*

Imperfect competition results in an inefficient allocation of resources. This is illustrated in Figure 13.1, which compares the output of offices under perfect competition and monopoly. Under perfect competition offices would be built up to the point *OM*, where the marginal cost of each firm equals its marginal revenue which equals the market price. This is the most efficient output, in that the cost of producing an extra office just equals the value which the community places on an extra office (as shown by the falling demand curve). The monopolist, however, restricts output to OM_1, where marginal cost equals his marginal revenue. The latter is less than price, i.e. what consumers are prepared to pay. Thus resources devoted to office-building are less than they would be under perfect competition. Furthermore, the prices of such resources are distorted, and this would have repercussions on other sectors of the construction industry, e.g. housebuilding and road construction (even though here

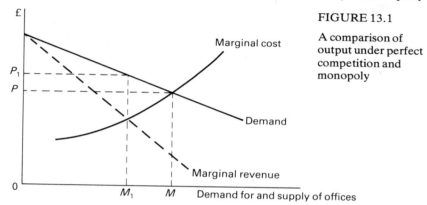

FIGURE 13.1

A comparison of output under perfect competition and monopoly

competitive conditions may exist), and, indeed, throughout the rest of the economy.

Nevertheless, two main qualifications to the above argument should be noted. First, the monopoly of office-building could lead to considerable economies of scale. Second, there is no *guarantee* that providing for a competitive output in one line of production will improve the allocation of resources unless perfect competition is general throughout the whole of the economy.

Usually, however, there are grounds for government action where the owner of a property right can, by his own influence, affect the market price. Thus compulsory purchase may be invoked when a site-owner exercises his monopoly power to hold up redevelopment, urban renewal, road-widening, etc. Even so, it is now generally considered that compensation should be paid at the current competitive market price, thus applying the constraints imposed by the price system. Similarly, legislation which covers security of tenure and compensation for tenants' improvements, e.g. the Agricultural Holdings Act 1948, the Landlord and Tenant Act 1954, and the Rent Act 1977, serves to protect tenants in their weak bargaining position as compared with landlords.

It should be noted, however, that government action may itself give rise to imperfect competition or create a monopoly situation. For instance, the favourable tax treatment afforded to building societies in borrowing funds produces an imperfect capital market for house purchase. By enabling loans to be granted at a comparatively low rate of interest, the societies can discriminate between borrowers (see pp. 212–13). Above all, land nationalisation, proposals for which are mooted from time to time, would create a state monopoly of land.

(3)   *Immobility of the factors of production*

It usually takes time for the supply of factors of production to respond fully to changes in the conditions of demand. And, in the case of real property, disequilibrium often persists for a considerable period. Thus, while the answer to a fall in the demand for existing buildings in a particular locality may be complete redevelopment, existing leases have to expire or tenants rehoused. Furthermore, some owners may refuse to co-operate in the over-all scheme. In the meantime the effects are cumulative, giving rise to 'twilight' zones and inner-city decay. Since these produce external costs, redevelopment may have to be speeded up by local authority action, with compulsory-purchase powers being used if necessary (see later).

Regional policy is also concerned with problems arising from the immobility of labour. On the one hand, unemployment does not lead to workers moving to more prosperous areas. On the other hand, wage rates do not fall sufficiently to attract firms into depressed areas. Thus the government has to act so that firms move to areas of high unemployment. Carrots are offered in the form of tax concessions, low-rent factories and a modernised infrastructure. Alternatively, the big stick may be applied in the form of physical controls. Thus firms wishing to expand or erect industrial buildings of over 50,000 square feet in the more prosperous regions such as the South-east need an Industrial Development Certificate issued by the Department of Industry.

(4) Externalities

Externalities occur where the activities of some individuals or groups give rise to spillover benefits and costs for others. Because the initiators are unable to collect payment from the beneficiaries or the sufferers to extract compensation for the extra costs imposed on them, it is generally assumed that externalities are ignored by private decision-makers, giving rise to a divergence between *private* net product and *social* net product. The situation is illustrated in Figure 13.2, where marginal social costs exceed marginal private costs (the costs to the developer of building higher) as more intensive living gives rise to external costs of smoke, noise, loss of open space, etc. Plot density should therefore be limited to M_1 instead of M in order to achieve the optimal development where marginal social benefit equals marginal social cost.

This does not mean, however, that all activities giving rise to externalities should be subject to public control. Where people live in close proximity, some spillover effects are inevitable. Thus town-dwellers limit the open space available to one another and suffer a continuous hum of traffic noise, but such costs have to be set against the advantages of town life. Furthermore, certain external costs are too trivial to bother with (e.g. slight traffic noise), but where the line should be drawn (e.g. as regards congestion) is often debatable.

Moreover, to some extent externalities may be accounted for by the

FIGURE 13.2

External costs and
plot density

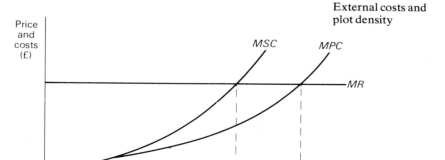

price system. For example, people will pay more for a house in neighbourhoods having good schools, open spaces, shopping facilities, golf courses and road and rail communications. On the other hand, shops will command a lower rent where traffic congestion is a serious problem, for trade will be adversely affected. Similarly with office rents: the necessity of having to pay employees an extra 'London allowance' to offset higher travelling costs, car insurance, etc., makes labour more expensive and induces some firms to seek alternative locations. We find, too, externalities being 'internalised' by private arrangements. Thus a developer will attract shops to a shopping centre by making prior agreements with key retailers, and arrangements are made to concentrate small firms on industrial estates where they have some mutual interdependence. With residential estates, houses and flats are sold subject to leases or covenants in order to secure external benefits (e.g. a satisfactory standard of upkeep, garden maintenance, etc.) or to avoid external costs, e.g. excessive noise, car-parking nuisance, etc.

However, leaving the price mechanism to deal with externalities is not a satisfactory solution to the problem. For one thing there may be heavy frictional costs before a new equilibrium pattern of land values is established. How much congestion has to be suffered, for instance, before the price-system solution is arrived at? For another, passively leaving the price system to deal with externalities may produce an inferior net social product (see below). Some positive means of dealing with externalities is therefore usually necessary.

Where transactions are costless, bargaining between the affected parties may be possible to mitigate divergence of interest. Assume, for instance, that a developer *X* has bought and intends to build on a

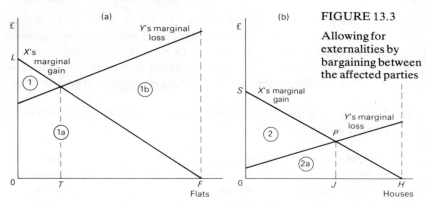

FIGURE 13.3

Allowing for
externalities by
bargaining between
the affected parties

considerable part of the garden of a Victorian mansion. Local residents, designated party Y, regard this development as a loss of amenity. X has two possible schemes. Scheme 1 is for a block of flats – and the higher the number of storeys (to increase the number of flats), the greater is the loss of amenity. Scheme 2 is for low-rise housing which still produces some loss of amenity according to the number of houses on the site.

In Figure 13.3 the area under X's curves shows the total gain to the developer; that under Y's curves shows the total loss to the residents. If there were no restrictions on development or no negotiation, X would adopt scheme 1, building OF flats, since the triangle LOF is greater than the triangle SOH. But the residents' loss, equal to 1a + 1b, is greater than X's gain. Thus it will pay them to 'buy off' X down to OT flats, where the net social gain equals area 1.

However, scheme 2 (limited to OJ houses) yields a larger net social gain, 2. To achieve this Y could offer up to 1a + 1b − 2a. X could also be better off since 2 is greater than 1, and would accept as little as 1 + 1a − 2 − 2a. The difference between the two, 1b − 1 + 2, represents the benefit which can be achieved by negotiation, for 1b equals a loss avoided (that is, a gain), − 1 equals a gain forgone (a loss) and 2 equals a gain achieved (a gain). How this benefit is actually shared between the two parties will depend upon their respective negotiating skills.

It should be noted that were X to be made legally liable to compensate Y for the amenity costs inflicted, he would still develop to OJ, where his marginal gain JP equals his marginal damages bill. But he would now be forced to pay for the full damages inflicted rather than possibly achieve something less by skilful negotiation.

Nevertheless, negotiation may be an impracticable solution, for a number of reasons:

(a) Costs of negotiation may be exorbitant relative to the benefits to be shared.

(b)   The costs (or benefits) are so far-ranging that all the losers (or beneficiaries) cannot be identified. For example, an incongruous block of flats would offend passers-by as well as the local residents.

(c)   Because 'free riders' cannot be excluded, it may be impossible to organise sufficient collective-bargaining strength to negotiate effectively.

(d)   Uncertainty and selfishness may prevent a satisfactory solution by private action (p. 261).

Usually, therefore, some form of government action is necessary.

First, the government may use the price system to bring externalities into the reckoning. For example, to deal with congestion, parking-meters may be installed and local residents charged for reserved parking permits.

Second, taxation and subsidies may take the idea of 'charging' a stage further. Thus a 'congestion tax' on road transport has been proposed to allow for the spillover costs of congestion and air pollution imposed by one motorist on all other road-users when he takes his car on the road. Thus in Figure 13.4 real congestion occurs when the traffic flow reaches OF, mainly in the peak morning and evening hours. While the private cost of congestion to the motorist is shown by the curve PP', there is an additional marginal cost to all other road-users which gives a total opportunity cost – the marginal social cost – depicted by the curve PS. The motorists' demand curve, DD', shows that they will use their cars at higher traffic flows only as the cost falls. The equilibrium traffic flow, if no allowance were made for external costs of congestion, would be OM, where net benefit, $DOPN$, the difference between total benefit and total private costs, is greatest. However, if we allow for external costs, total costs at OM exceed benefits by ENR. Thus efficiency in the allocation of road space is secured with a flow of OM'. This could be achieved by imposing a tax of ET on motorists, and this would yield $VWTE$ in revenue.

Similarly, the rating of empty houses can also be regarded as a tax imposed partly to offset the external costs resulting from the inadequate availability of accommodation.

On the other hand, external benefits may be allowed for by subsidies. Government help towards slum clearance and housing falls under this heading (although, alternatively, it could be regarded as offsetting external costs). Other examples are the contributions and tax concessions made to the repair costs of ancient monuments, listed buildings and historic mansions where, because private costs of upkeep exceed private benefits, rapid deterioration and eventual demolition would otherwise result (see Chapter 7).

Third, and frequently in the field of land resources, externalities may be covered by controls. Most evident are the consents required under the

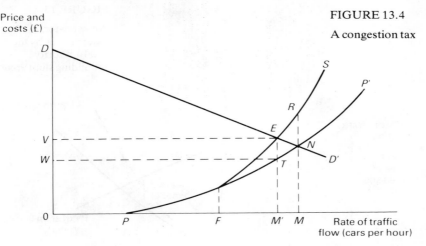

FIGURE 13.4

A congestion tax

Town and Country Planning Acts. Thus, in our earlier example of the flat development, scheme 2 with *OJ* houses could be secured by planning requirements, an essential device where there are insurmountable obstacles to voluntary negotiation. Consequently, planning and building regulations must not be regarded as being negative. By imposing conditions on proposed development, they seek to minimise external costs arising, for example, from road congestion, fire hazards or a building out of harmony with its surroundings. Indeed, planning can secure benefits additional to those estimated for by the private developer. Thus it may arrange for shops to have complementary locations (see pp. 263–4), a new road system to be incorporated in a major redevelopment scheme, or a green belt to ring an urban conurbation.

Fourth, the externalities may be 'internalised' by widening the area of control. The National Trust, for instance, harmonises both the interests of farmers and walkers in order to secure maximum benefits from the Lake District. Similarly, Water Authorities have been formed to co-ordinate drainage, water supply, waste disposal and angling interests in order to maximise net benefits.

Fifth, the government may itself assume responsibility for providing certain goods and services. This is usual when externalities are: (i) of national importance, e.g. a nationalised shipbuilding industry can allow for defence requirements and a reduction of unemployment when deciding the level of activity; (ii) so extensive that only government authority can adequately allow for them, e.g. providing a major airport; (iii) cumulative, e.g. a slum area. Thus, if left to private enterprise, the clearance of a slum would take place in year *P* in Figure 13.5. However, a local authority could allow for the external benefits of such complete rebuilding – better health, less juvenile deliquency, an improved road

FIGURE 13.5

Allowing for
externalities by the
local authority
rebuilding slum areas

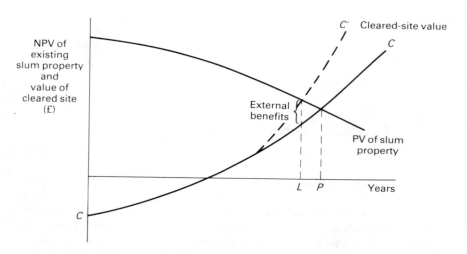

lay-out, etc. The capital value of such benefits would be added to the private enterprise's value of the next-best use, moving the cleared site value curve from *CC* to *CC'* and thus bringing redevelopment forward to year *L* (see also pp. 96–8 and pp. 100–1).

(5) *Public provision of goods and services*

It may be necessary or desirable for certain goods and services to be provided by the government. To explain the reasoning behind this it is usual to classify such goods as 'community', 'collective', 'public' and 'merit' goods.

Community goods and services are those, such as defence, police protection, roads, street-lighting, common land and national parks, where 'free riders' cannot be excluded. Here the state has to assume responsibility, covering the cost of the goods and services out of taxation.

Collective goods and services are those which have to be provided by the state because they satisfy people's collective needs, e.g. parks, National Trust properties, motorways, bridges, water supply, refuse collection and drainage, but where 'free riders' can be excluded (though this may incur spillover costs). The important point, however, is that because heavy initial fixed capital investment is required, production takes place under conditions of decreasing cost. In such circumstances

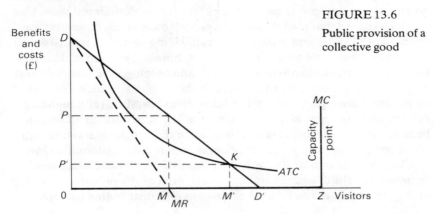

FIGURE 13.6

Public provision of a collective good

public provision is the most satisfactory method of securing the optimum allocation of resources.

We can illustrate with reference to a public garden in the centre of a town. Let us assume: (i) people derive pleasure from the flower gardens and would be willing to pay for this benefit; (ii) the garden can be fenced round so that, by excluding 'free riders', a price can be charged; and (iii) the only cost is the initial price, which includes a capitalised sum for future maintenance, giving marginal cost of zero up to the capacity of the gardens to take visitors. The situation is depicted in Figure 13.6, where the *ATC* curve is a rectangular hyperbola and the capacity of the gardens is *OZ*. Thus production, in terms of number of visitors, takes place under conditions of decreasing cost. As a result, some form of imperfect competition is inevitable.

If the gardens were provided privately by a monopolist, he would charge an admission price of *OP*, limiting visitors to *OM*, where marginal cost equals marginal revenue and where elasticity of demand equals unity.

Suppose now that the gardens were taken over by the local authority. By lowering the price to *OP'*, a larger number of people *OM'* could enjoy the gardens at no extra cost, and total costs would be covered.

Public goods and services are those where their enjoyment by an extra person imposes no sacrifice on others – often referred to as the *principle of non-rivalry*. In short, marginal cost is nil. Thus, in the above example of the garden, limiting admission to *OM'* visitors would not be a Pareto-optimal situation. If no charge were made, benefits could be increased by *KM'D'* at *no extra cost*, but the total cost would have to be covered out of taxation. The gardens are now provided in exactly the same way as community goods.

In practice, provision by the public sector has been extended to *merit* goods. These are goods and services which it is considered would be 'inadequately' demanded through the market mechanism largely because people have insufficient income or are unwilling to devote a satisfactory proportion of income to buying them, e.g. housing, education, libraries. Decisions on public involvement in providing such goods, however, rest on subjective judgements and thus lie in the realm of politics. First, what constitutes 'inadequate' is largely a subjective view, since (although cost – benefit analysis may help – see Chapter 10) it is difficult to measure benefits when consumers are not bidding for them in the market. Second, when charges are below market price, as with housing, alternative forms of allocation have to be devised; these, unlike market decisions, tend to be arbitrary. Third, where taxation covers, either fully or in part, the cost of the service, taxes can be used as a means of redistributing income.

IV   THE TAXATION OF REAL PROPERTY

Objectives of taxation

As we have seen, taxes can be levied to raise revenue, stabilise the economy, reallocate resources and redistribute income and wealth. But different taxes vary in the extent to which they achieve these different objectives, being strong on some and weak on others. For example, while local rates are efficient in raising revenue, they tend to be defective in redistributing income more equitably since the amount which has to be paid in rates may not reflect a person's ability to pay (see p. 253).

Some taxes, notably local property taxes and development land tax, are levied specifically on real property. Their main objective is to raise revenue, and they must be judged principally on their efficiency in this. But, being selective, they are unlikely to be neutral in their allocative effects, tending to divert resources from real property to other forms of spending. Our analysis will therefore have to pay particular attention to this aspect of such taxes. Furthermore, general taxes, such as capital gains tax and capital transfer tax, can in practice be selective as regards real property. Capital transfer tax, for instance, may force the liquidation of a landed estate. Not only will this tend to depress land values in a particular locality but fragmentation of the estate may be detrimental to efficient management.

Since real property is both a source of income and a form of wealth, it is subject to all the taxes levied on income and wealth generally – income tax, corporation tax, capital gains tax, capital transfer tax, stamp duties, etc. However, tracing the incidence of all these taxes on real property would be too lengthy a task for us here. We therefore confine our discussion to an examination of the merits and demerits of the two taxes which are specific to real property – local property taxes (with particular reference to the British rating system) and development land tax.

Merits of a local property tax

It is against the background of local government that local property taxes have to be examined. If it is judged that in providing certain services local *government*, as opposed to mere local *administration*, has advantages, then local people must be allowed to make their own decisions as to the type of service they prefer. This means that they must be responsible for raising the revenue required to meet the cost without being dependent on central government grants. In practice, as a source of revenue for local authorities, taxes on property have many advantages.

First, they promote local autonomy and accountability. By being reserved to the local authorities, property taxes afford a degree of financial independence from central government. Moreover, by being raised on a local basis with the rate determined annually, they make *local* authorities responsible to *local* people. However, such accountability is limited in that only residential property is directly linked to the electoral process: no local voting powers are enjoyed by commercial and industrial property, though political influence may be exercised through pressure groups, such as the local Chamber of Commerce.

Second, local property taxes are generally acceptable. Having been levied for nearly 400 years, they conform to the view that 'an old tax is no tax'. Moreover, in form they are simple, easily understood and appear equitable, in that property benefits from local services, and those occupying the largest properties tend to be the richer members of the community.

Third, there is certainty of yield. Not only are property taxes difficult to evade, but being based on fixed property any increase in the rate of tax cannot be shifted geographically (unlike a sales tax where people can shop in a cheaper area). Only in the long period can occupiers respond to high rates by moving to another area.

Fourth, property taxes have administrative advantages in that once rateable values have been assessed the rate is easily calculated and can be adjusted when additional revenue is required. Furthermore, costs of collection are relatively economic, being less than 2 per cent of yield.

Demerits of a local property tax

In spite of the above advantages, however, local property taxes have, particularly in recent years, been subject to considerable criticism.

First, because domestic rates are a *selective* tax on a particular good, there is a loss of welfare compared with a direct tax which raises the same

FIGURE 13.7

The effect of the
imposition of rates on
rents and the supply
of housing in (a) the
short period, and (b)
the long period

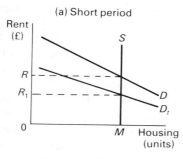

(a) Short period

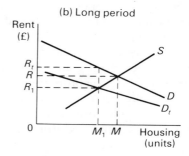

(b) Long period

amount of revenue (see p. 220). Furthermore, a tax on housing services is illogical in the light of the government's policy of subsidising housing as a merit good.

Second, local property taxes, like all selective outlay taxes, distort market prices and thus, at least in the long period, have reallocative effects. In order to show this, we will assume: (i) there is a competitive free market in housing; (ii) houses are homogeneous; (iii) all houses are rented on a weekly tenancy; (iv) no rates are being levied initially; and (v) the demand for rented housing is depicted by the D curve in Figure 13.7.

Initially the rent paid is OR in Figure 13.7(a). If rates are now imposed on the tenant on an *ad valorem* basis, the demand curve shifts to D_t. In the short period the stock of rented houses is fixed, and the new rates will be borne by landlords, for net rent will fall from OR to OR_1 – unless the tenant is under a long-term contract to pay rent exclusive of rates. In the long period, however, the supply of houses is more elastic since owners will, assuming no planning consent is required, adapt them to other uses or simply not replace them as they wear out, switching to lower-taxed and more profitable forms of investment. This means that some of the burden can now be passed on to the tenant, the extent depending upon the relative elasticities of supply and demand. Thus in Figure 13.7(b) RR_t of the rate burden is shifted forward to the tenant, and RR_1 backwards to landlords, the total rates paid being $R_tR_1 \times OM_1$. Furthermore, rented housing decreases by MM_1.

It should be noted, however, that if the new rates result in improved local services, especially education, roads and transport facilities, there could be an increase in the demand for property in the area, the demand curve shifting to the right. As a result, the impact of the rates on the landlord is partly offset by a rise in rents, so that rented housing will not decrease by as much as MM_1.

Furthermore, when the rate system itself is made selective by varying the poundage between different types of property (as, for instance, when agricultural land pays no rates and domestic buildings pay at a lower rate than shops, offices and factories), there are additional allocative effects.

Third, the yield from property taxes lacks buoyancy – the result of the narrowness of the tax base together with its rigidity in the face of inflation. Concentrating on a single form of wealth – property – allows other types, e.g. pictures, jewellery and antiques, to escape tax. Consequently, a rise in local government expenditure results in a considerable increase in the rate poundage. While, as we have seen, this promotes accountability, it hampers progressive authorities who wish to extend their services. Again, while the yield from such taxes as income tax and VAT automatically increases with inflation, the rise in property prices takes time to be reflected in higher rateable values, because quinquennial revaluations have, through administration difficulties, been continually postponed (and indeed have now ceased to be a statutory requirement). Worse still, local government services tend to be labour-intensive, so that the yearly rate poundage increase tends to be proportionately higher than the over-all rate of inflation. Since the half-yearly rate demand makes the rise so obvious, there are periodic outbursts of discontent and political repercussions in local government elections.

Fourth, local property taxes tend to be regressive and inequitable. Not only do poor people tend to spend a higher proportion of their income on housing but also the tax levied may be unrelated to ability to pay. For example, a single pensioner may live in an identical house to a family containing many wage-earners. Nor is there any direct link between the property tax and local services used. A pensioner, for example, has little call on education or refuse collection. Nevertheless, rent rebates can help to offset the rate burden for poorer people. In any case the rating system must be viewed in relation to the over-all national fiscal structure where more progressive taxes and certain other free social benefits can compensate.

Similar considerations of equity apply to business undertakings. Agriculture enjoys the advantage of being *de*rated. On the other hand, small firms probably find what is virtually a lump-sum tax more onerous than large firms which have a higher turnover, while a rate increase imposes a heavier burden on those forms of production which are building-intensive, e.g. retailing, compared with those which are labour- and machinery-intensive, e.g. light industry.

Fifth, groups bearing the lowest rate burden, e.g. farmers and householders, tend to press for more goods and services to be provided by local authorities rather than through the market.

Sixth, local property taxes accentuate relative differences in the ability of local authorities to finance their essential services. Often the authority having a low rateable value has more to spend on new infrastructure, housing and education, and is thus forced to levy a high rate poundage. This means that the rates paid on similar properties can vary from one part of the country to another, and even between different parts of the same urban concentration. Such 'fiscal zoning' has allocative consequences, households and firms tending to move to those areas where the rate poundage is lowest – areas, in fact, where the infrastructure could even be superior. And although inequalities between districts may be corrected by central government equalisation grants, it may only be at the expense of undermining local autonomy.

Different forms of local property tax

It is usual for local property taxes to be levied *ad valorem*; but the tax base can vary between net annual value, capital value and site value.

(1) *Net annual value*
In Britain the basis of assessment is *net annual value*, determined as follows. First a gross annual value – the yearly rent that the property might reasonably be expected to let for on a determined date – is given to the property, and then statutory deductions are made for maintenance and insurance to give the net annual value (NAV).

Compared with a site-value base, NAV has certain advantages. First, because the base includes buildings as well as land, the yield is higher, especially for property where the building cost is a high proportion of the total cost. Second, it is easier to assess, since in a free market rentals can be calculated by comparison with similar properties.

On the other hand, NAV has significant defects. First, because the tax falls on buildings as well as on land, it tends to be more regressive as regards houses, which are occupied by poor as well as rich people. Second, NAV is not neutral as regards building improvements, for these are taxed. In the long period, therefore, capital tends, as we have already seen, to move to untaxed uses, an owner-occupier, for example, preferring to buy antique furniture rather than build a garage. Third, NAV is not without practical difficulties, particularly in assessing rentals for dwellings. Rent control and the loss of the private sector has meant that evidence of *free-market* rentals is confined to about 2 per cent of the privately rented sector (which itself accounts for only 14 per cent of total dwellings). Fourth, anomalies occur. Not only is agricultural land derated with a severe loss of possible revenue to rural authorities, but relieving charities of rates penalises those authorities (such as Westminster, Oxford and Cambridge) containing a high proportion of charities within their boundaries, especially as the NAVs are included in the 'valuation list' which the central government uses in assessing its 'needs' grant.

(2) *Capital value*

Here the tax base is the value of the premises if sold freehold on the open market, given a willing buyer and a willing seller. Provided the capital value is equal to the NAV capitalised at the relevant rate of interest, it will produce a base for taxation equivalent to NAV.

In practice, however, marginal divergences between the two methods may have allocative effects. If potential use value is included in capital value, vacant and underdeveloped sites will pay more tax than under NAV, thus accelerating redevelopment, discouraging unoccupation of buildings and stimulating greater use of existing property.

Other variations in assessing capital values may affect the rate of renewal of property, particularly dwellings. Capital-value assessments in the USA, for example, allow for the state of repair and length of life of the property and risk of rental default. Such factors lower the capital value of such property as slum housing even though net returns relative to gross yields are high since little is spent on upkeep. Thus the tax base is smaller than it would be if *net* returns were capitalised to obtain the capital value, and it is suggested that the resulting tax advantage tends to retard urban renewal.

Even the British NAV system, however, can discourage maintenance and improvement, especially of houses. Instead of the tax being levied on *actual* net returns (receipts less costs, including maintenance), they are based, as explained earlier, on an estimated gross rental less statutory deductions which decrease in relative proportion at high gross rental values. Nor are tax allowances granted for improvements. Thus a change to a capital-value assessment based on capitalised *actual* net returns should result in higher standards of maintenance if, as it has been estimated, the demand for better housing is price-elastic.

(3) *Site-value rating*

The idea behind site-value rating (SVR) as the basis of rent assessment is that the tax falls only on the *land* element of real property, i.e. the open-market value of the site on the assumption that it is currently available for its most profitable use. Thus, compared with a NAV or capital-value base, the buildings are not taxed, but, rather, potential value is taxed (see Figure 13.8).

As the basis of a property tax, SVR has certain advantages.

First, it has strong moral backing, in that it is closely associated with taxing 'betterment' – the increase in land values resulting from community projects, e.g. roads, railways and public parks, and, more controversially, from the growth of population. The argument is founded on Ricar-

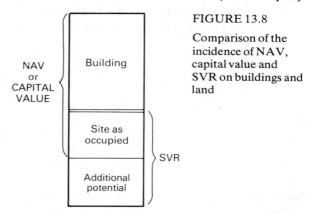

FIGURE 13.8

Comparison of the incidence of NAV, capital value and SVR on buildings and land

do's theory of economic rent: since land is fixed in supply, its value is determined solely by demand, not by any activity on the part of the owner. SVR is a tax on this demand-determined value and is thus a means by which 'betterment' can be returned to the community. Moreover, because sites are, for spatial reasons, fixed in supply, the tax falls entirely on economic rent with no effect on supply.

Second, SVR should improve the efficiency of land use. Since site value is the sole tax base, it is in effect a lump-sum tax which is levied irrespective of how the site is used, the value of the building on it, or whether the buildings are improved. That is, SVR is neutral as regards the type of use, intensity of use and any improvements made. There is thus an incentive to develop sites to their most profitable use, since the burden of the given tax would then be spread over higher gross receipts. Even if speculators continued to hoard land – vacant central sites and agricultural fringe land – SVR would ensure that they had to pay towards the cost of public services provided. Furthermore, the improvement of existing buildings would be encouraged. Thus SVR should speed up the renewal of inner-city areas.

Third, SVR could have benefits for housing. In the short period the rate burden would tend to shift to central sites and away from suburban houses. Figure 13.9 shows that, under SVR, (a) will pay rates on one-half of the original base, whereas (b) will pay on only one-quarter. In the long period the more intensive use of central sites should, given no change in the demand for land resources, reduce the demand for, and thus the price of, peripheral land, the main outlet for new housing.

Fourth, SVR should produce external benefits. The impetus to the redevelopment of central sites would, given no change in the demand for land resources, reduce city sprawl with its high infrastructure cost and long journeys to work. On the other hand, this could be accompanied by external costs – increased city-centre traffic congestion and the loss of

FIGURE 13.9

The incidence of site-
value rating

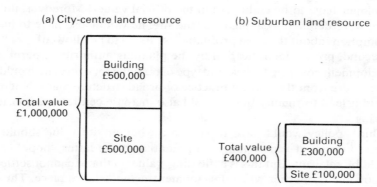

(a) City-centre land resource   (b) Suburban land resource

open space such as large private gardens and centrally situated recreational facilities which could be taxed out of existence. In the SVR pilot
study of Whitstable, for instance, it was estimated that the local golf
course's rate bill would increase seventyfold. Indeed, such external costs
would be reflected in lower site values of surrounding properties, with a
corresponding reduction in the tax base. Such costs, however, could be
partly dealt with by planning controls.

Fifth, SVR would reduce 'fiscal zoning' since, in the long run, the
movement of business and people to 'low-rate' areas would be self-
defeating in that it would simply raise site values there.

Sixth, SVR should promote objectivity in making planning decisions.
Because the NAV system rates both buildings and land, the higher
rateable value which would result becomes a factor influencing the
decision of the local planning authority regarding a proposed development. With the building element removed by SVR, planning decisions
can follow a consistent policy based solely on amenity and environmental
considerations.

Nevertheless, while SVR has certain advantages, it does face objec-
tions on principle and runs into difficulties in implementation.

First, the true site value can only be ascertained when a *vacant* site is
being *competed* for, because only then will the most profitable use under
present conditions be indicated. At other times indirect methods of
valuation have to be used, and these give rise to difficulties in ensuring
accuracy and uniformity. Comparability is the safest method, but even so
the personal judgement of the valuer cannot be eliminated when allowing
for differences in the size and position of sites. Moreover, the difficulty of
isolating the site element from any value resulting from improvements or
the enterprise of the owner could provide scope for challenge, appeals

and litigation. In contrast, the residual method means that the valuer has to assess the most profitable use and, ultimately, the cost of the building which will secure this. Thus the specialised expertise of *all types* of developer have to be embodied in the official valuer! Moreover, unless there were detailed local plans for the site, he would also have to make assumptions about the most profitable use likely to be allowed!

Second, precise identification by the planning authority of permitted development covering the use and type of building for every site would be a departure from the current practice of broad structure plans. Not only would it lead to rigidity but it would also increase centralised decision-making.

Third, policy would have to stipulate whether site value should be assessed on short-run or long-run potential. If the latter, 'hope' value would be relevant. But this is a 'floating' value, in that it cannot settle on *all* possible properties when development *actually* takes place. Thus to attribute a long-term potential value to *all* properties would involve double-counting. Furthermore, it would in effect be a tax on income – since the owner could do nothing to recoup that part of the tax based on potential. The site-value assessment would be greater than the capitalised, *current* net return from the site. In short, the incidence of the tax is no longer falling entirely on betterment, and, by impinging on current resources, exaggerates a defect of the net annual value system in that it may be unrelated to the taxpayer's present capacity to pay.

Moreover, by assessing potential site values, SVR would not only tax increased value before it was realised but might even tax an 'increase' that might *never* be realised. For one thing, there could be several interests in the land resource, with no individual owner being able to redevelop because of failure to acquire the other interests. For another, although the land resource was taxed for a number of years on potential development value, that potential might be lost before it could be realised owing to a change in planning policy or development elsewhere (e.g. a new hypermarket).

In the above ways, therefore, SVR could penalise the owner who postpones development in order to acquire adjoining land or complementary interests which will produce a comprehensive scheme. In so doing, it could encourage piecemeal development detrimental to satisfactory town planning.

Fourth, apart from planning restrictions, such encumbrances as rent control, long leases and private covenants would have to be allowed for in estimating site value.

Fifth, assessment of site value can only be provisional when the environment is constantly changing. For instance, a new motorway would improve accessibility, but site values may not rise if the motorway increased the supply of sites. In any case the betterment may be thinly spread and accompanied by 'worsement' in the areas from which people move. Thus a period of at least five years would have to elapse following the completion of the motorway before there was reliable evidence of the resulting change in site values. Once site values have, however, been determined they would not be subject to the many assessment changes which, under NAV, follow structural alterations and additions.

Sixth, while the inclusion under SVR of the potential value of vacant and underdeveloped sites may provide an initial tax base equal to NAV, this might not be achieved if building costs increased relatively to site values, e.g. because of a shift in shopping from city centres (where sites are fixed in supply) to out-of-town hypermarkets (where alternative sites are available) (see p. 27). If as a result the rate poundage had to exceed 100p, the site-value tax would no longer fall entirely on economic rent and would thus cease to be neutral as regards land use. Moreover, methods of avoiding a high rate poundage have their own disadvantages: increased government grants may involve a loss of local autonomy, while additional tax sources may erode local accountability.

Seventh, while the tax would be paid by owners instead of occupiers, in the long period its incidence as regards particular uses can be passed on to occupiers according to the relative elasticities of demand of occupiers and the elasticity of the supply by owners. Inasmuch as the tax would be paid by owners but hidden in rents, SVR tends to weaken the links between local taxation and representation and local accountability. However, against this must be set the fact that owners are fewer in number than occupiers, making the tax administratively easier to collect.

Finally, in weighing up the pros and cons of the proposed introduction of SVR into Britain, we have to remember that, because the uncertainties associated with the assessment of site values would give rise to considerable challenge by owners, a period of transition of some years would have to elapse before it could become fully operative. In the meantime it might not provide a firm and predictable basis for financing local services.

The strength of SVR (already operative in such countries as Denmark, New Zealand and Tanzania) is the incentive it provides towards development and improvement. It has particular merit, therefore, for underdeveloped countries. In Britain, on the other hand, the main need is to direct development into the best channels, an aim which is probably more effectively achieved by planning requirements. Moreover, as regards the other objective of appropriating betterment for the public purse, it must be remembered that much is already secured through development land tax and capital gains tax.

The future of local property taxes

The defects of local property taxes – particularly their lack of buoyancy – have led to frequent demands for their abolition or augmentation from other sources of revenue, e.g. increased government grants, charges for certain services such as education, and new local taxes, particularly a local income tax, sales tax or motor-vehicle-licence tax. Alternatively, the central government could accept full financial responsibility for services of national importance, such as education, police and social services.

The real difficulty of abandoning the local property taxes is finding from other sources a comparable yield which, for instance, is equivalent to a 10p rate of income tax. Increased government grants or switching financial responsibility for certain local services to the central government would undermine local autonomy and accountability. Imposing charges could be politically difficult. Introducing new local taxes would either deprive the government of its own much-needed revenue or increase the rate of tax on income and on spending to unacceptable levels.

A local property tax is therefore likely to continue. The most that can be hoped for is that local authorities are given some additional income to relieve the ever-increasing rate burden, for then the deficiencies of the tax become less acute. The only other alternative is to reduce the scope and scale of services provided by the state in general and local authorities in particular.

V PLANNING CONTROLS

The case for planning controls

Before a development can proceed the formal permission of the local planning authority – the district council – has usually to be obtained. While actual decisions are made on a case-by-case basis, proposed developments are normally required to conform to the over-all structure plan drawn up by the county council for its area. General building regulations also have to be complied with. In many respects, therefore, structure plans and building regulations represent control by general regulation.

Planning consents can be regarded as a form of physical control for dealing with certain aspects of market failure, mainly those arising because the conditions necessary for the efficient allocation of resources do not hold. The appropriateness of planning as a method of control can be examined in the context of how it deals with the causes of market failure.

(1) *Improved knowledge*
Decisions influencing the allocation of land resources through the market may be based on inadequate knowledge. At times, it can be argued, people may not be the best judges of their own welfare. For instance, their preferences expressed through the market could make inadequate provi-

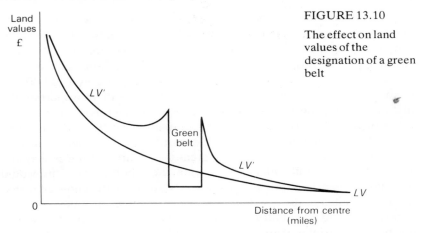

FIGURE 13.10

The effect on land values of the designation of a green belt

sion for open space, such as parks and playing-fields. Through planning, a paternalistic policy is followed by allocating land to such uses. On the other hand, permission to build on cheap land near a motorway may be refused because the authorities consider that prospective purchasers of houses would underestimate the noise nuisance.

Again, in their present utilisation of land resources, individuals might make insufficient allowance for future needs. Thus, as we saw in Chapter 7, there may be a case for taking measures to preserve buildings having special architectural or historic interest. Indeed, the designation of green belts around towns may not only be necessary to safeguard amenity land for unborn generations but it could also increase land values in the present. In Figure 13.10 original land values, shown by the curve *LV*, decrease regularly from the city centre outwards. With the introduction of the green belt, the land-value curve shifts to *LV'*, showing that the fall in the average value of land in the green belt is more than compensated for by the rise in values elsewhere – even in the city centre, since accessibility to recreation and amenity land is now guaranteed.

Uncertainty arising from imperfect knowledge of the intentions of others in a similar position can affect land-use decisions. This can be explained in terms of *the prisoner's dilemma*. The police suggest to prisoner *A* that, in return for confessing and implicating his accomplice *B*, they will do their best to ensure that *A*'s sentence is limited to one year's imprisonment, though *B* will get five. However, prisoner *A* senses that the police do not have a strong case and that, if neither confesses, there is a chance that they will both be acquitted. He has no means of communicating with *B*, and so his problem is to assess how *B* is likely to react to the same offer. Will he remain silent, relying on *A* to do likewise in order to give them both a good chance of going free? Or will he act selfishly and settle for one year, leaving *A* to do five years? This 'prisoner's dilemma' can be related to owners' decisions on whether to improve their property in a rundown inner-city area. One owner is contemplating spending £20,000 on improving his property. If the owners of adjacent properties do likewise, there is a beneficial spin-off because the value of all properties would each increase by £30,000. On the other hand, if fellow-owners neglect to renovate their properties, the first owner's expenditure could be largely wasted in terms of adding to the value of his property since it may eventually have to be demolished. While the planning authority also does not have knowledge of owners' intentions, it can, however, create greater certainty by policy action – announcing a definite plan to renovate the whole area. This would stimulate owners to improve independently, secure in the knowledge that those who failed to do so would be brought into line. A similar situation occurs if individual retailers could be induced to move from a central position to a peripheral area more accessible to shoppers (e.g. a shopping centre) provided they were sure that external benefits of concentration would be retained by fellow-retailers making the same move.

Inaccurate forecasts of future demand may also affect the efficient allocation of land resources. For example, in building on a particular site the developer has to estimate the extent to which demand is likely to grow through population expansion or a rise in incomes. If he underestimates future demand, the site will not be developed intensively enough; if he overestimates, it may be difficult to let units at an economic rent. Since planners control future growth, the better information available to them may avoid such mistakes – through a policy of density control. The same applies to shopping space, planning controls perhaps being necessary to prevent too much being provided.

Imperfect knowledge may take the form of having to make decisions without being able to ascertain the investment plans of competitors. This can result in over-supply by the industry concerned and the inability to sell at the expected price. We can illustrate by looking at office development in a city area. In Figure 13.11 D, D_1 and D_2 represent the demand curves for offices at different time periods, and S is the long-period supply curve. In period 1 demand increases from D to D_1 but, because it takes some time for supply to expand to OM_1, the number of offices remains fixed at OM. Competition therefore leads to higher rents, which rise to OP_1. Office developers respond to this higher price, starting to build offices irrespective of the fact that others are doing likewise. When all their building programmes have been completed supply has increased to OM_2. In order to clear the market, price has to fall to OP_2 – unless demand increases to D_2 or inferior office accommodation is taken off the market. Here, again, planning can impose a scheme which co-ordinates the proposals of separate developers.

Finally, it should also be noted that general regulations covering

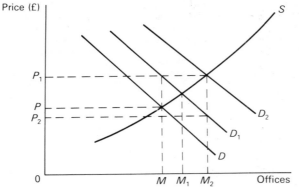

FIGURE 13.11

The effect of time lags
in the supply of
offices

structure plans and building requirements also serve to eliminate much
uncertainty, thus providing a framework within which developers can
formulate their particular schemes.

(2) *Allowance for externalities*

The activities of individuals or groups may, as shown earlier, give rise to
spillover benefits or costs to others. In certain circumstances externalities
may be dealt with by 'internalisation', agreement, or through the market
mechanism. A large communal garden space can be made exclusive when
all the residences that benefit are provided by a single developer (as with
the London squares built some two centuries ago). Or, within a local
community, rules may be drawn up governing car-parking, standards of
house maintenance, children's play areas, etc. Alternatively, such matters
may be covered more rigidly by covenants in the leases of the same estate.
Finally, external benefits result in certain firms congregating in particular
areas, e.g. offices in the City of London, because through the market they
can exclude other types of business by offering higher rents.

But where the total effect of the externality is important but spread so
thinly that persons affected cannot be identified for purposes of co-
ordinated action, state intervention is necessary. These conditions apply
in particular to land use. The type of building erected and the use to which
it is put affect the welfare not only of neighbours but also of passers-by.
Thus both the design of the building and its use are subject to public
intervention through planning control.

In practice, such control tends to concentrate on dealing with undesirable external effects. For instance, it seeks to eliminate competitive uses of
adjacent land, e.g. factories in residential areas and the erection of
buildings which do not harmonise with their surroundings, or to prevent
loss of variety in shopping centres or in employment outlets. But planning
can also be positive, arranging complementary uses, e.g. siting dwellings,
schools, shopping facilities and bus termini in strategic proximity, or by

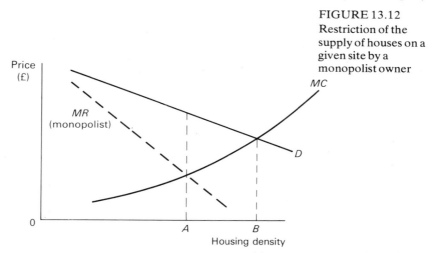

FIGURE 13.12
Restriction of the
supply of houses on a
given site by a
monopolist owner

encouraging the preservation of a listed building by granting a change of use.

(3)   *Dealing with imperfect competition*

Local authority planning backed by powers of compulsory purchase provides an overriding authority when the owner of a particular site stands in the way of a comprehensive development by using his monopoly position to demand an extortionate selling price. Indeed, once the need for planning has been established, the logical step of allowing the planning authority to exercise powers of compulsory purchase makes coercion more acceptable.

Planning powers may also be used to deal with underdevelopment of a site. For instance, the owner of a vacant half-hectare site in a built area may find it more profitable to restrict building to three executive town houses (*OA* in Figure 13.12), whereas the need of the district is for a more intensive development of smaller houses, a development which would result if building were pursued to the perfect competition position where price equalled marginal social cost, *OB*.

(4)   *The provision of public and collective goods*

The deficiencies of the market in supplying public and collective goods have already been examined. Since the provision of these goods, such as roads, bridges, car-parks, commons and national parks, must be the responsibility of the state, and because they cover large areas or have location significance, some central planning is inevitable. Indeed government bodies are also responsible for other infrastructure services, such as parks, sewerage, schools and water supply, and these, too, have to be integrated into a land-use plan for the area.

An over-all planning authority has other advantages for dealing with public services and land use. Thus if a private firm is entirely responsible for a development, it is restricted to working within the existing road scheme, the pattern of which was probably established before the coming of motor transport. In this way the road lay-out becomes ossified in an inefficient form. In contrast, co-operation between the private developer and a local authority having planning powers would allow the road system to be altered to meet the needs of modern transport and the environment generally.

(5)   *Improving the mobility of resources*

For various reasons resources may be sluggish in responding to changes in the conditions of demand or supply as indicated by the market. For instance, there may be an increase in industrial activity in a given area, but there is a bottleneck in the supply of the necessary labour to increase output, the main cause of which may be the shortage of suitable housing in the district. Here the planning authority can help by ensuring that development proceeds in a balanced way with housing being provided parallel to permission being given for new factory buildings.

Similarly, in a depressed area labour may not wish to move because of social ties. The latter should be regarded as a benefit to be taken account of by the planners, who should thereby encourage the development of new employment opportunities by making it easier for growth firms to be established in the area as regards obtaining sites and having an up-to-date infrastructure.

(6)   *The redistribution of income*

As explained in Chapter 1, income redistribution is a political decision rather than an economic one. But problems of income distribution may be inherent in planning decisions. For instance, a householder who sells a part of his garden for development does so because he gains a net benefit. But, by imposing uncompensated costs on his neighbours, they suffer a loss of welfare. Thus while the planning authority may consent to a development on environmental grounds, there can be distributional implications.

Indeed, planning may go further, redistributing income as an active policy. For example, while there may be economic grounds for earmarking dwellings for essential workers in city centres where the price of land is high, it also allows the poorer member of the community to occupy dwellings at a lower rent than would be established in a free market.

Furthermore, planning decisions may redistribute income in favour of future generations, for example by providing land for parks and recreation, preserving green belts and protecting historic buildings. This involves value judgements concerning the marginal utility which will be derived from future income and the fact that this is likely to be larger than that of the present community.

Justification of planning regulations

As we have seen, the defects of the price mechanism may be offset by the government intervening in the market by adjusting its own supply and demand (e.g. by stockpiling of agricultural produce and basic materials, locating its own offices in Development Areas, placing orders with firms in areas of high unemployment), by taxing or subsidising certain activities (e.g. imposing a higher rate poundage on commercial and industrial buildings than on dwellings, subsidising agriculture through rate relief) or by making regulations on a general basis (e.g. rent control, general building and fire-precaution regulations). Why, therefore, should it interfere by planning control, which relies on a *case-by-case* assessment?

First, a centrally determined rate of tax would be general in its application and might not be appropriate for particular cases. Thus the external costs of a proposed development, e.g. extracting minerals in an area of outstanding natural beauty, may in total be so great that any tax imposed ought to be so high as to prevent such a project from being economically viable. But is it certain that this would happen? It is possible that the *rate* of tax decided centrally on an average basis would be so low as to enable the mineral extraction to proceed. In this particular case, therefore, the rule that an activity should proceed to the point where marginal social benefit equals marginal social cost (see p. 276) would be breached. The difficulty is that the external costs incurred can vary in magnitude from one beauty spot to another, for each differs in character and in the number of visitors attracted. Taxation, however, would be applied to each on the same basis, perhaps even preventing mineral extraction where the beauty spot is of no outstanding quality and so remote that it is hardly likely ever to attract many visitors.

Parallel criticisms apply to minimum standard regulations, e.g. room height, window space, ventilation and safety precautions. Not only do the minimum requirements tend to become the accepted normal standard of provision, but being decided centrally they impose rigidity. With buildings there must be flexibility to cover individual cases, e.g. a historic building, where special features have to be preserved. Indeed, because all developments tend to be heterogeneous in character, there is much to be said for controlling on a case-by-case basis rather than by general regulation.

Second, when granting planning permission, the local authority can impose special conditions covering the provision of public services, such as access roads and open spaces, a community centre, low-income housing units, etc. Obviously the extent of such possible 'planning gain' varies from project to project, and planning on a case-by-case basis permits flexibility in the conditions imposed.

Third, while (as we have seen) some distributive effects are often inherent in planning decisions (e.g. countryside recreation facilities involving high transport costs and low-density housing standards benefit the rich more than the poor), intervention by taxation would be far more favourable to the rich since they are in a better position to pay in order to proceed with a scheme.

Difficulties of control by planning

First, compared with taxation (where this is possible), planning lacks flexibility as regards individual preferences. This applies particularly to zoning through structure plans. For instance, part-time married women workers might be excluded from employment by transport costs and the time taken in travelling to a factory in an industrial zone. Thus a firm classified as 'industrial' and relying heavily on such labour might be prepared to pay additional rent (including a tax) for a site convenient for its employees, and this would be justifiable if the extra benefits to the firm exceeded the external costs. Moreover, structure plans may impose rigidity over time since the highest and best use of a land resource can alter with income changes and transport developments.

Second, planning may not take sufficient account of certain benefits which exist in the current land-use situation. Thus in the past structure plans to deal with the environmental problems of inner-city areas have not fully allowed for the loss of job opportunities in small firms which existed through low rents, the higher travelling cost to work, the extra cost and inconvenience of obtaining odd-job services, the destruction of social contacts, the loss of community spirit, and the elimination of variety, e.g. in employment, shops and architecture.

Third, planning tends to overlook certain repercussions of the controls imposed. For instance, low-density housing requirements may mean that building for the poorer members of the community is confined to those parcels of land available for high-density development, with the result that its price per hectare exceeds that of land for rich people's housing. Similarly, design guides, such as the Parker–Morris standards, impose an additional strain on maintaining the stock of second-hand dwellings. Secondary effects also occur when commercial developments are restricted in intensity, e.g. by plot ratios, in order to limit congestion. In practice, the reactions of firms may actually increase movement. For instance, storage may be decentralised and the space vacated occupied by employees, while usually extra vehicles are needed to maintain contact between decentralised offices and the centre. In addition, public transport has to overcome the difficulty of serving more scattered destinations.

Fourth, planning tends to be negative in character. Thus, while it may prevent undesirable results, e.g. the despoliation of a beauty spot or excessive urban sprawl, planning controls in themselves do not lead to market forces initiating those schemes that the authorities would like to promote.

Fifth, case-by-case examination of applications for planning permission leads to delays in arriving at a decision, delays which are both frustrating and costly to the developer and wasteful in the use of land resources. Such delays are more significant when the application is for the development of a large site, since then alternative schemes have usually to be considered and objectors may force a public enquiry. For instance, although the Surrey Docks closed for business in 1970, no plan for the 400-acre site in central London has yet (1980) been agreed, nor has any start been made in providing the necessary infrastructure. It seems, too, that it takes longer to obtain all the necessary permits to develop in Britain than in other countries. A survey of factory building published by Slough Estates Ltd in 1979 showed that for Britain the period was thirty-five weeks, compared with only four weeks in Canada and five in the USA. Even in France, where planning constraints are fairly severe, it was only fourteen weeks. Only Australia, with thirty-two weeks, came near the British period.

VI BETTERMENT AND LAND NATIONALISATION

Reasons for land nationalisation

Land nationalisation may be undertaken for a variety of reasons – to satisfy political ideology, to allocate land more effectively, to facilitate planning, and to collect 'betterment'.

The first objective lies outside the field of the economist since it rests almost entirely on subjective judgement. If the electorate chooses a government which proposes to bring all land into public ownership, so be it. Nevertheless, public ownership may be misguided if alternative methods of securing the other objectives – allocating land, facilitating planning and collecting betterment – have significant advantages.

As regards the allocation of land, state ownership, it is often argued, is necessary to remedy the defects of the price mechanism, which (because of the high cost of land) fails to provide adequately for public uses, takes insufficient account of external costs and benefits, lends itself to monopoly influence and is sluggish in overcoming the immobility of resources. On the other hand, allocating land resources by central decision-making ignores the main strengths of the market economy: demand is indicated through the price mechanism, private enterprise acts to satisfy this demand – both current and future – and efficiency is stimulated by competition and the profit motive. Can public ownership, its opponents ask, be so effective in allocating resources? For one thing, while the integrity of officials is not challenged, they are not directly subject to the discipline of the market, such as the interest charges which accumulate as land is kept vacant. Nor are they by nature sufficiently enterprising to formulate bold and imaginative policies, especially as regards future development. For another, public ownership does not completely eliminate the weaknesses of the market economy. Public bodies themselves become monopolies, possibly exercising greater power than those existing under private enterprise, and their economic policies often vacillate with the swing of the political pendulum, thereby hampering consistent long-term planning for future development. In any case, it is argued, the government can act through subsidies, taxation, planning regulations and, if necessary, by means of compulsory purchase to ensure that land is secured for public uses and externalities provided for. This would allow most land resources still to be allocated by a process of decentralised decision-making operating through the market.

Of course, such an allocation is only efficient if a single price rules for land in the market, and private and public uses have to compete on equal terms. Usually, however, proposals for nationalisation envisage public bodies being able to acquire their land at a lower price than private developers. We return to an examination of this dual-price system later, looking at it in terms of what was proposed under the Community Land Act 1975.

The planning case for the public ownership of land rests mainly on the advantages enjoyed by a public body in assembling large sites for comprehensive development rather than allowing development to proceed piecemeal in response to market forces as individual sites become available. As we shall see when discussing the proposals of the Community Land Act, the argument is not wholly convincing.

We now proceed to consider the 'collection-of-betterment' argument.

The logic of 'betterment'

The White Paper *Land* (Cmnd 5730, 12 September 1974) set out two main objectives of the Labour government's policy of bringing all development land under public ownership: (i) to enable the community to control the development of land in accordance with its needs and priorities; and (ii) to restore to the community the increase in value of land arising from its efforts. The first objective has already been referred to and will be considered later in the context of the Community Land Act 1975. It is with the second objective that we are concerned here.

The White Paper's view is quite clear:

> The growth in value, more especially of urban sites, is due to no expenditure or capital or thought on the part of the ground owner, but entirely owing to the energy and enterprise of the community . . . it is undoubtedly one of the worst evils of our present system of land tenure that instead of reaping the benefit of the common endeavour of its citizens, a community has always to pay a heavy penalty to its ground landlords for putting up the value of their land.

But can this argument stand up to economic analysis? Or do its foundations rest solely on an emotional appeal?

The values of all goods and services are the result of the interaction of demand and supply in the market. It is through the demand of the community that all values are created: if demand increases relative to supply, the price of a commodity rises. This principle is generally applicable, but it is most noticeable when supply tends to be fairly fixed, as it is with vintage cars, stamps, antique furniture, houses and land. Under a system of private property rights and market allocation of goods, the possessor of a commodity where demand increases relative to supply will obtain a higher price and thus a windfall gain – known in economics as 'economic rent'. But to label the windfall gain which accrues to landowners through increased demand for land as 'betterment', and to appropriate it entirely, is to select a special form of ownership for punitive treatment. The value of all goods which are not in completely elastic supply will increase as demand increases as a result of higher incomes, a change in tastes, a growth in the population, and so on. Land and buildings are no exception to this general rule. To call this gain 'betterment' and to tax it at a higher rate rests solely on a political decision made possible because landowners are a comparatively small group in the community, with a correspondingly small voting strength.

Again, the extent to which an increase in the value of a particular piece of development land arises from the 'efforts of the community' can be queried. Development involves laying down fixed capital equipment for a future demand that is by no means certain. Only in the present can the community signal its demand. Thus one developer may be able to offer a much higher price for a piece of land because he can foresee a more profitable type of development arising from the future demand of the community. So a part of 'betterment' arises from the skill of the developer rather than the efforts of the community. It is here submitted that capital gains tax would be the most consistent way of dealing with such a rise in the value of land.

Is the situation basically different when the increase in land values stems from the provision of infrastructure – schools, communications, water supply, a sewerage system and other public-utility services? In principle, the provision of such services represents investment which should earn a stipulated return either through the charges levied or the proceeds of taxation, mainly rates. Even where the return consists largely of social benefits, e.g. public parks, they should eventually be manifested in higher house prices, which would give a high net annual value and thus a high rate yield. There may be extra spillover benefits to the investment in infrastructure which arise through agglomeration factors, e.g. an increased variety of job opportunities, which add still further to the value of land in the vicinity. But it is hardly consistent for the owner of land to be charged a 'betterment' tax which is additional to the taxes paid by other forms of business whose extra profitability arises partly from different types of external economy, e.g. radio weather forecasts for shipping, daily market prices for farmers. Furthermore, gains from agglomeration economies may be accompanied by losses elsewhere through dispersal.

The third type of 'betterment' arises through the grant of planning permission. Here there is a strong case, resting on the nature of planning permissions, for a special tax to appropriate such 'betterment'. For the reasons given earlier in this chapter, the community may decide that land can only be developed if it has the necessary planning permissions, which act to restrict the possible supply. For instance, only certain parts of the agricultural land surrounding a town are given planning permission for housebuilding. Restriction of supply leads to a considerably increased value of that land which is granted planning permission, but through the very method by which they are granted permissions may benefit one landowner and handicap another. There is justification, therefore, for appropriating some of the windfall gains secured by the lucky landowners – and possibly a case for compensating those landowners who have been refused! Whether the whole of the gain should be taken is a matter for debate.

To sum up, then, 'betterment' can be applied to: (i) a capital gain arising from increased demand; (ii) the enhanced value of land resulting from community infrastructure; and (iii) a windfall gain due to the grant of planning permission. Subjecting (i) and (ii) to an additional special tax discriminates against the ownership of land as opposed to other forms of enterprise. Only with (iii) is there a logical case for such a tax.

A basic problem is how the community is to collect such betterment – by taxation, or through the wider policy of public ownership of all development land. A survey of the three post-war schemes which have been tried will indicate some of the difficulties.

Town and Country Planning Act 1947

This Act was partly based on the recommendations of the Uthwatt Committee (1942). Although development rights were vested in the state, land was still to be allocated by market forces. To collect betterment, therefore, a *development charge* of 100 per cent was levied on development value – the difference between the value of a site in its current use and its value for development resulting from the grant of planning consent. Since existing development values were estimated to be worth £300 million, a fund consisting of £300 million-worth of government stock was set up to compensate existing owners.

In this way all betterment was to accrue to the state, while cheaper land would be available for public projects since it could now be obtained at current-use value. But the Act failed, chiefly because the 100 per cent development charge gave owners no incentive to make their land available for development. Indeed, if owners developed themselves, they were subject to the heavy tax levy before they started to reap the rewards of their development. In 1953, therefore, the development charge was abolished.

Land Commission Act 1967

This Act established a Land Commission having two main functions.

First, it had to assess and collect a new *betterment levy* on the development value of land. However, the Labour government, heeding the major cause of the failure of the earlier development charge, fixed the new levy at 40 per cent. But to deter owners from delaying bringing land forward for development, the levy was eventually to rise to 50 per cent and even higher.

Second, the Commission would influence the allocation of resources by actively participating in the land market. Armed with compulsory-purchase powers, it was to buy land ripe for development and resell it to developers, with public authorities and small house builders enjoying concessionary rates.

In practice, the scheme ran into difficulties. Not only did the cost of collecting the levy prove heavy but also land did not come forward for development. On the one hand, owners of land were prepared to take a chance on a Conservative government, committed to the abolition of the Land Commission, being returned to power. On the other, in three years the Land Commission accumulated only 2,000 acres of land for development (as against an expected 50,000 acres per annum) largely because local planning bodies proved to be a drag on its activities.

Hence, when a Conservative government took over in 1970, the Land Commission was abolished. Betterment was to be collected at a rate of 30 per cent through the capital gains tax which had been introduced in 1965.

As a result of the public outcry against the profits made by land speculation between 1970 and 1972, a development gains tax was introduced in 1974. The tax was levied at corporation-tax rate for a company or at the marginal income-tax rate (excluding the investment surcharge) for an individual on an increase in the value of land arising from planning permission for a new use, and was payable on first lettings. It remained in force until replaced by the development land tax in 1976.

Community Land Act 1975

The Community Land Act 1975 provided for the ultimate ownership of all development land by local authorities. The time-table for the full implementation of the scheme was divided into two stages.

Stage 1 covered the transitional arrangements. Initially local authorities in England and Scotland and the Land Authority for Wales were simply given the power to acquire land needed for development within the next ten years. The idea was that land would be earmarked for development ten years in advance and that within such land there would be a five-year rolling programme for actual development. Acquisition was by agreement or, with the authority of the Secretary of State, by compulsion. Certain developments, chiefly land already held by builders on 12 September 1974 and small developments, were either 'exempted' or 'excepted' from the main provisions of the Act. Later, the *power* of the local authorities to acquire was, by order of the Secretary of State, to be transformed into a *duty*. It was envisaged that at least ten years would elapse before all local authorities in Britain were subject to this duty. In the meantime betterment would be collected by a development land tax.

Stage 2 represented the permanent scheme. When all local authorities were covered by the duty to acquire land, the Secretary of State would fix a date when there would be no private ownership of development land: henceforth development would take place only on land owned by local authorities. Compensation for land acquired would be at current-use value. Since there would be no 'betterment' to the private owner, development land tax would come to an end.

In practice, the scheme proved to be misconceived and mistimed. First, it suffered from the defects of its predecessors – the basic rate of 80 per cent development land tax discouraged development proposals, landowners preferring to take a chance on a Conservative government, committed to its repeal, being soon returned to power. Second, and more disastrous, its introduction coincided with the property slump of 1974–7, when development virtually came to an end. This should have relieved the pressure on local authorities as they accumulated land for development. But the economic difficulties of 1976 enforced a cutback in public-sector spending, thus depriving local authorities of the finance necessary to acquire land even at current-use value. The result was that the municipalisation of land scheme hardly got under way (only 2,300 acres were acquired by local authorities in the two years ending 31 March

1978) before it was dropped by the Conservative government in 1979. But the Land Authority for Wales, which had exercised its functions effectively, was retained.

Nevertheless, we cannot assume that this will end attempts to bring land under public ownership. We therefore examine the respective merits of land nationalisation and the development land tax in the context of the proposals contained in the Community Land Act.

Public ownership and the allocation of land resources

Public ownership of land achieves simultaneously the two objectives of (i) increased planning control, and (ii) the return of betterment to the community. But is it likely to be more efficient than a system which acts chiefly through the market? In other words, can it ensure that, at the correct point in time, land will go to its highest and best use when all costs and benefits, both private and communal, are taken into account. If it facilitates planning to deal with externalities, it can be an improvement. If it delays desirable development or distracts it away from its highest and best use, it will be detrimental. In that case, the 100 per cent return of betterment which public ownership achieves may prove less over all than a smaller percentage of the larger betterment which would result from a superior project.

Relating the discussion to the Community Land Act scheme, the first question that has to be asked, therefore, is in what ways would the acquisition of development land by local authorities assist planning? The White Paper *Land* criticised the existing position in the following terms: 'The community does not at present have sufficient power always to plan positively, to decide where and when particular developments should take place.' While the White Paper made no attempt to explain and enlarge on this statement, it seemed to intend that in future local authorities, not private developers working through the market, would initiate development, deciding the allocation of land resources to their highest and best use and *when* the development should take place. Would such local authority decision-making be likely to improve allocation?

We can envisage a situation where the power of local authorities to acquire land for development in order to concentrate ownership in a single body might be helpful in planning comprehensive schemes. Previously, for instance, a private developer might have requested permission to redevelop a single site. Instead, the local authority can, by acquiring adjacent interests, ensure that a potentially better development, involving a much larger area, could be undertaken.

Certain qualifications, however, should be noted. First, had the private developer the power to command the amount of capital required, he could have carried out the larger and superior development by purchasing adjacent interests in the open market provided he did not run up against a monopolist seller. Only by being able to purchase at current-use value, being armed with compulsory-purchase powers, and possessing access to larger sums of capital, would the local authority be in a better position.

Second, large and comprehensive developments can be, and have been, completed through partnership schemes between local authorities and private developers. Here the expertise of the private developer, the financial strength of the institutions and the powers and responsibilities of the local authority are integrated to the advantage of the community (see Chapter 9).

Third, there is a distinct possibility that where land is owned by local authorities it could influence planning decisions. Until now, the planning authority has held the balance between the proposals of the private developer and the interests of the community at large. When the local authority owns the land, judge and plaintiff are rolled into one. Planning decisions could well be affected by this combined function, just as *Concorde* has been allowed to exceed the desired noise level at Heathrow in order that it can become operational.

Fourth, local authorities, even county councils, may be too small for effective planning. For instance, a private developer may feel that only one recreational centre would be economic for an area covering the boundaries of three county councils. He therefore initiates a scheme which is central to the area, and planning permission is granted by the appropriate council within whose boundaries it happens to fall. When these three councils represent at least three *developing* authorities, it might happen that each decides to have a recreational centre, with the result that not one is economically viable.

Last, there is the overriding question of whether local authority officials would have the drive, incentive and expertise of the private developer in initiating development schemes. This doubt was expressed in a report by the Royal Institute of Chartered Surveyors in 1974 entitled *The Land Problem: a Fresh Approach:*

In our view there are four prerequisites for successful development: the will to develop, the professional and technical expertise, the financial resources and the availability of suitable land. The mere ownership of land cannot by itself cause development to take place. Without the will to develop, without the expertise and financial resources, land will simply lie undeveloped ... One of the most valuable aspects of the system hitherto has been the vigilance of the entrepreneur over development opportunities and his vigour in pursuing them. Under the system envisaged that initiative would be lost. In its place, identification of suitable land would depend on the political will of local authorities, members of which are often under pressure from ratepayers to resist development, even where it is socially necessary . . . We believe that the conflicting pressures referred to, and the bureaucratic problems with which public bodies are beset, would seriously retard the pace of development.

To sum up, the case for the public ownership of land to improve development is inconclusive. Local authorities already have extensive planning powers through broad development structure plans and detailed development control. If they are also to be responsible for *initiating* development, there are grave misgivings as to whether they would prove as efficient as private enterprise. In essence the policy choice seems to lie between the dogma of nationalisation and the pragmatic solution whereby the advantages of development through private enterprise are combined with securing a high proportion (but not 100 per cent) of betterment through a development land tax.

The allocative effects of a dual land price for private developers and public uses

In a competitive pricing system one price rules for the same good. The market price secures an optimum allocation of resources, for it equals both the value which the community puts on an extra unit of the good and the additional cost of supplying that good.

What the Community Land Act did was to allocate land at two prices: to private developers at the full current market price, to local authorities at the current market price *less* development land tax (DLT). Take an example of agricultural and housing land, selling respectively at £1,000 and £20,000 an acre: the private house builder would have to pay £20,000 an acre for his land, but on the other hand the local authority would have paid £20,000 *less* DLT. Indeed, as DLT was to be increased, the price differential between the private developer and the local authority would also have increased.

Such a price differential would have had important results:

(a)   It would favour the building of local authority housing compared with owner-occupied and other private housing.

(b)   It would favour those local authorities who had agricultural land at low current-use value compared with those authorities whose land was almost completely built on and who therefore could only carry out future development on land with a comparatively high current-use value.

(c)   Since local authorities could buy land at a relatively low price, their developments were likely to use land more extensively than if it had to be bought at the current market price, as with the private developer.

(d)   Because of the lower capital cost, the penalty to the local authority of holding undeveloped land over time would have been reduced.

(e)   If the local authority were to carry out a commercial development, it would have obtained the land at a much lower price than would have had to be paid by the private developer. Indeed, the price differential could have been so large that it would have virtually eliminated competition from the private developer. Where the latter still managed to compete, the only reason would have been the relative inefficiency of the local authority. Thus, in practice, the land-price differential would tend to mask any inefficiency of local authorities in carrying out developments.

The only grounds upon which a lower land price for a local authority development could be justified would be where such a development confers external benefits to society which do not occur with private development.

Only if the local authority paid the current market price for development land would the situation be remedied. This could have been achieved by requiring it to hand over to the central government the full amount of DLT saved. This was not envisaged. Instead it was suggested that the sum would be divided as follows: 40 per cent to the central government, 30 per cent to local authorities having little development land, and 30 per cent to be retained by the acquiring authority. The latter would still ensure that it enjoyed a pretty hefty price advantage if it decided to develop itself, say for housing or commercial uses.

Indeed, the financial arrangements of the scheme produced a further disadvantageous allocative effect. From what they saved on the DLT element, local authorities were expected to build up a land-account surplus to finance purchases in the future. Obviously, the land-account surplus would be larger if the local authority acquired land where the DLT element was the greatest: that is, where the difference between market value and base value was the highest. But base value rested largely on current-use value plus 10 per cent or cost of acquisition plus 10 per cent. Two problems therefore arose: (1) How were local authorities to ascertain the cost of acquisition? This is known to the Board of Inland Revenue but is regarded by them as confidential information. (2) The land most suitable for development around towns, e.g. as regards nearness to the centre and the provision of suitable infrastructure of roads, sewers and schools, tends already to have planning permission or to be in the hands of developers. It was thus 'excepted development' as regards the Act. In order to obtain cheap land which would yield the largest land-account surplus the local authority would have had to acquire and develop land *further* from the desirable facilities, i.e. inferior land incurring external costs of development. Full social costs would therefore have been higher when the infrastructure costs were allowed for!

The nature of the development land tax (DLT)

From the point of view of economic analysis a high rate of DLT should have no effect on the supply of land for development since the tax falls on economic rent. This is the return over and above the 'transfer price' which accrues to a factor through fixity of supply. Transfer price covers what the factor can earn in its best alternative use plus any return (often termed 'normal profit') required by the owner to overcome his inertia or inconvenience in effecting such a transfer. This can be illustrated both arithmetically and diagrammatically.

Suppose undeveloped farmland surrounding a town is required for housing. The current-use price is, say £1,000 per acre; this is the transfer price, i.e. what another farmer would be prepared to pay for the land for agricultural use. Planning permission is now given for a housing development on twelve acres of a particular farm. As a result the price of these twelve acres rises to £20,000 an acre. Thus development value for the purposes of DLT would equal current market price *minus* current-use value, *plus* 10 per cent, i.e. £240,000 – (£12,000 + £1,200) = £226,800. DLT payable would be 60 per cent on all realised development value above £50,000 in any one year, i.e. 60 per cent of £176,800, or £106,080. The farmer is thus left with £133,920, and by taking his gain he can obtain almost 134 acres to replace the twelve sold.

The above argument can be shown diagrammatically as follows. If no planning permission were required and all the agricultural land surrounding the town were suitable for housing, we can assume that any price above the agricultural price will secure the land for housing. In other words, the supply (S_a) of land is perfectly elastic at OY in Figure 13.13, i.e. at £1,000 an acre. Demand for agricultural land is given by the demand curve D. Any increase in demand for land for housing, XX_1, can be supplied without any rise in price. In other words, because supply is perfectly elastic, the increase in demand to D_1 has no effect on price.

In practice, however, planning permission is restricted to twelve acres, OX and supply curve S_b. Thus the price of these soars above their agricultural-use value to £20,000 an acre, OY_1. There is a windfall gain, or betterment, to the farmer of Y_1YPQ. The whole of this windfall gain can be taxed away without making any difference to the farmer's willingness to supply the land for housing, assuming that his inertia costs were included in the price OY. DLT could thus rise to almost 100 per cent.

In theory, the argument is neat; in practice, it runs up against snags. The first is that we do not know for certain how much the farmer will

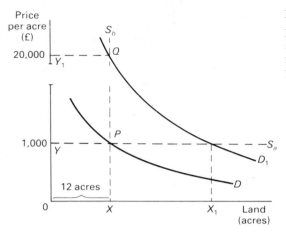

Price per acre (£)

20,000

1,000

12 acres

0   X   X₁   Land (acres)

S_b

Q

Y_1

P

Y

S_a

D_1

D

FIGURE 13.13

Economic rent arising from restricted planning permission

actually require to cover his inertia and upheaval costs. Subjective valuations cannot be ignored. He may feel, for instance, that the £133,920 left to him is insufficient compensation for land which has been in the possession of his family for generations. Or he may refuse to sell, illogically in view of the above analysis, unless he can add the amount of the tax to the price. This would imply that previously the market was functioning imperfectly, with housing land being sold at a price less than buyers were prepared to pay. A second is that the theory is essentially static, making no allowance for expectations. The farmer may speculate against a future rate of DLT, refusing to sell if he thinks it might be reduced in the near future, or being more ready to sell if he fears an increase. Where there is a lack of voluntary sales, the price of development land will rise (other things being equal), while if compulsory purchase has to be invoked, development will be delayed by the time-consuming procedures of a local public enquiry.

The present position

The three post-war attempts of Labour governments to deal with the problem of betterment have foundered largely because they incorporated the ultimate public ownership of all development land. Apart from the weaknesses inherent in allocating land by public agencies, the lack of inter-party agreement on policy produced instability in the land market chiefly because the Conservative party was committed to repeal the measures if returned to power. As a result, development land was withheld from the market following nationalising measures, while uncertainty deterred development by adding to the risks involved.

But there is now an opportunity for bipartisan agreement. The Conservative party has accepted the need to collect betterment through DLT and has pitched the rate at a realistic level (60 per cent on development value above £50,000). Can the Labour party face up to the economic consequences and administrative difficulties of public ownership, dropping this commitment and settling for the collection of betterment through DLT? The answer may well depend on which wing of the Labour party emerges triumphant from the current internal power struggle.

FURTHER READING

Community Land Act (London: HMSO, 1975).
A. J. Harrison, *Economics and Land Use Planning* (London: Croom Helm, 1977) chs 1–9.
J. Harvey and M. K. Johnson, *Introduction to Macro-economics* (London: Macmillan, 1974) chs 11–15, 19, 20.
V. W. E. Moore, *The Community Land Act, 1975* (London: Sweet & Maxwell, 1975).
Report of the Committee of Inquiry on Local Government Finance (Layfield Report), Cmnd 6453 (London: HMSO, 1976).

Index